An Integrated Approach to
BUSINESS STUDIES

LECTURER'S GUIDE

BRUCE R JEWELL

Longman

Edinburgh Gate
Harlow, Essex

Pearson Education Limited
Edinburgh Gate
Harlow
Essex CM20 2JE
England and Associated Companies throughout the World

ISBN 0582 40543 2

First edition published 1990
Second edition published 1993
Third edition published 1996
Fourth edition published 2000

Printed in Italy by G. Canale & C.S.p.A Borgano T.se – Turin

The Publisher's policy is to use paper manufactured from sustainable forests.

Contents

Curriculum 2000 and Business Studies

The Qualifications and Curriculum Authority (QCA)

QCA acts as the regulator for GCE A level and other examinations taken by students in schools and colleges in England (there are sister bodies for Wales and Northern Ireland).

The QCA has been charged with the responsibility of introducing Curriculum 2000, the umbrella term used for the major changes to the 16–19 curriculum introduced in time for students embarking on a 16–19 course in and after September 2000. These changes include:

*   major revision to the specification and assessment of GNVQs;
*   the introduction of a single award GNVQ (equivalent to a single A level);
*   the introduction of a three-unit award GNVQ (equivalent to an AS level);
*   the introduction of a key skills award for all 16–19 students;
*   the creation of Advanced Subsidiary level (the new AS level);
*   the revision of GCE Advanced level;
*   the introduction of Advanced Extended to stretch the ablest candidates (and replace the rather neglected special paper examination).

It is to the A and AS level changes to which we now turn.

The new A and AS levels

Advanced Subsidiary level (the new AS) is introduced to replace the Advanced Supplementary level (the old AS). The old AS was introduced in an attempt to broaden the sixth-form curriculum, but the national take up of the old AS was disappointing. Many students correctly estimated that the time commitment for a package of two A levels and two old AS levels would exceed that of the traditional three A levels package. The new AS level, however, is pitched at a standard below A level – in fact, the standard that is expected of an A level student after one year of A level study.

The new AS consists of three units and is available both to students committed to a full A level in the subject and those who merely seek an AS in it. The new AS will be a success because all candidates for A level will take the AS examination en route to the A level. To obtain the full A level, it is necessary to combine three AS units with a further three units at full A level standard (known as A2). The AS is a qualification in its own right, whereas A2 is merely the second (and more demanding) half of the A level. The full A level therefore consists of six units.

Notice that these changes bring A levels into line with single award GNVQs, which also each consist of six units. The aligning of the two qualifications (A level and GNVQ) is also seen in changes in terminology (such as 'unit' rather than 'module') and in the A to E grading systems (with the abolition of the old 'near miss' N grade).

Assessment can either be staged or at the end of the course. Staged assessment is, in effect, the new name for modular assessment, where candidates are assessed after completing each unit. End-of-course assessment is, in effect, the traditional linear model for A level. It is assumed that the majority of candidates will opt for at least some staged assessment during a two-year course. It is likely that the main candidates opting for all examination at the end of the course will be students taking a subject over a year rather than the more common two years.

The QCA ruled that, to reduce the disruption to school and college life caused by examinations, this assessment will be confined to two periods – January and June. This decision preludes the three times a year assessment scheme developed by the OCR in its 'Cambridge Modular' A level. With six units to study, it inevitably means that students will have to prepare for two units simultaneously, rather than concentrate on a single unit/module as in the past.

The QCA has tightened up the rules on resitting particular unit examinations. Whereas under the old system candidates could retake a module examination as many times as they liked within their period of registration, under the new system candidates can retake examinations only once, and the final, or synoptic, examination can only be taken once. If a candidate is dissatisfied with his or her result after the completion of all units, the only recourse is to retake all units in a subsequent year. The restriction to a single retake is unlikely to seriously harm candidates. It is my experience that most students make progress at first resitting of a unit/module, but that progress is far less common when candidates take an examination a third or subsequent time.

The rules on synoptic assessment have been considerably strengthened by the QCA. Pre-Curriculum 2000, synoptic assessment was only a requirement in modular schemes and in practice was not too demanding. Curriculum 2000 A level schemes must include a minimum of 20 per cent synoptic assessment, which must occur at the end of the course. This precludes the 'Foundation followed by options' model found in the OCR's Cambridge Modular scheme. Synoptic assessment requires an integration of Business Studies themes at the end of a course of study. The QCA's definition of synoptic assessment in the context of Business Studies is as follows:

- synoptic assessment should address the requirement that A level Business Studies specifications should encourage students to see the relationships between different aspects of the subject;
- synoptic assessment involves the explicit integration of knowledge, understanding and skills learned in different parts of the A level course;
- where a specification contains options, synoptic assessment should focus on the elements contained within the compulsory content.

It is important to remember that synoptic assessment is more than a series of questions on discrete topics combined in a single end-of-course examination. Synoptic assessment involves the questions that cover a range of topics and themes within the subject. It is, therefore, important for teachers to include within their scheme of work, time and activities designed to develop in their students a synoptic rather than compartmentalized view of the subject.

The QCA's criteria

The QCA lays down criteria for A level specifications drawn up by the awarding bodies. Pre-Curriculum 2000, the QCA's documents were known as subject 'cores' as they focused on the topics that candidates were required to study. The switch to the word 'criteria' reflects the fact that:

- the QCA's statement is the criteria for approval of a specification;
- the criteria refer to more than the factual content of a specification – as well as laying down mandatory topics, they also include statements concerning the aims and objectives of A level Business Studies.

AS and A level specifications in Business Studies should encourage students to:

- develop a critical understanding of organizations, the markets they serve and the process of adding value, which should involve consideration of the internal workings and management of organizations and, in particular, the process of decision making in a dynamic external environment;
- be aware that business behaviour can be studied from the perspectives of a range of stakeholders – including customer, manager, creditor, owner/shareholder and employee – and of the economic, environmental, ethical, governmental, legal, social and technological issues associated with business activity – students should also understand that Business Studies draws on a variety of disciplines and that these perspectives and disciplines are interrelated;
- acquire a range of skills, including decision making and problem solving in the light of evaluation and, where appropriate, the quantification and management of information.

AS and A level specifications in Business Studies should:

- emphasize the nature and process of decision making within organizations;

- focus on organizations in different business sectors and environments, recognizing that they face varying degrees of competition, and that they can be large and small, local, regional, national and multinational, and run for profit or not for profit;
- be firmly rooted in the current structure of business and business practice;
- enable students to understand the importance of seeing business problems and situations from different perspectives;
- emphasize that information management affects all functional areas of business – students should understand that the efficient use of information depends on the establishment of effective IT-based information management systems;
- enable students to identify business problems, plan appropriate investigations into such problems and make justifiable decisions consistent with their analysis of primary and/or secondary material in order to suggest solutions.

The mandatory subject content is arranged in five areas:

- **objectives and the business environment**
  - business objectives;
  - stakeholders;
  - organizational culture;
  - the market;
  - competition;
  - labour market;
  - market failure;
  - macroeconomic variables;
  - macroeconomic policy;
  - legal, political and social environment;
- **marketing**
  - the role and nature of marketing;
  - market research;
  - segmentation;
  - marketing plans;
  - the marketing mix;
  - sales forecasting;
  - responsiveness to demand;
- **accounting and finance**
  - budgeting;
  - cash flow forecasts;
  - final accounts;
  - costing;
  - contribution;
  - break-even analysis;
  - investment appraisal;
- **people in organizations**
  - human resources planning;
  - organizational design;
  - motivation and leadership;
  - employment law;
  - employee relations;
  - employee participation;
- **operations management**
  - efficiency;
  - capacity utilization;
  - production methods;
  - stock control;
  - waste management;
  - pollution control;
  - decision making;

– quality assurance;
– continuous improvement;
– R&D;
– new product design.

These mandatory topics are present in all A and AS specifications, although awarding bodies have discretion over other topics that they might wish to include or emphasize in their particular specification. This provides an element of diversity and therefore choice while at the same time some standardization of the essential elements.

Differentiating AS from A2

In previous statements of the subject cores, the QCA differentiated AS from A level in terms of:

• a list of mandatory topics for inclusion;
• the quantity of topics for inclusion.

The distinctions used in Curriculum 2000 criteria (and, therefore in specifications) are not in terms of subject content, but on the focus for the divisions of the subject. The distinctions are seen in the focus statements included in the document. These are summarized in Table 1.1.

It should be emphasized that the A2 specifications take the study of business to a new and greater depth. This involves understanding of the:

• interrelationships between topics;
• development of strategies for a dynamic environment;
• strategy and strategic considerations.

Table 1.1: The distinctions between AS and A2

AS focus	A2 focus
1 Objectives and the business environment	
In AS specifications, the emphasis should be on the strategic importance of clear objectives. In particular, there should be an awareness of how the business environment provides opportunities and imposes constraints on the pursuit of short- and long-term objectives.	A level specifications should, in relation to various business situations, require students to recognize potential conflict between the objectives of different stakeholder interests and suggest and evaluate resolutions to such conflict. Students should be required to recognize the interrelationships between objectives and an uncertain business environment and devise and evaluate strategies that aim to anticipate, respond to and manage change.
2 Marketing	
In AS specifications, the study of marketing should focus on the processes of finding and satisfying customers, with an emphasis on marketing objectives, strategy and tactics.	A level specifications should require students to analyse and evaluate the potential of different marketing strategies, tactics and techniques for enabling businesses to identify and adapt to changing market opportunities and achieve their objectives.
3 Accounting and finance	
AS specifications should emphasize the use of accounting and financial information as an aid to decision making and financial control.	A level specifications should require students to use a range of performance measures critically and evaluate the appropriateness of different financial techniques in shaping decision making in the context of the wider strategic objectives of businesses.

4

	Table 1.1: (contd)	
AS focus		**A2 focus**

4 People in organizations

AS focus	A2 focus
AS specifications should require students to understand the significance of various management and organizational structures for a business and its employees. Students should recognize the opportunities and constraints, in relation to people in organizations, created by the business/legal environment and appreciate the contributions of selected management theories.	A level specifications should require students to understand the interrelationships between organizational structure, leadership style and motivation in a business and evaluate the implications of these for the effective planning and management of human resources.

5 Operations management

AS focus	A2 focus
In AS specifications, the study of operations management should focus on the ways organizations use inputs and manage business processes efficiently to satisfy customers.	A level specifications should require students to analyse and evaluate the use of different operations management tools to enhance decision making in order to improve efficiency and quality.

The other distinction between AS and A2 level lies in the weighting given to assessment objectives. Knowledge, application, analysis and evaluation all feature in the assessment objectives at both levels, but, as we move from AS to A2, we find that there is a reduced emphasis on the lower-order skills and an increased emphasis on the higher-order skills. It is therefore important for candidates to have an understanding of the objectives and their relative weighting.

Table 1.2: Weighting of assessment objective for AS and A2

	Assessment objectives	Weighting (%)		
		AS	A2	A level
AO1	Demonstrate knowledge and understanding of the specified content.	25–35	15–25	20–30
AO2	Apply knowledge and critical understanding to problems and issues arising from both familiar and unfamiliar situations.	20–30	20–30	20–30
AO3	Analyse problems, issues and situations.	20–30	20–30	20–30
AO4	Evaluate, distinguish between fact and opinion, and assess information from a variety of sources.	15–25	25–35	20–30

The specifications

The criteria drawn up by the QCA provide a set of rules to which the awarding bodies work in devising their specifications. Note the change in terminology – 'examination boards' are now awarding bodies to reflect:

- a more positive approach;
- the fact that examinations are merely one form of assessment;
- GCE and GNVQ being brought more closely into line.

Also 'specification' replaces the former word 'syllabus' partly to reflect the shift from factual content towards a statement of what candidates are required to be able to do in relation to the topic.

Awarding bodies have considerable discretion when drawing up specifications, although they must conform to the QCA's criteria. In practice, this means that:

- topics identified in the criteria must be included in the specifications;
- the approach to subject topics identified by the QCA focus statements must be reflected in the specifications and subsequent assessment.

Subject topics not identified in the QCA's criteria can be included, however, provided they do not overload the specifications. This provides awarding bodies with some discretion about topics.

The QCA's criteria also impose some constraints in relation to assessment regimes. As noted above, at least 20 per cent of assessment must take the form of synoptic assessment, in which candidates are required to explore the interrelationships between subject topics. The other constraint in terms of assessment methods relates to internal assessment (which usually means coursework, although the two terms are not synonymous). There is a 30 per cent ceiling on internal assessment, although no minimum is imposed. This means that awarding bodies can award up to 30 per cent of the total marks or choose to make it optional. This represents a significant raising of the ceiling on coursework, but, interestingly, the Curriculum 2000 specifications show a shift towards optional coursework. Hence, awarding bodies such as the OCR and Edexcel that previously had a compulsory coursework element now allow a choice of coursework or an additional examination paper. At this stage, it is difficult to see if coursework will increase in importance as a result of the QCA raising the ceiling or if coursework will decline in importance as centres opt for the extra paper.

The Assessment and Qualifications Alliance (AQA)

The AQA has introduced a Curriculum 2000 specification that builds on the highly successful AEB syllabus. This scheme of assessment is summarized in Table 1.3. The first three units are assessed at the new AS standard and constitute the Advanced Subsidiary in Business Studies. During the A2 year, students revisit the same topic areas to explore them in greater detail, as well as covering a wider variety of subtopics within the particular area.

Table 1.3: The AQA's scheme of assessment

Unit	Topics covered	Nature of assessment	Weighting (%)
1	Marketing and accounting and finance	1¼-hour exam 2 compulsory stimulus questions	15 (30)
2	People and operations management	1¼-hour exam 2 compulsory stimulus questions	15 (30)
3	External influences and objectives and strategy	1½-hour exam based on a case study	20 (40)
4	Business decision making in functional areas shown in 1 and 2	1½-hour exam based on a case study	15
5w	Business report and essay	1½-hour exam	15
or 5c	Project	3000-word project	15
6	External influences and objectives and strategy	1½-hour exam based on a case study	20

Note: The figures in brackets refer to the AS level weighting

Edexcel

Because the awarding bodies are working to the same specifications, it is not surprising that the specifications of different boards cover broadly similar material and bear similarities in their assessment schemes. However, the packaging of the material as well as the titles given to units do vary, as we can see from Edexcel's scheme, summarized in Table 1.4.

Unit	Topics covered	Nature of assessment	Weighting (%)
1	Business structures, objectives and external influences	Structured questions 1¼-hour exam	15 (30)
2	Marketing and production	Unseen case study 1¼-hour exam	20 (40)
3	Financial management	Structured questions 1¼-hour exam	15 (30)
4	Analysis and decision making	Structured questions 1¼-hour exam	15
5	Business planning	Unseen case study 1½-hour exam **or** coursework (3000 words)	20
6	Synoptic: corporate strategy	Pre-seen case study 1½-hour exam	20

Table 1.4: Edexcel's scheme of assessment

Note: The figures in brackets refer to the AS level weighting.

Assessment takes the forms of:

* optional coursework;
* structured question (including data and stimulus response);
* an unseen case study;
* a pre-seen case study.

Unit 6 is clearly labelled as a synoptic unit that can only be taken at the end of a course of study, but it is not immediately clear from some unit titles what is included in the unit. Unit 1 includes the people and human resource management elements of AS level. This involves the study of internal organization, communications and motivation as well as the external environment.

Units 2 and 3 are self-explanatory from their titles. Unit 4, Analysis and decision making, focuses on eight areas:

* sales forecasting;
* new product development;
* probability and decision making;
* critical path analysis;
* costing;
* ratio analysis;
* investment appraisal;
* industrial relations.

Unit 5, in which there is a choice regarding the form of assessment, involves business planning, including SWOT and PEST analysis, human resource, marketing and financial planning.

Finally, the synoptic unit 6 focuses on strategies to cope with a dynamic environment, together with a study of corporate culture and the management of change. The topics selected for this unit are themselves all-embracing, integrative topics that explore the links between the main areas of the specification.

OCR

The OCR's specifications represent a major modification of the OCR's 'Cambridge Modular' examination. In contrast with the old scheme:

* coursework is now an option rather than being compulsory;
* a reduction in the use of pre-seen case studies;

Table 1.5: The OCR's scheme of assessment

Unit	Topics covered	Nature of assessment	Weighting (%)
1	Business structure, objectives and environment	1¼-hour exam based on an unseen case study	15 (30)
2	Business decisions	1½-hour exam data response questions	20 (40)
3	Business behaviour	1¼-hour exam based on a pre-seen case study	15 (30)
4 to 7	Option modules: • marketing • accounting • people in organizations • operations management	1¼-hour exam based on an unseen case study	15
8 or 9	Business thematic enquiry Project	1¼-hour exam involving a report on an unseen case study a 4000-word project	15
10	Business strategy	1¼-hour synoptic exam based on a pre-seen case study	20

Note: The figures in brackets refer to the AS level weighting.
Units 2 and 3 cover the same material.

• the choice of option areas for study in depth is reduced from two out of four to one out of four;
• the integrative unit is scheduled for the end of the course, thus replacing the 'foundation plus options' that have traditionally been a feature of the Cambridge Modular scheme.

Table 1.5 summarizes the scheme of assessment.

Unit 1, Business structure, objectives and environment, covers the material that one would expect from the first section of the QCA's criteria. Units 2 and 3 cover the same content. The focus is on the activities of the organization in the four functional areas of marketing, operations, accounting and human resources management. The OCR stresses that in the delivery of the unit, the emphasis should be on how businesses acquire and use resources in the areas of:

• the definition, targeting and satisfaction of the market;
• the acquisition, management and use of human resources:
• the process of adding value via production;
• accounting for business activity.

In business decisions the emphasis is on the ways decisions are made within each functional area and between them. This includes appropriate methods of analysis and business planning techniques. Study should focus on the pursuit of objectives within a framework of opportunities and constraints. Decisions should be perceived by means of the expectations of the full range of stakeholders in businesses activities. The overall approach considers the importance of business objectives and culture to the effective working of an organization, the need to plan effectively and the ways in which decisions are made and problems tackled. Emphasis is placed on the interrelationships between activities within the organization as a whole.

The A2 components commence with an in-depth study of one of the four functional areas of management. The optional project unit requires the submission of a report of about 4000 words that must:

• be investigative in nature, showing evidence of problem-solving skills;
• be based either on a single organization or a more general business-related issue;

- use, analytically and with evaluation, business studies knowledge drawn from more than one element of the whole business studies core, as studied in Units 1, 2, 3 and 10.
- be presented as a report with a clear definition of the problem and objectives in pursuing it.

The topic chosen could arise from any form of personal or school- or college-organized contact with any type of organization. The only requirement is that the topic should clearly be a business one, enabling the rigorous and effective use of the candidates' knowledge.

The alternative to submission of a project report is to sit the unit 9 examination, entitled Business thematic enquiry: 'This is based upon an unseen case study. The central theme of the case study is known to teachers in advance in order to permit preparatory study around that theme. The theme is always one which enables candidates to use knowledge from many parts of the specification. Candidates are expected to write a report which is problem-solving/evaluative in nature using both the evidence presented in the case and the understanding gained from previous study of the theme. No materials of any kind can be taken into the examination' (OCR).

As with the two preceding awarding bodies' specifications, synoptic unit (10) focuses on business strategy: 'Unit 10 is a compulsory and synoptic module, designed to complete the A level in Business Studies and to be covered at the end of the course.

The content of this strategy unit is:

- setting corporate objectives
- tools for corporate planning
- external influences
- devising and implementing strategy
- reviewing strategy
- managing strategic change.

Delivering objectives and the business environment

The QCA's criteria require that AS and A2 level specifications must include the following topics relating to objectives and the business environment:

- business objectives;
- stakeholders;
- organizational culture;
- the market and competition;
- market failure;
- labour markets;
- macroeconomic variables;
- macroeconomic policy and its impact on business;
- the international environment;
- the legal, political and social environment;
- business strategy in pursuit of objectives;
- business planning;
- methods of analysis.

Each of the above topics will be found in the specifications of the awarding bodies, although each has chosen to place its own particular emphasis on topics and has packaged them in different ways.

As noted earlier, the distinction between AS and A2 is contained in focus statements that, regarding objectives and the environment, are as follows (quoted from the QCA's subject criteria):

'In AS specifications, the emphasis should be on the strategic importance of clear objectives. In particular, there should be an awareness of how the business environment provides opportunities and imposes constraints on the pursuit of short-term and long-term objectives.

A level specifications should, in relation to various business situations, require students to recognize potential conflict between the objectives of different stakeholder interests and suggest and evaluate resolutions to such conflict. Students should be required to recognize the interrelationship between objectives and an uncertain business environment and to devise and evaluate strategies which aim to anticipate, respond to and manage change.'

The AS specifications should, therefore, focus on the role of objectives, the nature of the environment, constraints and opportunities (that is, the threats and opportunities identified in SWOT analysis) and the distinction between the short and long term. At A2 level, there is likely to be a greater emphasis on the conflict between different stakeholders' objectives. There is also a stress on the changing environment and its consequences for the management of resources. Managing change in an uncertain environment is a particular feature of A2 specifications. These topics, which are so closely bound up with the four functional areas of business, are not only essential lead-in topics before we deliver the rest of the course, but prime candidates for inclusion in a synoptic unit.

Of the five areas identified in the QCA specifications, objectives and the business environment represents the one where treatment in the specifications seems to vary to the greatest extent. Moreover, the nature of the material is both introductory (and, therefore, rightfully located at the start of the course) and synoptic (thereby providing opportunities to draw together the threads at the end of the course).

Let us see how the material is treated in the various specifications.

Objectives and the environment at AS level

The AQA's specifications

This material is contained in unit 3 of the AQA's specifications in a unit entitled External influences and objectives and strategy. Candidates taking the course on a staged assessment basis will already have been introduced to Marketing and accounting (unit 1) and, therefore, must have become familiar with the concept of the external environment, objectives and strategy. The AQA's unit 3 takes this a stage further, with a full treatment of the topic.

The 'external influences' part of the specifications deals with the following as opportunities for business organizations and constraints on their ability to achieve their objectives:

- conditions in the market with reference to capacity utilization and the degree of competition;
- the causes, nature and implications of the business cycle;
- the consequences of changes in interest rates (including their effects on exchange rates);
- the impact of changes in the exchange rate;
- the measurement, causes and consequences of inflation and the importance of expectations of inflation on business behaviour;
- causes and consequences of unemployment;
- UK and EU law regarding health and safety, employment, consumer protection and competition;
- social responsibility;
- morality in decision making;
- ethical issues;
- technological change.

The 'objectives and strategy' part of the specifications commences with 'starting a small firm', dealing with the following:

- identifying a market opportunity;
- legal structure of business organizations;
- practical problems, such as raising finance, cash flow, establishing a customer base;
- writing a business plan;
- the role of objectives in decision making;
- short- and long-term objectives;
- conflicting objectives and stakeholders;
- SWOT analysis.

The Edexcel specifications

Unlike the AQA, the Edexcel specifications include this material in unit 1 (Business in context), where it is combined with an introduction to internal organization, communication and motivation. The 'objectives and external environment' part of the specifications covers the following:

- the mixed economy;
- the role of the entrepreneur;
- types of business organizations and the implications of these for raising finance, control and decision making;
- the role and importance of objectives;
- hierarchy of objectives;
- stakeholders and the role of profit;
- adding value;
- microeconomic factors;
- macroeconomic variables;
- the impact of interest and exchange rates;
- the law as a constraint;

- the political environment;
- demographic trends;
- the changing social structure;
- changing lifestyles.

The OCR's specifications

Like Edexcel, the OCR places 'objectives and the environment' at the start of the course, unit 1 being so entitled. The OCR includes material on:

- the nature of business with reference to stakeholders, legal structures, classification and role;
- objectives as the basis of strategy and behaviour;
- planning;
- microeconomic factors;
- the legal environment;
- changing technology;
- social change;
- ethical and environmental issues;
- State participation in the economy.

Objectives and the environment at A2 level

One of the differences between the treatment of this material at AS and A2 levels is that at AS level the focus is on a static situation in which the environment is either a constraint or an opportunity. At A2 level, the focus is more on a dynamic and uncertain situation in which business organizations adapt their strategies to cope with these changes.

The AQA's specifications

The final AQA unit, entitled External influences and objectives and strategy returns to this material, but at this more sophisticated level. The focus is on the implications for business strategy of:

- changes in macroeconomic variables;
- international competitiveness;
- EU policies;
- changes in export markets (with an explicit mention of the emerging markets in Eastern Europe and elsewhere);
- governments' economic policy;
- social responsibility, culture and ethics;
- environmental pressures;
- political changes;
- pressure group activities.

The unit also includes a study of:

- social audits;
- the financing of growth and the problems of overtrading;
- changes in ownership;
- mission statements;
- management reorganization in the wake of growth;
- decision-making models, including decision trees;
- corporate planning;
- contingency planning.

The Edexcel specifications

Edexcel includes this material in a combination of its A2 units. For instance, unit 4, which has a decision-making theme, includes decision trees. Unit 5 focuses on planning, including the following types:

- strategic;

- corporate;
- functional;
- business start-up;
- SWOT and PEST.

However, the bulk of the material is found in the synoptic unit, Corporate strategy. This returns the student full circle to the themes of the pursuit of objectives against the background of a changing environment.

In its notes for guidance, Edexcel states that 'The focus has moved from unit 1 to strategies designed to take advantage of favourable changes in the environment or to reduce the problems resulting from adverse changes in the environment.' This includes coping with the problems of 'seasonality' in either supply or demand. Edexcel has placed international considerations in this unit:

- export opportunities;
- competitiveness;
- entry in to overseas markets;
- the EU;
- multinational corporations.

The social responsibility and ethics section covers the same material as the AQA's specifications. Edexcel has also placed market failure in this unit. Market failure is an economics concept and covers a variety of situations in which the free market fails to allocate resources efficiently. It provides the rationale for government intervention in the economy.

Strategic decisions relate to the future development of the business, including:

- mergers and acquisitions;
- direction of growth;
- the Ansoff Matrix;
- synergy
- Porter's generic strategies;
- position maps.

Finally, the synoptic unit incorporates matters relating to corporate culture and the management of change – two topics that lend themselves to synoptic treatment.

The OCR's specifications

The topics contained in 'objectives and the environment' will obviously play a key role in unit 8 (Project) and unit 9 (Business thematic environment), candidates choosing one or the other. Neither has any explicit content, but is based on material covered up to that point.

The OCR's synoptic unit is entitled Business strategy (unit 10). It covers the:

- setting objectives;
- objectives, culture, organizational structure;
- strategic environment – namely, the external environment, but now including a larger content of macroeconomic factors;
- tools for corporate planning – information gathering, SWOT, portfolio analysis, break-even analysis, forecasting critical path, Gantt charts, decision trees, sampling, financial analysis, investment appraisal, costing, management styles, Ansoff's matrix;
- operational constraints, such as environmental ones;
- external influences, involving a revisiting of the external environment;
- devising strategy, including budgets and teamwork;
- implementing strategy – planning, delegation, responsibility, authority, motivation, value analysis, effectiveness, the market and production processes;
- controlling strategy – forecasting, budgets, variance analysis, cash flow, waste management;
- managing strategic change.

Approaching the topics

The review of the specifications shows that the subject of objectives and the environment features both at the start of the course and as an integrating theme at the end of the course. The same topics are dealt with at both levels, but there is an important distinction to be made. At AS level, the environment is accepted as a given fact and as a constraint on (or opportunity for) business organizations. At A2 level, the focus turns to developing strategies to prosper in an uncertain and changing environment.

Objectives

Candidates should understand the role of objectives in the determination of strategy and in the planning process. They should be aware that all business decisions are designed with the pursuit of objectives in mind. Organizations have different objectives and within each organization there is a hierarchy of objectives cascading down from the overall corporate objective through departmental/divisional objectives down to operational objectives at the section or individual level. Management by objectives reminds us that all sound objectives should be SMART – that is, Specific, Measurable, Agreed/Achievable, Realistic and Time-related.

Stakeholders

They have differing interests and differing ways in which they evaluate company performance. Candidates should be aware of the various and conflicting objectives of the stakeholders (profits for shareholders might seem to clash with higher pay for employees, for example). The concept of stakeholders provides an introduction to organizational behaviour with a contrast between the notion of maximizing (favoured by neo-classical economists) and that of satisfying. A related concept to explore is that of divorce of ownership from control.

Organizational culture

This is, in part, human resources management topic, but its presence in this section is related to the determination of an organization's mission statement. Unlike objectives, mission statements are written in qualitative terms and should guide the decision-making process.

Social responsibility, ethics and environmental considerations

These topics are inserted in the course to remind us that, as well as studying the impact of the environment on an organization, we should also be concerned with the impact of the organization on the environment.

It is relevant to consider the arguments for and against socially responsible and ethical behaviour. Always bear in mind that free market economists argue that the prime, even sole, duty of managers is to shareholders, not to the other stakeholders. These economists would argue that socially responsible behaviour, which conflicts with the profit-seeking motive, leads to inefficiency. Against these arguments, we should consider the impact (favourable and adverse) of a large organization on the community and the physical environment.

Ethical issues tend to be concerned more with individual actions than those of an organization as a whole. Business studies must always be taught within a legal and ethical framework. Students should understand how profits can be achieved while not only conforming to the law but also behaving ethically and with integrity.

In approaching environmental, or green, issues, it is useful to stress that 'environmentally friendly' activities assist in the marketing of products (so-called 'green marketing'). Moreover, environmental policies, which reduce waste and lead to recycling, can reduce a firm's costs. This notion of 'environmentally friendly' policies being in organizations' interests contrasts with the view found in economics that, as firms seek to minimize private costs, they convert internal costs into external costs by polluting the environment. Economists tend to see the solution in terms of internalizing the externalities and tend to ignore the idea that environmental policies can be beneficial for business organizations.

The economic environment

This subject can be subdivided into micro- and macroeconomics. Microeconomic forms of analysis that should become familiar to students includes:

- demand theory;
- price elasticity of demand (PED) – students need to understand the concept, be able to calculate PED, be able to apply the factors that determine PED and know that when demand is inelastic, price and revenue move in the same direction, but when demand is elastic they move in opposite directions;
- income elasticity of demand;

- cross-elasticity of demand;
- supply theory;
- the price mechanism;
- the market structures of perfect competition, monopoly, monopolistic competition and oligopoly – Business Studies students are not required to understand the graphical analysis of these models, but should have an understanding of the major conclusions from the theory of the firm, which are that:
  - product differential increases the firm's discretion when setting price;
  - perfectly competitive firms are pricetakers;
  - monopoly leads to higher prices, lower output and inefficiency;
  - oligopolists are interdependent and are naturally inclined to collude.

The study of microeconomic factors is especially important as a background to marketing (for example, regarding pricing policy).

Macroeconomic variables and policies also feature in this section. The key variables are national income (gross domestic product, GPP), unemployment, inflation, economic growth and fluctuations in the economy. The Business Studies focus should not be on the causes of changes in these variables. Instead, we should concentrate on the impact changes in them have on organizations and consequences of policies designed to eradicate problems.

The policies can be classified as fiscal, monetary, direct/supply-side policies. Although there is still a tendency to teach Keynesian fiscal policy, it should be remembered that monetary policy in the form of interest rates constitutes the prime macroeconomic policy in the world today. Direct policies tend to be seen as interventionist, whereas the term 'supply-side policy' tends to be reserved for policies designed to free up the market. Removing regulations represents a business opportunity.

Exchange rates are a key factor, in terms of both the domestic and international environments. For example, at the time of publication, sterling floats freely against other currencies and the Euro is merely one foreign currency among many others. A depreciation of sterling raises the cost of imports and, as such, increases business costs in the UK. However, by making UK exports cheaper abroad, depreciation will boost UK exports.

The labour market is also specifically mentioned in the specifications. It links up with human resources management and, in particular, with human resources planning and determining pay. Candidates should be aware of trends in the labour market, the analysis of pay by means of supply and demand and wage-push as a cause of inflation.

The alleged unwillingness of some private-sector firms to provide training in case employees are poached by rivals represents a form of market failure; a failure of the market to supply goods and services at the right price, right quantity and to the people who demand them. Other market failures include the:

- failure of the market to provide goods the public want;
- failure of the market to provide sufficient quantities of merit goods;
- provision of harmful, demerit goods;
- failure of private enterprise to take external costs and benefits into account;
- overpricing and underproduction of goods by firms enjoying monopoly power over the market.

Market failure is the economists' rationale for intervening in markets. After all, if markets did not fail, then government would not, and should not, intervene.

Business organizations

All the specifications refer to the distinction between the private and public sectors in a mixed economy. It should be appreciated that the distinction is not just in terms of ownership (privately owned versus government owned), but also in terms of the mechanism for allocating goods. The remaining parts of the public sector allocate goods mainly by non-market means – that is, the goods are free at the point of consumption. The debate over privatization/nationalization is now largely historical, although reference to this topic provides an entry into the question of share issues, control and differing objectives.

As well as the public and private sectors, we should also refer to the voluntary (charities) and not-for-profit sectors. It has always been accepted that Business Studies analysis applies to all organizations, but that what distinguishes the sectors is the question of ownership and objectives.

In terms of types of business organizations in the private sector (sole trader, partnership and companies), there is a vast amount of rather dull material that candidates should know – even if only as background to other aspects of the subject. Candidates are required to know the mechanism for establishing each of these business types and to be able to argue the advantages and disadvantages of each. However, the focus should be placed on the implications of the type of organization for decision making and control, raising finance, size of undertakings, and legal and financial liability.

The legal environment

This is another crucially important area in all the specifications. Employment and consumer law are particularly important, but reference should also be made to health and safety, equal opportunities, competition, environmental and planning law. Candidates are required to have a broad understanding of these areas of law and be able to apply them in given situations. A detailed knowledge of case law has never been required in this subject, but students should have some understanding of the concept of judge-made law.

EU law should also be covered in the course. Students should understand the nature of an EU directive and the impact of the treaties (EU primary legislation) on law in the UK.

The international environment

An understanding of the international environment is also required. Economic prosperity abroad creates market opportunities, while recession abroad acts as a constraint on exporters. To compete with foreign rivals (whether in the UK or in overseas markets) UK firms must be competitive in terms of price, quality, reliability and delivery dates. This opens the door to a study of marketing and operations management.

The EU

Europe is not fully appreciated by students who persist in seeing the UK as somehow detached. The UK is a full member of the EU (including the Social Charter) – the single currency is the only policy to which the UK is not committed. The implications of the EU to stress are that:

*   the UK can no longer impose import controls against her EU partners nor against the rest of the world in a unilateral manner;
*   the single market eliminated not only tariff barriers, but other barriers as well, such as technical barriers relating to laws on product specifications;
*   there is free movement of labour and capital within the EU;
*   the UK is subject to EU laws that are passed by a system of qualified majority voting;
*   the EU provides the UK with its largest export market and is the major source of imports;
*   EU laws provide protection for UK citizens and are not just interference.

The social environment

This topic can be subdivided into demographical factors and lifestyles. The former deals with the various numbers of people and is therefore important in terms of both recruiting labour and marketing goods. The latter deals with culture, patterns of living and behaviour. The major aspects of behaviour that we are concerned with are types of buying behaviour.

The technological environment

This is somewhat neglected in our subject area. Its main impact concerns the development of new products and new processes. In both cases, new opportunities are created, but there are also threats to existing products.

Decision making

This topic has always been at the heart of Business Studies. The scientific, quantitative approach to decision making has been stressed in all schemes. This involves objectives, gathering data, analysis, the devising of alternative solutions, evaluation, choice of solution and, finally, implementation and review. The process should include the key analytical techniques, such as:

*   critical path analysis;
*   investment appraisal;

- decision tree;
- ratios;
- portfolio analysis.

Students should be reminded that these techniques are not discrete parts of the course, but are for possible use in all aspects of business.

Planning

Planning should be introduced both early in the course and as a synoptic topic. Students should be aware of the different types of plans, the importance of the planning process and the format of any plan (objectives, situational audit, plan of action and monitoring and review). They should be able to produce a business plan and integrate functional plans into an overall one.

Planning provides an opportunity to integrate material by means of SWOT and PEST analysis.

Strategy

All specifications focus on strategy in the synoptic module. Candidates are required to:

- understand the concept of strategy;
- distinguish between strategy and tactics;
- relate strategy, culture and objectives;
- undertake SWOT and PEST analysis;
- understand the constraints on strategy;
- understand how strategy is communicated to employees;
- understand how strategy is implemented and controlled.

Delivering marketing

The QCA's criteria require that AS and A2 level specifications must include the following topics relating to marketing:

- the nature and role of marketing, including its interfaces with other business activities;
- market research;
- segmentation, market share, market growth;
- marketing objectives, planning and strategy;
- strategies in relation to the elements of the marketing mix;
- sales forecasting.

Each of the above topics will be found in the specifications of the awarding bodies, although each has chosen to place its own particular emphasis on the topics and has packaged it in different ways.

As noted earlier, the distinction between AS and A2 levels is contained in focus statements that, for marketing, is as follows (quoted from the QCA's subject criteria):

'In AS specifications the study of marketing should focus on the processes of finding and satisfying customers with an emphasis on marketing objectives, strategy and tactics.

A2 level specifications should require students to analyse and evaluate the potential of different marketing strategies, tactics and techniques for enabling business to identify and adapt to changing market opportunities and achieve their objectives.'

An interpretation of the distinction between these levels would suggest that the following would feature at A2 level:

- evaluation of alternative strategies rather than an analysis of a single strategy;
- a greater emphasis on quantitative and other analytical techniques (such as sales forecasting) to enable marketing decision making;
- a greater appreciation of the dynamic environment and the need to respond to changes;
- a greater degree of appreciation of the interface between marketing and other business activities.

Marketing at AS level

The AQA's specifications

Unit 1 of the AQA's specification links marketing with accounting and finance. The marketing content consists of:

- market analysis, including segmentation, market research and qualitative understanding of sampling;
- marketing strategy, including objectives, niche versus mass marketing, product lifecycle, product portfolio analysis (such as the Boston matrix) and adding value to create a unique selling point;
- marketing planning, incorporating strategies in relation to the marketing mix;
- applications of elasticity of demand.

The Edexcel specifications

This awarding body links marketing with production in unit 2. The marketing element consists of:

- the nature and role of marketing;
- marketing objectives;
- the marketing mix;
- market research;
- analysis of the product element of the marketing mix;
- pricing, including elasticity;
- promotion;
- channels of distribution.

The OCR's specifications

The OCR places marketing in units 2 and 3 (Business decisions and Business behaviour) with the three other functional areas of management. Again, the topics consist of:

- the nature of marketing;
- objectives;
- segmentation;
- market share/market growth;
- market research techniques;
- sampling;
- sales forecasting;
- marketing planning;
- marketing strategy for each element of the mix;
- responsiveness of demand (that is, elasticity).

Marketing at A2 level

The AQA's specifications

A level candidates will revisit marketing in unit 4 of the AQA's specifications. Again, it links up with accounting and finance. The unit will require candidates to look into the subject in more detail by exploring the following:

- assets versus market-led marketing;
- sales forecasting using moving averages and correlation using scatter graphs;
- marketing models and scientific marketing decision making;
- marketing plans (in greater detail);
- marketing budgets.

The Edexcel specifications

Unlike the AQA, this awarding body has not devised an A2 unit, which is wholly or substantially marketing. Instead, candidates revisit marketing topics in each of the A2 units:

- sales forecasting and sales budgets are a feature of unit 4, Analysis and decision making;
- new product development (NPD) is also included in unit 4 – although this is primarily a 'production topic', it is impossible to fully understand NPD without reference to marketing and market research;
- marketing planning features in unit 5, business planning – this requires candidates to revisit marketing strategy and the marketing mix;
- international marketing features in the synoptic unit 6, Corporate strategy.

The OCR's specifications

Alone, of the three English awarding bodies, the OCR offers an option paper at A2 level. Further marketing is one of the options available. Candidates choosing this option are required to revisit the subject, but in greater detail and depth. New topics appearing in the A2 option include:

- social and psychological factors influencing buyer behaviour;

- marketing and the law;
- quantitative understanding of sampling;
- sampling error;
- questionnaire design;
- Dagmar and Aida models;
- Ansoff's matrix;
- forecasting;
- international marketing.

Candidates not taking the marketing option will not be able to opt out of marketing altogether in A2. They will need to demonstrate their understanding of, and skills in, marketing analysis in their Business thematic enquiry (unit 8) or project (unit 9), which will cover topics from various parts of the subject. In addition, marketing strategy is one aspect of the overall strategy that is the subject of unit 10, the synoptic unit.

Approaching the topics

We can see that, at AS level, at least there is considerable overlap in topics and approach. The major differences between the specifications is in terms of the topic(s) with which marketing is linked. When linked with accounting, there is the possibility of hybrid question on, say, costing and pricing or on budgets. When linked with production, there is a possibility of hybrid question that links production runs with satisfying the customer. The other major difference at AS level concerns the inclusion of some topics (such as forecasting) at AS level in some specifications but not in others.

At A2 level, there are considerable differences in the coverage of marketing in the different specifications. The OCR has an in-depth option on marketing as one unit, but students who do not take this option will only revisit marketing in terms of those parts of the course that are designed to be integrative and synoptic. All the candidates studying courses designed for the AQA's specifications will revisit marketing for a unit that appears to be a repeat of an AS unit, but in fact covers the subject in greater depth. The Edexcel scheme's candidates will not revisit the topic in terms of a discrete paper, but will find that marketing topics will feature in each of their second-year units.

Allowing for the inevitable differences in content or emphasis or stress, the following is offered as advice on the approach to take for each topic within marketing.

The nature of marketing

Candidates can expected to be tested on:

- the marketing philosophy – what marketing is;
- market versus sales orientation;
- asset-led marketing – a concept especially stressed by the AQA;
- the interfaces with the environment;
- the interfaces with other functional areas of business;
- marketing as the integrative function within the organization.

Market share and market growth

Candidates should:

- be able to define these terms;
- understand the problems of defining and measuring both the market and share in the market;
- know that opportunities exist in a growing market;
- understand that in a static market, expansion is only possible at the expense of rivals;
- link up these concepts with portfolio analysis (such as the Boston matrix).

Marketing objectives

Candidates can expect questions on:

- the nature of objectives;
- the role of objectives in decision making and planning;

- marketing objectives within the hierarchy of the corporate objectives;
- the link between objectives, strategy and tactics;
- objectives and elements of the marketing mix.

Segmentation of the market

Candidates should prepare for questions on:

- ways in which to segment the market;
- what constitutes a viable segment;
- the advantages and disadvantages of segmenting the market;
- undifferentiated, differentiated and concentrated strategies;
- segmentation and market research;
- segmentation and marketing strategies in relation to price, product, promotion and distribution.

Market research

Candidates can expect questions on:

- the role of market/marketing research;
- the types of information sought;
- the roles and limitations of secondary research;
- the roles of primary research;
- primary research techniques (including, but not confined to, surveys);
- the advantages and disadvantages of each method;
- questionnaire design;
- survey methods;
- sampling methods.

At AS level, candidates are required to have a qualitative understanding of sampling methods. This means that candidates need to understand probability and non-probability methods and their limitations. In addition, it is necessary to know about sampling error and level of confidence, but candidates will not be required to undertake calculations involving standard deviation. At A2 level, a greater knowledge of the mathematics involved in sampling will be required of candidates.

Forecasting methods are included in all specifications at A2 level. It is important to realize that sales forecasting is not confined to moving averages used in time series analysis. In addition to times series analysis, it is important to introduce students to other quantitative techniques (such as correlation via scatter graphs) and to non-quantitative methods (such as the Delphi or panel methods).

Questions on forecasting are likely to stress:

- the methods and their limitations;
- their role in terms of marketing planning and budgeting (as well as cash flow forecasting and investment appraisal in other parts of the subject).

Marketing planning

Plans and the planning process can be seen as the umbrella topic for other topics. These other topics include objectives, budgets and strategies. Specifically regarding marketing plans, candidates should prepare for questions on:

- the roles and nature of plans;
- the relationships with the overall business plan;
- marketing strategy in relation to the elements within the marketing mix.

The marketing mix

Superficially known as the 4Ps – Product, Promotion, Place, Pricing – we should see the marketing mix as a checklist for devising strategies for each of the elements. In addition, blending is needed to ensure internal consistency within the mix.

Product

Candidates should expect questions on:

- the nature of products, including the augmented product;
- the product lifecycle – not just for its own sake, but for the analysis of strategies at the different points along the product lifecycle;
- limitations of the product lifecycle model;
- the role of branding;
- positioning and position maps;
- portfolio analysis, especially the Boston Matrix and Ansoff Matrix;
- new product development (NPD);
- factors to consider in NPD.

Promotion

Candidates should prepare for questions on:

- the promotional mix;
- objectives of promotion;
- choice of appropriate promotional techniques;
- choice of advertising media;
- evaluating the effectiveness of promotion;
- linking promotion with other aspects of the marketing mix and product lifecycle.

Place (distribution)

This is the rather neglected element of the marketing mix. Candidates should be able to answer questions on:

- the variety of different channels;
- the role of channel intermediaries;
- the appropriateness of direct or indirect channels;
- choice of distribution outlets, such as selective, exclusive or intensive distribution;
- physical distribution.

Pricing

Candidates should understand:

- the different types of pricing policies;
- pricing policies and pricing tactics;
- skim versus penetration pricing;
- cost-based pricing;
- costing;
- mark-ups;
- competition-based pricing;
- pricing and market structure;
- pricing and product differentiation;
- price elasticity of demand.

If demand is elastic, the product is homogeneous rather than differentiated and the market is competitive – then individual firms have little discretion over price.

International marketing

This is an A2 topic and its importance varies from specification to specification. It is important to stress that international marketing is affected by, but its study is not confined to, exchange rates, the EU and the single market. International marketing as a topic within marketing exists because people abroad represent a distinct segment of the market. Undoubtedly, a single currency and the completion of a single market reduces the differences between the UK and our EU partners. However, there are still differences of language and culture to consider. The issues to stress in international marketing are:

- choice of foreign markets to enter;
- entry strategies – exporting, licensing, multinational production and so on;

- standardization versus adaptation to the overseas market;
- the greater risks and problems involved;
- the EU and the World Trade Organization;
- exchange rates and their impact on volume and profit margins.

Delivering accounting and finance

The QCA's criteria require that AS and A2 level specifications must include the following topics relating to accounting and finance:

- budgets and variance;
- cash flow forecasting;
- interpretation of balance sheets;
- interpretation of profit and loss accounts;
- the limitations of final accounts;
- ratio analysis;
- costing and decision making;
- contribution as an aid to decision making;
- break-even analysis;
- investment appraisal;
- qualitative factors in investment decisions.

The distinction between AS and A2 level is contained in the focus statement (quoting from the OCR's subject criteria):

'AS specifications should emphasize the use of accounting and financial information as an aid to decision making and financial control.

A2 level specifications should require students to use a range of performance measures critically and to evaluate the appropriateness of different financial techniques in shaping decision making in the context of the wider strategic objectives of business.'

As with the two previous subject areas, this distinction can be interpreted to be that, at AS level, the focus should be on the relatively static and certain environment. At A2 level, on the other hand, the application of a greater range of techniques (which are then identified in the specifications) is required, together with a greater emphasis on the higher-order skill of evaluation, a greater understanding of the interrelationships with the other aspects of business and a greater appreciation of the problems associated with uncertainty.

Accounting and finance at AS level
The AQA's specifications

Accounting and finance is included in unit 1 (where it is combined with marketing). The AS level treatment of accounting and finance consists of:

- classification of costs, including contribution and break-even analysis;
- cash flow management;
- the distinction between cash and profits;
- sources of finance;
- budgeting – its roles, benefits and drawbacks;

- interpreting variances;
- responsibility accounting, with specific reference to cost centres and profit centres.

The Edexcel specifications

Edexcel requires candidates to take a dedicated unit – unit 3 – on financial management. The title should not lead teachers and students to think that it is based purely on financial accounts. In fact, it covers both the financial and cost and management part of the AS level course. Moreover, this particular unit also features the descriptive aspects of statistics that would have been positioned elsewhere in other schemes.

The unit covers material similar to that of the AQA's specifications, namely the:

- purpose, structure and interpretation of final accounts;
- limitations of final accounts;
- working capital management;
- distinction between profit and cash statements;
- ratio analysis;
- sources of finance;
- budgeting and simple variances;
- cash flow forecasts;
- classification of costs;
- contribution and decision making;
- break-even analysis.

The OCR's specifications

Accounting and finance as an aid to decision making and control features in units 2 and 3, Business behaviour and Business Decisions. Again, accounts topics covered within this unit consist of:

- the use of financial information;
- budgets;
- cash flow forecasting;
- structure and interpretation of final accounts;
- functions, and limitations, of accounts;
- classification of costs, break even analysis;
- contribution;
- investment appraisal (payback and APR).

However, break-even analysis is not explicitly mentioned.

Accounting and finance at A2 level

The AQA's specifications

Candidates following courses designed according to the AQA's specifications revisit accounting and finance in unit 4, which builds on unit 1. In addition to further development of AS topics, the A2 unit requires:

- understanding of the implication of the distinction between capital and revenue expenditure for final accounts;
- analysis of accounts over time;
- working capital management;
- the window dressing of accounts, which goes further than the mere limitations of accounts as window dressing implies a cynical manipulation of accounts;
- straight line depreciation;
- liquidity, efficiency, gearing profitability and shareholder ratios;
- the limitations of ratio analysis;
- special order contracts and contribution;
- break-even analysis;
- forecasting cash flows for investment appraisal;
- quantitative techniques of investment appraisal (but not the internal rate of return);
- qualitative aspects of investment decisions.

The Edexcel specifications

Edexcel's candidates revisit various aspects of accounting and finance in each of the three A2 units. Unit 4, Analysis and decision making, includes:

* cost analysis, including standard costing, contribution as an aid to decision making, cost and pricing and responsibility accounting (cost and profit centres);
* ratio analysis;
* investment appraisal.

Unit 5, Business planning, includes:

* sources of finance;
* debt versus equity finance;
* the role of budget accounts in the planning process.

The synoptic unit, 6, has little explicitly on accounting and finance, but clearly an understanding of accounting and finance is essential in any synoptic understanding of business.

The OCR's specifications

Unit 5 is a specialist but optional unit in accounting and finance. It requires an in-depth look at the topic as well as the AS and A2 topics found in other specifications. It stresses:

* the roles of accounting and financial decision making;
* accounting concepts;
* full absorption and marginal costing;
* valuation of assets;
* accounting as a basis for decision making;
* investment appraisal (including IRR);
* sources of finance;
* budgets;
* ratio analysis.

Students not opting for accounting and finance will find that both the Business thematic enquiry (unit 8) and Project (unit 9) will require an understanding of accounting and finance. The synoptic unit, 10, makes explicit reference to cash flow, liquidity, profitability and variance analysis.

Approaching the topics

As we have seen, the specifications cover broadly the same material, although there are differences in:

* the ways it is packaged;
* where the emphasis is placed;
* particular details (such as the inclusion or not of IRR).

Leaving aside the particulars, the accounting and finance part of an AS or A2 level course should cover the following.

The role of accounting and finance in businesses

In this area, the following should be covered:

* analysis of cost and benefits;
* the provision of evidence for decision making;
* the limitations of financial data for decision making;
* provision of information for stakeholders.

Accounting concepts

Here, the following should be understood:

- the implications of the concepts for the construction and interpretation of accounts;
- accounting rules and the protection of stakeholders.

Profit and loss accounts

It has never been the practice to ask questions involving the construction of accounts, but, to enhance learning, it is useful for students to be able to do just this. Candidates can be asked to manipulate accounts to answer 'What if ... ?' questions, and they are often asked to interpret profit and loss accounts with reference to:

- sales revenue;
- cost of sales;
- overheads;
- gross and net profit;
- the appropriation of profits.

Ratio analysis is a feature of A2 level, although at AS level the number and types ratios candidates are required to know is limited.

Balance sheets

Similar comments apply to balance sheets, with particular emphasis being placed on:

- fixed assets;
- working capital;
- liquidity ratios;
- sources of finance.

Candidates should also understand the linkages between the two accounts – for example, that retained profits shown in a profit and loss account are transferred to the corresponding balance sheet.

Special care should be accorded to reserves on balance sheets, for two reasons:

- many students continue to believe that reserves represent a pool of cash to finance investment, when, in fact, this is merely a technique to ensure that assets net of all liabilities equate with shareholders' equity;
- most students understand retained profits are a reserve, but few seem to remember revaluation and share premiums are also reserves.

Ratio analysis

The range of ratios candidates are required to know is one distinction between AS and A2 level. At AS level, the emphasis is on liquidity and profitability, whereas, at A2 the list is extended to include efficiency, gearing and shareholder ratios. The mechanical calculation of a ratio might not prove difficult, but remembering formulae and extracting the data often proves troublesome. In addition to calculating ratios, candidates should be able to:

- draw conclusions about their findings;
- set their findings in context;
- use historical and/or inter-firm comparisons;
- understand the limitations of ratio analysis.

Asset valuation

This includes stock valuation, the depreciation of fixed assets and valuation of a business. It is noticeable that the LIFO/FIFO methods of stock valuation have been reduced in importance in recent syllabi and this is also the case in the new specifications (they are even explicitly excluded in the AQA's). Nevertheless, it is important for candidates to realize that the way stock is valued has implications for cost of sales, profits as stated in the profit and loss account and the value of stock in the balance sheet.

This topic should be a way of reinforcing students' understanding of the limitations of accounting information. A similar comment can be made about depreciation of fixed assets. The straight line method is present in all specifications, although the reducing balance method should also be taught.

Most candidates understand depreciation in relation to the balance sheet, but greater stress needs to be placed on the fact that:

- net book value is not necessarily the current market value of an asset;
- depreciation is a provision, not a cost;
- depreciation is not part of a cash statement;
- depreciation is a negative item in a profit and loss account.

Candidates should realize that the choice of method has implications for the profit and loss account and the balance sheet.

The evaluation of a business as a going concern is a useful exercise in terms of student appreciation of the limitations of a balance sheet. It is also an opportunity to introduce the notion of goodwill and other intangible assets.

Cash statements

Cash flow forecasts are an essential part of any AS and A2 level course, but 'after the event' cash flow statements tend to be rather neglected, both in terms of specifications and their treatment in A level courses. However, candidates should understand the:

- distinction between sales revenue and cash inflow;
- distinction between purchases of inputs and cash outflow;
- methods of forecasting cash flow;
- role of cash budgets in working capital management;
- role of cash budgets in raising finance;
- link between cash flow and successive balance sheets;
- reason for depreciation not involving a cash flow.

Sources of finance

Examiners and specifications designers are always anxious that 'sources of finances' is not just a descriptive list of the same. It is essential that the topic be approached from the following perspectives:

- the implications of sources for the balance sheets;
- the implication of sources for gearing and, therefore, control and profits;
- the cost of capital;
- matching sources to uses;
- factors affecting choice of finance;
- evaluation of sources of finances.

Cost and management accounting (CMA)

Although it might not feature explicitly in questions, it is useful for candidates to understand how CMA differs from financial accounting. They should be aware of the purpose of CMA, its role and the different conceptions and rules. As CMA is accounting for decision making, it is especially relevant in a Business Studies course.

Costing

This is both an AS and A2 topic. Candidates are required to understand:

- the classifications of costs;
- the behaviour of costs with respect to changes in the level of production;
- methods of costing;
- allocation of overheads;
- the concept of contribution and its importance in decisions relating to special order contracts, deleting the unprofitable product and the 'make or buy' decision;
- break-even analysis, its roles and limitations;

- the relationship between costs and pricing policy;
- the behaviour of costs and budgets;
- responsibility accounting, with particular reference to cost and profit centres.

Budgets

Candidates should understand the nature of a budget account and the assumptions on which it is based. They should be introduced to cash budgets (cash flow forecasts), budget profit and loss accounts, budget balance sheets, sales budgets, production budgets and marketing budgets. They should place budgets in the context of planning, monitoring and control. They should be able to:

- construct and manipulate a simple budget;
- calculate simple variances and draw appropriate conclusions;
- describe the roles of budgets in terms of management responsibility and accountability.

Variances

Candidates should be able to calculate simple variances against either standard costs or budgets. The detailed variance analysis that was a feature of the original UCLES (Cambridge) syllabus seems not to be a feature of Curriculum 2000 specifications, but candidates should still be able to draw conclusions about the nature and possible causes of variances. They should be viewed in the context of a monitoring and review process for the next planning cycle.

Investment appraisal

This is a key Business Studies topic as it is about decision making using quantitative analysis and qualitative factors. Not only is it important at both levels, it is one of those analytical techniques that distinguish a good student project from a merely average one.

We have seen that the choice of techniques varies from one specification to another (with IRR being left out of some). Payback, accounting rate of return (ARR) and net present value (NPV) feature in all specifications and, in relation to each, candidates should:

- be able to employ the techniques to reach a decision;
- understand the nature of the data on which the techniques are based;
- understand the limitations of the techniques;
- be able to evaluate the techniques, especially when they produce conflicting results;
- understand the non-financial factors that should be taken into account.

Delivering operations management

The QCA's criteria require the following topics to be included in all specifications:

*   operational efficiency with respect to scale, capacity utilization and methods of organizing production;
*   stock control and resource management;
*   waste management and minimization;
*   pollution control;
*   quality assurance;
*   continuous improvement;
*   training;
*   research and development;
*   new product development and design;
*   the use of decision-making techniques in operations management – although it is not specified, this refers to critical path analysis and other techniques of operational research.

The distinction between AS and A2 levels is expressed in terms of the following focus statements (quoted from the QCA's subject criteria):

'In AS specifications the study of operations management should focus on the way organizations use inputs and manage business processes efficiently to satisfy customers.

A2 level specifications should require students to analyse and evaluate the use of different operations management tools to enhance decision making in order to improve efficiency and quality.'

Notice that the AS statement seems to focus on 'efficiency' in a static sense, whereas at A2 level there appears to be a greater emphasis on analysis and evaluation, on improvements in efficiency and quality, and on the use of analytical techniques to aid decision making.

Operations management at AS level

The AQA's specifications

Operations management is combined with people in organizations in unit 2 of the AQA's specifications. The specifications are divided into three parts: productive efficiency, controlling operations and lean production.
   Productive efficiency combines the following:

*   economies and diseconomies of scale;
*   capacity utilization, underutilization and ways of increasing usage;
*   capital versus labour-intensive methods;
*   job, batch and flow;
*   the trade-off between productivity and flexibility, such as standardized products and mass production.

Controlling operations unites stock control (graphical representation, but not calculations) with quality control and assurance. Benchmarking is also included in this section.

Lean production incorporates:

- cell production – linking with people;
- just-in-time – linking with IT, suppliers, purchasing policy and people;
- waste minimization;
- time-based management – shorter product development times and simultaneous engineering;
- continuous improvement and Kaizen groups.

The Edexcel specifications

Production (rather than 'operations') is included in unit 2, where it is combined with marketing. The Edexcel specifications cover similar ground to the AQA's, including:

- methods of organizing production;
- lean production;
- capacity utilization;
- economies and diseconomies of scale;
- resource management;
- stock control;
- just-in-time versus just-in-case;
- quality assurance and control;
- quality circles and Total Quality Management (TQM);
- *Kaizen*;
- improving quality by training.

Combining marketing and production in the same unit opens the way for questions on the interfaces between these two areas of management. This could involve questions on production runs, batch sizes and product variations. Shorter product development times will give a firm a competitive advantage. Quality is clearly both a production and a marketing issue.

The OCR's specifications

Operations management is included with four other functional areas of management in units 2 and 3, Business behaviour and Business decisions. The operations management part of the unit specifications includes the same material as is contained in the AQA's and Edexcel's specifications, namely:

- job, batch, flow and cell;
- lean production;
- productive efficiency;
- scale of operations;
- capital utilization;
- stock control;
- just-in-time;
- waste;
- quality;
- training to improve quality;
- continuous improvement;
- bench marking;
- efficiency to satisfy customers.

In a unit in which it is combined with all four other functional areas of management, there are endless possibilities for hybrid questions linking two or more areas. In addition to the links with people and marketing mentioned above, there is also a possibility of questions linking production and cost accounting.

The students return to operations management in the decision-making unit, unit 3. The awarding body has identified the following production decisions:

- production objectives and their relationships to marketing objectives;
- decisions relating to production methods;
- capacity utilization and capital intensity;

- the importance of cost–benefit analysis in decision making;
- reconciling the interests of stakeholders.

Operations management at A2 level

The AQA's specifications

Students revisit operations management in unit 4, which builds on material covered in AS unit 2. The prologue states that 'candidates are required to analyse and evaluate the use of different operations management tools to enhance decision making in order to improve efficiency and quality.'

In particular, candidates at A2 level develop their understanding of productive efficiency with reference to research and development and critical path analysis. The former should be linked to product design, product lifecycles and market research. The latter requires an understanding of the business implication of critical path analysis for 'efficiency in business decision making, time-based management and working capital control.'

Students enhance their understanding of controlling operations by a study of the applications of IT within and between businesses. Stress is laid on stock control, computer-aided design (CAD), computer-aided manufacturing (CAM), communications, budgetary control and teleworking.

The final section relates to geographical location (within and outside the UK) and facilities. The specifications state that the 'focus must be on business-based decision making using methods such as break-even analysis or investment appraisal.' These two techniques of analysis will have been carried over from previous units.

Edexcel's specifications

The coverage of production at A2 level is found mainly in unit 4, Analysis and decision making. This includes:

- research and development;
- new product development;
- adding value;
- CAD;
- value analysis;
- technological change;
- lean production, including time-based competition.

Production plans are mentioned in unit 5, Business planning, but it is noticeable that it is not given the emphasis in these specifications that is accorded to financial, marketing and human resource plans.

There is no explicit reference to production in the synoptic unit, 6, but clearly the main themes in the study of operations must be present in a synoptic unit. These themes include efficiency, capacity utilization, quality and waste minimization.

The OCR's specifications

Unit 7 is a specialist, but optional, unit on operations management. The main areas covered are the:

- management of the production process, including production planning, location, scale, division of labour, production methods and information management (management information systems);
- constraints on production, including the environment, resources, waste management/pollution control and the law;
- costing, including approaches to costing, standard costs and break-even analysis;
- productive efficiency, including productivity, capacity utilization, production control (such as critical path), employees, work study, stock control, quality control and value analysis;
- technology, including the use of IT in operations;
- research and development.

Candidates choosing one of the other optional units should not neglect their study of operations management in the A2 level year. The operational management themes might appear in the synoptic unit 10, Business strategy.

Approaching the topics

The review of the specifications shows that there are major differences between awarding bodies in terms of the extent and depth of coverage and the ways in which operations management is packaged. The most extensive coverage is in the optional unit of the OCR's specifications, although it is likely that most candidates will not be taking the operations option. Candidates following the AQA's specifications will cover operations management in one paper at each level, whereas candidates following Edexcel's will cover it mainly at AS level, but will visit some operations/production topics in various A2 level units.

We can identify the main topics and themes as being the following.

Production processes – job, batch, flow

This topic must go beyond mere description to an analysis. The job, batch, flow model should be used to analyse the implications of choice of process for:

- the level of investment required;
- production planning and control;
- capacity utilization;
- scheduling;
- labour requirements;
- quality control;
- variations in the products;
- flexibility.

Scale of production and costs

Again, it is necessary to go beyond a description of the types of economy of scale towards a higher level of analysis. This involves the calculation of average costs and understanding the implications of a minimum efficient plant size any one scale of operation. One misconception that it is important to dispel is that economies of scale result from an increase in the level of production. In other words, spreading overheads over a larger volume of production is not economies of scale. The latter result from an increase in the scale of production and is, therefore, a long-run, rather than a short-run phenomenon.

The well-known diseconomies of scale tend to have their origin in people management. One idea to stress is that diseconomies of scale are not inevitable – management strategies can be developed to ward off the onset of diseconomies of scale.

Lean production

This is a very popular topic within the operations management part of the course. It should be stressed to students that just-in-time techniques are merely one part of lean production. Moreover, just-in-time approaches to stock purchases and holding are well known, but less well known is just-in-time manufacturing by the firm itself. The ideas to stress are:

- the ways in which just-in-time production is organized;
- the implications of just-in-time production for relationships with outside suppliers;
- its implications for human resources management;
- its benefits;
- how production is organized in cells and the implications of this on the layout of equipment and for the workforce;
- how lead times can be reduced by time-based competition strategies;
- the implications of shorter product development times for firms' competitive strategies;
- the concept of 'waste' and how it can be reduced;
- the philosophy of continuous improvement, its advantages, how it differs from improvement in the Western model and how it can be achieved.

Productive efficiency

'Efficiency' should be distinguished from 'effectiveness' in that efficiency involves both input and output. This is a topic that lends itself to quantification and an analysis of how it can be improved. The next four topics should be taught in terms of improving efficiency.

Capacity utilization

Underused capacity represents a waste and, therefore, a failure to achieve maximum efficiency. Students should understand that both supply and demand factors often cause producers to operate at less than full capacity. Underutilization because of bottlenecks or production problems provides a lead into issues relating to production planning, scheduling and control.

Critical path analysis (CPA)

This is the one operations research technique that is common to all specifications. In addition to the quantitative aspects of critical path analysis (that is, minimum times, earliest start, latest finish, total and free float), students should understand CPA in terms of planning and deployment of resources. The critical path diagram can be analysed in conjunction with Gantt charts, which, surprisingly, are not mentioned in some specifications.

Work study

Arising out of Taylor's scientific management, work study should be seen as a technique to improve efficiency. Students should understand that it involves both work measurement (the basis of piece-work rates and costing) and method study (to improve operations). They should have some understanding of the methods employed, the benefits and the human implications of work study.

Training

From the operations management perspective, training should be approached in terms of the acquisition of skills and improvement in efficiency and quality. Training represents investment in human capital and has implications in terms of cost and efficiency.

Pollution control and waste management

These topics should not be confined to legal and ethical considerations. Although pollution laws do act as constraint on firms, we should also approach the topic positively, as reducing costs by recycling or as a way of creating marketing opportunities. Waste minimization reduces costs when the products are recycled. 'Environmentally friendly' products also appeal to green consumers.

Stock control

This topic should not be divorced from production planning and from the purchasing of inputs. A graphical analysis of stock movements will identify re-order levels, re-order quantities, lead times and buffer stocks. Calculations of economic order quantities are not required, but the topic is a useful point of entry for a consideration of the problems of managing in times of uncertainty. Comparisons could be made between a textbook stock graph and real-life movements of stock.

So as to integrate it with accounting, stock control can be linked with the appearance of stock in both balance sheets and profit and loss accounts.

Research and development (R&D)

New product development is a topic that links operations with marketing. It should be emphasized that there are several stages in new product development and that all kinds of factors (both marketing and production) need to be taken into account in the design of a product or deciding to abort the product before it reaches the launch stage. R&D can also be the basis for understanding intangible aspects and is another source of competitive advantage.

Quality management

Students should understand the:

- differences between quality control, quality assurance and Total Quality Management (TQM);
- mathematical basis of sampling;
- implications of end-of-the-line quality control compared with concurrent quality management;
- requirements for, and benefits of, a successful quality assurance programme;
- philosophy of TQM;
- implications of TQM for human resources management and an organization's culture;
- roles and benefits of quality circles.

Information technology

The IT part of the operations management specifications stress that it is an aid to planning and control. Reference should be made to CAD, CAM, robotics and management information systems. Students are not required to know how it works or develop their IT skills. Instead, IT should be seen as a source of competitive advantage, as it enhances planning and control, provides for greater flexibility, increases the productivity of labour and reduces lead times.

Delivering people in organizations

The QCA's criteria identify people in organizations as the fourth area to be covered in an AS and A2 level course in Business Studies. In the student text, this material can be found mainly in Part VI, People in organizations. To some extent, this is merely another name for the same thing, although it could be argued that HRM focuses on the use of human resources to achieve organizational objectives, whereas 'people in organizations' suggests that students also consider the issues from the employees' perspective (the views of those who are the human resources). At its most superficial, this could be confined to what it is like to work in a particular organization. Alternatively, it could involve a more analytical look at organizational behaviour.

The QCA's specification lays down the following list of mandatory topics:

- human resource planning (formerly known as manpower planning);
- organizational structure and design;
- motivational theory;
- leadership and management styles;
- employment law;
- employee relations, both collective and individual;
- employees' participation in decision making.

The relevant focus statements distinguish between the two levels as follow (quoted from the QCA's subject specifications):

'AS specifications should require students to understand the significance of various management and organizational structures for a business and its employees. Students should recognize the opportunities and constraints, in relation to people in organizations, created by the business/legal environment and to appreciate the contributions of selected management theories.

A2 level specifications should require students to understand the interrelationships between organizational structure, leadership style and motivation in a business and to evaluate the implications of these for the effective planning and management of human resources.'

The AS level, focus, therefore, is on structures, opportunities and constraints, as well as selected theories (such as those of Elton Mayo, Douglas McGregor and Frederick Herzberg). At A2 level, a more rounded look at the topic is required, linking organizational structure, management (or leadership) styles and motivation. In addition, there is a greater stress on evaluation and applying ideas in the practical management of human resources.

People in organizations at AS level
The AQA's specifications

At AS level, people in organizations constitutes half of unit 2, People and operations management. This involves full coverage of the 'people' topics that feature in the QCA's criteria, namely:

- management structures, incorporating culture and change;

- organizational design;
- management by objectives (MBO);
- delegation;
- consultation, including quality circles;
- motivation theory;
- motivation in practice;
- financial incentives;
- leadership and management styles;
- human resource planning;
- recruitment and selection;
- induction;
- training, including reluctance to train staff as a market failure, in economists' usage of the phrase.

Edexcel's specifications

Alone of the three English awarding bodies, Edexcel has not produced a unit that wholly, or even mainly, is 'people in organizations'. Instead, the 'people' material occurs in a number of separate units at the two levels. At AS level, unit 1, Business in context, incorporates key HRM material:

- functional areas of management;
- internal structure of organizations;
- communications theory;
- communication nets;
- failure of communications;
- motivational theory;
- job design.

Edexcel's specifications leave other aspects of HRM to A2 level, although participation in the form of quality circles and training to improve quality feature in unit 2 where this material is integrated into the operations management part of the specifications.

The OCR's specifications

People in organizations constitutes one-quarter of units 2 and 3, Business behaviour and Business decisions. The people section includes a useful focus statement that is included as a prologue:

'The study should focus on understanding the significance of various management and organizational structures for a business and its employees. Candidates should recognize the opportunities and constraints in relation to people in organizations, created by the business/legal environment. They should appreciate the contributions made by selected management theorists.'

The material covered consists of:

- workforce planning, linked to the objectives of organizations;
- organizational design;
- organizational principles;
- motivational theories and practices;
- leadership;
- money as a motivator;
- recruitment and selection;
- training;
- severance;
- labour turnover.

Students return to some of this material in the AS level unit 3 in which 'The acquisition, management and use of human resources' features in the topics of planning and decision making.

People in organizations at A2 level
The AQA's specifications

Candidates return to people in organizations in unit 5, People and operations management. At A2 level, emphasis is placed on:

* communications;
* the relationships between communications and morale;
* problems with communications;
* employer and employee relations at both the individual and collective levels;
* participation of employees;
* trade unions and ACAS;
* industrial disputes and their resolution;
* new unionism;
* principles of employment law;
* 'soft' and 'hard' HRM;
* workforce planning;
* pay as part of an HRM strategy;
* personnel effectiveness – productivity, turnover, absenteeism, health and safety.

Edexcel's specifications

Candidates study the following people topics in unit 4, Analysis and decision making:

* industrial relations;
* collective and individual bargaining;
* ACAS and employment tribunals;
* participation of employees;
* employment law, including EU law.

In unit 5, Business planning, candidates study:

* the labour market;
* recruitment and selection;
* job specifications and descriptions;
* induction;
* payment to labour;
* training and development;
* leadership and motivation;
* leadership and human resource planning.

The synoptic unit, 6, entitled Corporate strategy, includes sections on organizational culture and the management of change.

The OCR's specifications

As with the other functional areas of management, the OCR offers a specialist optional paper on people in organizations (covered in unit 6). Interestingly, the equivalent optional paper in the pre-2000 syllabus was called Human resources management, but, in keeping with the QCA's criteria, the unit has reverted to its former title of People in organizations. This specialist option provides comprehensive coverage of 'people' topics, including:

* communications and their impacts;
* group behaviour;
* organizing and controlling the activities of people at work;
* motivation and morale;
* leadership styles;
* management of change;
* recruitment and training to acquire skills;
* anti-discrimination legislation/equal opportunities policies;

- contracts of employment;
- legal aspects of employment;
- health and safety;
- employee relations;
- health and safety;
- employment tribunals;
- dismissal;
- trade unions;
- individual and collective bargaining;
- the Social Chapter and EU directives;
- ACAS;
- participation of employees;
- remuneration.

For those students not taking the People in organizations option, it should be remembered that HRM is likely to feature heavily in the synoptic unit.

Approaching the topics

The review of the content suggests that the material is packaged in different ways by the various awarding bodies. It is noticeable that, in the case of Edexcel (and to a lesser extent the other bodies), the distinction between AS and A2 levels in the case of people in organizations is not just in terms of the depth of the coverage, but also in terms of the content itself. Consequently, these considerations must impact on the treatment of at least some of the topic.

Defining the topic

The title given to the topic in the QCA's criteria is significant. As observed above, 'people in organizations' at its simplest could be a rather descriptive account of what it is like to work within an organization. At its most complex, it could take the form of a sociological or psychological analysis of organizational behaviour. Whatever the depth of the analysis, the phrase 'people in organizations' suggests that we approach the topic from the perspectives of both the employer and employees.

The approach of personnel management or human resource management is from the perspective of the organization. Employees are resources (in fact, the most important resources for modern service-sector organizations) deployed in order that the organization achieves its objectives. The HRM approach places people at the centre of strategic management. The old term 'personnel management' tends to have a 'welfareist' ring to it, whereas HRM (hard or soft) links people with objectives and strategies. HRM is not just a new name, it is a new philosophy. Moreover, personnel management is a specialist function, whereas everyone who manages a person is a human resources manager.

The aspects of HRM to stress are the:

- HRM philosophy itself;
- link between HRM, objectives and strategies;
- distinction between personnel management and HRM;
- distinction between hard and soft HRM.

Human resources planning

This is a useful umbrella topic that can include detailed human resources strategies and policies such as recruitment and selection, training, downsizing and pay. Human resources planning also provides a useful link with overall corporate planning and, consequently, is a likely candidate for any synoptic question.

The particular aspects of human resources planning to stress are:

- supply and demand in the labour market;
- forecasting human resources requirements;
- formulation of human resources strategies to acquire, retain and develop human resources;
- legal and other constraints.

Organizational structure and design

The organizational principles part of a Business Studies course should start with the writings of classical theorists, such as Henri Fayol. It should then look in turn at organizational concepts, such as the various designs of organizations (by type, by height), looking at issues such as the span of control, tall versus flatter organizations, delayering and centralization versus decentralization. This is clearly not the most enjoyable part of the course, but can be re-invigorated by linking up structures with planning, organisational culture and change.

The modern trend is towards:

- flatter structures;
- delayering;
- flexibility;
- maximizing the use of human resources;
- releasing the potential of human resources.

By linking organizational issues with objectives, strategy and planning, it is possible to make what could otherwise be a dull topic enjoyable.

Motivational theories

The key aspects of this popular topic are the:

- definition of motivation;
- distinction between motivation and morale;
- ideas of the key theorists, which usually include Frederick Taylor, Elton Mayo, Abraham Maslow, Douglas McGregor and Frederick Herzberg.

It is important for candidates to understand what the theorists really said and meant. So, for instance, Taylor saw scientific management working for the benefit of workers as well as management. Equally, Maslow and Hertzberg did not dismiss the importance of pay in motivating the workforce for, as a hygiene factor, adequate pay is essential to avoid creating a dissatisfied and a demotivated workforce. However, although adequate pay is a necessary condition for a motivated workforce, it is not a sufficient condition. Finally, McGregor did not believe there were just two types of workers – X and Y. Instead, he argued that different managers held two competing sets of assumptions about workers and that workers responded according to the manner in which they were treated.

Motivation in practice

The emphasis in this subject is on practical methods of motivating the workforce – in other words, linking up theory with practice. This involves linking theory with:

- different systems of payment;
- job design, including job rotation, enlargement and enrichment;
- different ways to enrich a job;
- leadership and management styles;
- communications;
- participation and consultation.

Leadership and management styles

Although theories have moved on from the styles approach to leadership, the emphasis at AS and A2 levels is still very much on the styles approach. Hence, the advantages and disadvantages of authoritarian, democratic and *laissez-faire* styles should be emphasized, but should be set within the context of motivating the workforce and the achievement of organizational objectives. Students should also understand that the key is the appropriateness of the style to the particular situation. The OCR's specialist optional unit, People in organizations, includes a reference to the dilemma of meeting the needs of both the people and the task. This dilemma is especially well analysed in the Blake and Mouton management grid.

Employment law

The law relating to employment is given considerable prominence in the QCA's criteria and, therefore, in each of the specifications. Candidates need to understand the law relating to:

- contracts of employment;
- the rights of employees;
- dismissal;
- discrimination and equal opportunities;
- health and safety;
- pay – equal pay, the minimum wage;
- trade unions and labour relations.

In addition to UK law, attention must be paid to EU Law, especially as the UK has now acceded to the Social Chapter. It should be appreciated that this statement of high principles:

- acts as a constraint on the UK government and Parliament, whose laws can be challenged by UK workers if they are contrary to the Social Chapter;
- allows for the passage of EU directives on employment issues by a system of qualified majority voting at the Council of Ministers – to date, few directives have been issued under the Social Chapter, but there is the potential for wide-ranging measures.

The law is continually evolving and this is especially the case with the employment rights of part-time employees. The combination of EU law and the UK's own equal opportunities laws has meant that part-time workers (who are disproportionately female) now enjoy the same rights, pro rata, as full-time workers. This eliminates the common argument that employers appoint part-timers because the latter enjoy fewer legal rights.

On the topic of equal opportunities, it is important to stress that an understanding of the law should be combined with an understanding of equal opportunities policies developed by firms.

Employer employee relations

Again, this can be rather uninteresting if the focus is solely on types of unions and their structures. It is preferable to concentrate on the:

- bargaining process;
- trend towards local, and even individual, bargaining;
- rise of new unionism – single unions, no-strike deals, single table, single status;
- causes and resolution of disputes;
- role of ACAS;
- role of trade unions in the modern economy.

Participation

A description of the types of employee participation schemes should be set against a background of the:

- benefits of participation to an organization and its workforce;
- preconditions for successful participation;
- contrast with old-style labour relations.

Groups and teams

The starting point should be Elton Mayo's later studies at the Hawthorne plant. This can be taken further with later studies, such as those of the stages in the formation of groups (B. W. Tuckman), what makes for an effective group and roles within a team (R. Meredith Belbin). The stress should be laid on:

- the advantages of working together in groups and teams;
- motivation;
- group/team effectiveness.

This topic can be successfully integrated with operations management topics, such as lean production and production processes.

Communications

The HRM stress should be on:

- the role of communication in the management process;
- the interrelationships between communication and organization design/styles of leadership;
- communication and motivation;
- communication and working in groups;
- causes and consequences of communication failure.

Reward

Payments to employees tend to be rather neglected in A level courses. However, students should have an understanding of:

- the different types of payment systems;
- time rates versus piece-rates;
- how to set piece-rates – this links up with work study and work measurement, which should be included in the operations management part of the course;
- profit- or performance-related pay;
- broad-banding and other aspects of 'new pay' – this topic links up with motivation and organizational design;
- the non-pay aspects of reward management.

By emphasizing reward management (rather than employees' pay or remuneration), the topic is placed within a framework of strategies for HRM.

Organizational culture

Although in terms of the criteria and specifications, culture is placed in the 'objectives' section, it should be stressed that culture is reflected in leadership style, communications, motivation and other aspects of HRM. Organizational culture has, after all, been defined as 'how we do things around here'.

Schemes of assessment

We have seen that the awarding bodies approach the material in a variety of ways. In essence, the same topics occur in each, although there are differences at the margins and in emphasis. The main differences lie in the ways in which the material is packaged in the specifications and in the ways in which it is assessed.

The awarding bodies use different combinations of assessment techniques, as shown in the Table 7.1.

Table 7.1: Summary of the awarding bodies' assessment techniques

Awarding body	Level	Unit	Forms of assessment	A level weighting (%)
AQA	AS	1	Stimulus questions	15
	AS	2	Stimulus questions	15
	AS	3	Unseen case study	20
	A2	4	Unseen case study	15
	A2	5	Business report *and* essay *or* project	15
	A2	6	Unseen case study	20
Edexcel	AS	1	Structured questions	15
	AS	2	Unseen case study	20
	AS	3	Structured questions	15
	A2	4	Structured questions	15
	A2	5	Unseen case study *or* coursework assignment	15
	A2	6	Pre-seen case study	20
OCR	AS	1	Unseen case study	15
	AS	2	Data response	15
	AS	3	Pre-seen case study	20
	A2	4–7	Unseen case study	15
	A2	8	Project	15
	A2	9	*or* report based on unseen case study	15
	A2	10	Pre-seen case study	20

The table shows that the assessment techniques can be classified as:

• data response, stimulus response or structured questions;
• case study-based questions – this classification can be subdivided in pre-seen and unseen case studies;
• business report;
• essay (in practice, the free response question is now confined to AQA-specification courses);
• project or coursework assignments.

Preparing students for a pre-seen case study exam

The OCR and Edexcel issue some case studies in advance of exams. This provides an opportunity for students to investigate the issues identified in a case study. Question-spotting is natural in this situation, but always warn students that:

- additional information on the day might give a whole new slant to the material;
- although topics can be identified, the actual question they will be asked is far from predictable;
- they must not neglect their general revision.

Positive tips to offer are:

- use the key concepts in Jewell or a dictionary of terms to define all specialist words in the case study;
- undertake analysis of the case study using techniques such as SWOT and PEST;
- investigate business issues related to the market in which the firm operates;
- use quantitative data to rehearse answers to possible questions, but be prepared to respond to additional information on the day;
- the focus of any good case study is problems to be resolved, decisions to be made and providing an answer to the question 'What would you advise the firm to do? – in AS and A2 level exams the questions will not be as open-ended as that, but they are generally structured towards this end.

Every word in a case study can have great significance. Students are ill advised to ignore the meanings and nuances of words. However, be careful not to exaggerate the importance of some points in the case study and remember that the subject is Business Studies – not economics, government and politics, sociology or environmental science – so concentrate on business issues.

Unseen case studies

The kind of investigation that is a feature of pre-seen case studies cannot, of course, occur with unseen case studies. The advice that lecturers should offer candidates is as follows:

- read and re-read case studies before tackling the questions;
- explore the linkages between topics within the specifications;
- choose appropriate theories and techniques of analysis to answer the questions;
- answer the questions as set and reach a clear conclusion based on reasoning and evaluation.

Structured questions

Structured questions take the form of data response questions (where the answer is gathered from the evidence) and stimulus response (where the text is a stimulus). In practice, the distinction between the two is not clear-cut and they share the common characteristic that questions are linked to written text and/or numerical data and are not free response questions.

These types of questions provide the opportunity to study large, real-life businesses rather than focusing just on the hypothetical (and usually small) firms that feature in case studies. These questions provide the opportunity to look at general issues relating to business in the UK.

The advice to offer to students is as follows:

- read and understand the text before looking at the questions;
- answer all the questions, noting how the marks are allocated;
- consider linkages between topics in the syllabus;
- avoid answers that either paraphrase the text or are totally detached from it;
- demonstrate that you understand and can analyse the text;
- always consider the limitations of the data and take a critical view of data;
- take every opportunity to practise using past questions;
- show the workings for numerical questions;
- apply knowledge to the situation at hand;
- select appropriate knowledge and analytical techniques;
- integrate different areas of knowledge when answering questions;

- reach a clear conclusion by means of analysis and evaluation;
- compare students' answers with the published marking scheme.

Business reports

This approach is now becoming established in a variety of forms, in A level Business Studies. Although reports have some similarities to case studies in that material is presented and candidates analyse and evaluate it, reports have some distinctive features:

- they are more open-ended;
- candidates are required to write in a prescribed report format.

In terms of assisting preparation, the comments on unseen case studies are equally valid here, but candidates should be aware of the conventions of the report format and, in the case of the OCR, they should be made aware of the published assessment criteria contained in its specifications.

Projects

It is interesting that, despite the raising of the QCA's ceiling on coursework, there has been a reduction in the importance of coursework within the overall scheme of assessment of two of the awarding bodies. In each case, coursework is now optional and Edexcel's and the OCR's weighting has fallen compared with the syllabuses that preceded the 2000 specifications.

The first important piece of advice to give students relates to the nature of the task and the assessment criteria to be used.

The AQA requires students to produce a 3000-word project consisting of:

- a feasibility study for starting your own business;
- a study of a reorganization of the operations of a manufacturing or service business;
- a study of the effect on local firms of a significant external change;
- a study based on advertising;
- a case study of an entrepreneur;
- a study of operations management used in a local manufacturing business;
- a study of a firm's personnel performance indicators;
- a study of a firm's export performance and prospects;
  or
- an alternative that still 'allows candidates the opportunity to reach the higher levels of the assessment criteria' (AQA) (this is especially important advice that should also be taken on board by candidates of other awarding bodies) and the title should be chosen with assessment criteria in mind – always choose a topic that offers an opportunity to achieve the highest level of response in each category of the assessment criteria.

Edexcel's coursework is located in unit 5, Business planning. Edexcel prescribes two assignment questions, from which candidates select one title.

The awarding bodies all stress that the assessment criteria should inform the choice of topic for investigation and the structure of the report. Students should be given a copy of the criteria at the latest at the commencement of the coursework unit. As criteria are expressed in difficult language, it is important to interpret and explain the meanings of words such as 'application', 'analysis', 'synthesis' and 'evaluation'. It is also important that students understand the system of levels of response marking used in connection with both projects and examinations (see Table 7.2).

Table 7.2: Levels of response marking systems used by the awarding bodies

AQA	Edexcel	OCR
1 Knowledge and understanding (16) 2 Application of knowledge/ methodology (16) 3 Analysis of evidence (16) 4 Synthesis (10) 5 Evaluation (22) 6 Quality of written communication (4)	1 Demonstration of knowledge and critical understanding of specific content (20) 2 Application of knowledge and understanding to problems and issues arising from both familiar and unfamiliar situations (20) 3 Analysis of problems, issues and situations (20) 4 Evaluation, distinguishing between fact and opinion and assessing information from a variety of sources (20)	1 The skill with which the problem has been explained in context (5) 2 The skill with which appropriate and realistic objectives have been set (10) 3 Evidence of appropriate research method (10) 4 Evidence of appropriate primary and secondary research (10) 5 Evidence of understanding and use of appropriate Business Studies knowledge (15) 6 Selectivity, analysis and synthesis (15) 7 Evaluation, recommendation or strategy development (15) 8 Presentation (5) 9 Written communication (5)

The stated aims of the Edexcel assignment are as follows. Students will be involved in the process of primary research and data collection. The assignment will provide opportunities for students to collect and collate both primary and secondary information in a variety of ways. Students will be required to analyse and evaluate the information, including making judgements and drawing conclusions. Their findings should be presented in an appropriate form. It should encourage students to:

- investigate specific business activities by means of individual studies;
- collect, select and use business information in ways that are appropriate to the prescribed assignment;
- demonstrate awareness of a variety of solutions to business problems and the need to make reasoned statements and communicate these effectively;
- enhance underpinning knowledge.

The OCR states that there is no discrete subject content, but a report must:

- be investigative in nature, showing evidence of problem-solving skills;
- be based either on a single organization or on a more general business-related issue;
- use, analytically and with evaluation, business studies knowledge drawn from more than one element of the whole Business Studies core, as studied in units 1, 2, 3 and 10.
- be presented as a report, with a clear definition of the problem and setting objectives in pursuing it.

The topic chosen could arise from any form of personal or school-organized contact with any type of organization. The only requirement, in this respect, is that the topic should clearly be a business one, enabling the rigorous and effective use of the candidates' knowledge. The choice of project is for the candidate to make, but, in making that choice, reference should be made to:

- the requirements of the specification – the project should not require the candidate to use knowledge or techniques that are beyond the specifications, but should give clear opportunities to use knowledge from it;
- the assessment criteria – these give a strong indication of the requirement and of the basis on which the examiners will award marks.

The levels of response within each category are expressed in descending order. Candidates should be aware of the criteria so that they have the opportunity to reach the highest level. As an illustration of how this works, see Table 7.3, showing the marks for a single category taken from the AQA's assessment scheme. Up to 16 marks are available for analysis of evidence.

Table 7.3: The marks given for levels of response regarding analysis of evidence from the AQA's assessment scheme.

Levels	Marks	Quality of analysis of evidence
4	16–13	Substantial analysis of the data, selectively using various written and numerical techniques to identify causes and/or possible solutions and showing judgement in the use of the techniques.
3	12–9	Analysis of the data, selectively using various written and numerical techniques to demonstrate insight and depth.
2	8–5	Some analysis of the data, using various written and/or numerical techniques, showing some understanding, but lacking insight and depth.
1	4–1	Some analysis of the data presented, showing some understanding, but neither insight nor depth.
0	0	No analysis provided.

To reach the top level, there has to be 'substantial analysis', techniques must be used 'selectively', causes or solutions must be identified as a result of the analysis and judgement must be shown regarding how the techniques are used. Failure to conform to this descriptor will mean that examiners will look to the lower levels until they discover the descriptor that fits the way the project has been handled.

After fully briefing students on the requirements of the awarding body, it is then necessary to provide them with a framework for the structure of a report (see Table 7.4).

Table 7.4: How to structure a research report

Chapter/section	Content
Introduction	A precise explanation of what the research is about
Background	Background material on the company, its markets and competitors
Investigation	The methodology used Presentation of research findings
Analysis and evaluation	Analysis of results Evaluation of methods and results
Conclusion	A direct answer to the question posed Recommendations where appropriate
Bibliography	A list of all sources used
Appendices	Detailed data referred to, but not shown elsewhere

Advice on choosing a topic and title should revolve around the following questions.

- Is it legitimate within the specifications?
- Is it realistic for an A level candidate?
- Will information be available?
- Will it provide opportunities for candidates to score well on the criteria detailed in the marking scheme?
- Does it lead to a clear conclusion?

It is essential that candidates include some of the following techniques of analysis, where appropriate. These include written methods:

- SWOT (Strengths, Weaknesses, Opportunities, Threats) analysis;
- PEST (Political, Economic, Social, Technological) analysis;
- product lifecycles;
- the Boston Matrix;
- the Ansoff Matrix
- Porter's generic strategies.

Also, numerical techniques, such as:

- investment appraisals;
- break-even analysis;
- critical path analysis;
- decision trees;
- variance analysis;
- averages;
- correlations;
- costings;
- sampling theory.

Other vital points to impress on students are that:

- they must reach a clear conclusion that directly answers the questions in hand;
- there must be evidence, analysis and evaluation to back up their conclusions;
- they should evaluate and admit to any limitations of their chosen methodology;
- the report should be well presented with headings;
- there should be a 'flow' to the argument, with the candidate demonstrating that they are in control of the subject matter;
- the completion of successive drafts will improve the quality of the work;
- as the first line is the most difficult to write, they should get down to the task quickly, with the added bonus that it will get easier as they progress into the subject.

Table 7.5: Causes of failure

Poor titles	Marks lost
1 Too large	1 Objectives were not realistic, explained or followed
2 Vague and ill defined	2 Inappropriate methodology
3 Too descriptive	3 Failure to use theory
4 Little scope for analysis and evaluation	4 Absence of analysis or evaluation
5 Little scope for demonstration of business knowledge	5 Inappropriate analysis
	6 Absence of vital evidence for theory
6 Requires sensitive information	7 Failure to answer own question
7 Misunderstood by candidate	8 Evidence ignored
8 Divergence between title and project	9 Confusion – lack of control of subject matter
	10 Absence of conclusion
	11 Inappropriate conclusion
	12 Conclusion not backed up by evidence

The grades

Grades for each component of the A level are awarded at grading meetings held after the initial marking has been completed and the marks have been entered on computer files. The grading committee is responsible for identifying the scripts at the important grade boundaries (which are now A, C and E). In essence, they seek the weakest scripts that are still worthy of an A, a C and an E. To assist the members of the committee in their task, the QCA has drafted the following grade descriptors, which apply to all schemes of assessment. These descriptions apply to A level.

Grade A

Students will demonstrate in-depth knowledge and critical understanding of a wide range of business theories and concepts. They will apply this knowledge and understanding to analyse familiar and unfamiliar situations, problems and issues, using appropriate numerical and non-numerical techniques accurately. They will effectively evaluate evidence and arguments, making reasoned judgements to present appropriate and supported conclusions.

Grade C

Students will demonstrate knowledge and understanding of a range of business theories and concepts. They will apply this knowledge and understanding to analyse familiar and unfamiliar situations, problems and issues. They will use both numerical and non-numerical techniques. They will evaluate evidence and arguments to present reasoned conclusions.

Grade E

Students will demonstrate knowledge and understanding of a limited range of business theories and concepts. They will show some ability to use this knowledge and understanding in order to analyse familiar and unfamiliar situations, problems and issues. They will make some use of both numerical and non-numerical techniques. Students' evaluation of evidence and arguments will be limited.

Points to note

As a candidate moves up the grades, an improvement in performance is expected naturally, but not just in qualitative terms (a greater demonstration of higher-order skills) – in terms of frequency and appropriateness, too. Those awarded an A grade demonstrate:

- in-depth knowledge;
- critical understanding;
- application of appropriate techniques;
- accurate use of these techniques;
- evaluation of evidence and arguments;
- reasoned judgements;
- appropriate and supported conclusions.

The absence of one of these qualities in an individual question will not block students from achieving the grade, but examiners do expect to see that, on balance, these features are generally present in candidates' scripts.

At C grade, candidates are expected to demonstrate:

- knowledge and understanding (note the lack of 'in-depth');
- a range of theories and concepts (note the absence of 'wide');
- application (but note that 'Using ... techniques accurately' is left out);
- evaluation and conclusion (but note that the words 'effectively', 'reasoned' and 'supported' do not appear).

The descriptor for grade E uses the same structure as before, but note the reference to 'limited range', 'some use' and 'limited' evaluation.

These descriptors should become familiar to candidates as they strive for the higher grades. These can be achieved by increasing the depth of knowledge and understanding, demonstrating the higher-order skills more often and effectively, and reaching reasoned conclusions supported by evidence.

The grade descriptors can be used in conjunction with value-added data. For those not familiar with this, it should be explained that there are different methods of calculating input scores, but that the 'Greenhead' method is especially appropriate here. To calculate input scores, award:

- 4 marks for each A starred at GCSE;
- 3 marks for each A;

- 2 marks for each B;
- 1 mark for each C.

A value-added input score of 25 can be achieved with 8 A grades and 1 C grade in GCSE examinations. A score in single figures suggests that either the student did well in a small number of subjects or, more likely, gained a collection of C grades. Using the National Average Results Value Added Chart, it can be concluded that with:

- 23 points or more, the candidate should gain grade B in Business Studies;
- 16 points or more, they should gain a C;
- 12 points or more, they should gain a D;
- 4 points or more, they should gain an E.

These are based on past performance statistics. There clearly is a danger of demotivating candidates, however, if they discover that the best they can hope for is an E. The scores should be seen as an indication of the minimum target grade. Therefore, a 23 points plus candidate who achieves less than a grade B will have performed less well than they should have. Value-added input scores can also be used to motivate students to 'defy the statistics' and achieve a better-than-expected result.

Useful web sites

Qualifications and Curriculum Authority (QCA)	www.qca.org.uk
Assessment and Qualifications Alliance (AQA – formerly AEB, NEAB and City & Guilds)	www.aqa.org.uk
Edexcel (formerly ULEAC and BTEC)	www.edexcel.org.uk
OCR (formerly Oxford and Cambridge and RSE Examination Boards)	www.ocr.org.uk

Key skills

One feature of Curriculum 2000 is the extension of key skills from GNVQ courses to all courses aimed at the 16–19 age group. The key skills qualifications cover communication, application of number and IT, although students are also encouraged to develop and gain accreditation in the wider key skills of working with others, problem solving and improving their own learning.

Each of the AS and A2 level subjects is required to make a contribution to the development of key skills in students. Business Studies can play a key role in the delivery of key skills – especially for arts and social sciences students who have not chosen mathematical or computer-based subjects and for predominantly sciences students for whom AS or A2 Business Studies might be an invaluable opportunity to develop communication skills. Communication, IT and application of number (as well as the three wider key skills) are essential in business and are, therefore, essential to students of business. This is reflected in the specifications of the awarding bodies. For instance, the OCR's specifications (see Appendix A of the specifications) are designed to support the following objectives:

*   enabling candidates to appreciate the importance of working with others and contributing to the work of teams and, during the course, gain personal experience of this and develop their skill in these areas;
*   development of skills of communication, including those implicit in quality of language, and application of number, and the ability to use these in investigations in decision-making and in problem-solving situations;
*   develop knowledge and competence in the use of language, concepts, conventions, techniques, theories and decision-making processes appropriate to, and used within, business behaviour;
*   develop skills of primary research, presentation of data, analysis and evaluation;
*   develop knowledge and critical understanding of the contribution IT can make to every aspect of the Business Studies and develop skills of using IT and applying it where relevant and appropriate.

Business Studies can be seen as the vehicle for development of key skills, but:

*   it is important that the burden is shared with other subjects;
*   this must not distort study of the subject.

Assignments and exercises should be developed that, at one and the same time, develop and test understanding of the subject matter and the key skills of the student.

The key skills specifications

As stated above, the key skills qualifications focus on the original three key skills identified in the early GNVQ specifications. The QCA states that:

'The broad aim of the three key skills units is to develop and recognize your (the student's) skills in:

*   obtaining and interpreting different types of information;
*   using, developing and communicating information to meet the purpose of your studies, work or other activities;
*   effectively presenting the results of your work.'

These broad aims apply to all three key skills.

The Key skills qualification is available at three levels, but here we focus on level 3, as this is the appropriate level for A level students. The ascent from level 1 to level 3 is characterized by 'students taking more responsibility for decisions on how [to] use skills to suit different tasks, problems and situations' (QCA) and a move from straightforward to complicated subjects. Straightforward subjects are those that we 'often meet in work, studies or other activities. Content is put across in a direct way with the main points being easily identifiable' (QCA) – the sentence structures are simple and the vocabulary is familiar. Complicated subjects, on the other hand, involve a number of ideas that are likely to be abstract, very detailed or deal with sensitive issues – 'The relationship of ideas and lines of reasoning may not be immediately clear' (QCA). Moreover, specialist vocabulary and complicated sentence structures may be used.

The above definition can be interpreted by referring to a typical investment appraisal question, where a student is presented with data and required to calculate payback, average rate of return or net present value. Typically, there will be a follow-up question evaluating the technique of analysis and/or analysing other factors to be taken into consideration. This is not really evidence of operating at level 3 for application of number. This is because an instruction to, for example, calculate payback does not result in students demonstrating autonomy in choice of method and the subject matter is straightforward rather than complicated.

Before offering suggestions for Business Studies activities to develop key skills, it would be useful to summarize the elements for level 3 – see Table 8.1.

Table 8.1: Summaries of level 3 key skills

Communication

C3.1a	Contribute to a group discussion about a complicated subject
C3.1b	Make a presentation about a complicated subject using at least one image to illustrate complicated points
C3.2	Select and synthesize information from two extended documents that deal with a complex subject. One document must include images
C3.3	Write two different types of document about a complex subject. One piece of writing must be an extended document and include at least one image

Application of number

N3.1	Plan and interpret information from two types of sources, including a large data set
N3.2	Carry out multistage calculations to do with:
	• amount and sizes;
	• scales and proportions;
	• handling statistics;
	• rearranging formulae
	Work with a large data set on at least one occasion
N3.3	Interpret results, present findings and justify methods. Use at least one graph, one chart and one diagram

IT

IT3.1	Plan and use different sources to search for and select information required for different purposes
IT3.2	Explore, develop and exchange information and derive new information to meet two different purposes
IT3.3	Present information from different sources for two different purposes and audiences, including one example of text, one of images and one of numbers

Objectives and the business environment (Jewell, *An Integrated Approach to Business Studies: Student's Book,* Parts I and II)

The first two parts of the textbook cover business objectives, business organization, introduction to management and the impact of the external environment. The topic of business strategy reappears in the penultimate chapter as a lead into synoptic assessment. These parts of the textbook cover the QCA's section on objectives and the business. Like other sections of the subject, it is rich in areas for the development and demonstration of key skills. The ideas that follow are suggestions for key skills development.

C3.1a
Discussion on such business issues as:

- business and the physical environment;
- business and the community;
- ethical issues in business;
- government regulation of business;
- business and the EU.

C3.1b
A presentation on:

- fiscal or monetary policy;
- the Working Time Directive;
- the impact of the single currency on business;
- demographic trends;
- the organizational structure of an organization.

C3.2
Read and synthesize information from two extended documents:

- an article from the business section of a broadsheet newspaper and a theoretical account of the topic in a textbook;
- two newspaper accounts of a takeover;
- two conflicting pamphlets relating to the single currency;
- a comparison of two annual reports.

C3.3
Two documents about a complicated subject:

- an essay chosen from the textbook or from a past paper;
- a report on trends in the economic environment;
- a report on employment law;
- a project or research assignment (as the original is submitted to the Business Studies awarding body, a copy should be made for key skills accreditation);
- a report on an organization's structure.

N3.1
Obtaining and interpreting data relating to:

- population trends;
- trends in the economy;
- changes over time (time series);
- market growth and market shares.

N3.2
This is multistage calculation and there are fewer opportunities to demonstrate it in these two sections than in the later section, although data could be analysed in terms of measures of central tendency, spread and skewness.

N3.3
For this it is necessary to interpret, present and justify a method. A statistical analysis of trends involving interpretation of data could provide evidence of this element. It is essential that the methodology is explained and justified.

IT3.1
Search for and select information from IT-based sources, such as CD-ROMs and the Internet, on topics such as:

- inflation;

- interest rates;
- exchange rates;
- sources of assistance to business;
- trends in a particular market;
- movements in share prices;
- government policies.

It is essential that use is made of the material – the mere submission of a printout does not provide evidence of understanding.

IT3.2

Explore, develop, exchange information, This could include generating charts and graphs using spreadsheets, database and word-processing facilities to manage and present information relating to:

- market trends;
- economic trends;
- company statistics.

IT3.3

This is presenting information, so a word-processed report on any of the communications topics contributes evidence of this skill. The criteria require candidates to produce two pieces of work, but at least one must include images and one include numbers. In addition to the reports (with illustrations on economic trends), candidates could consider a report on organizational structures, incorporating organizational charts and appropriate illustrations for staffing organizations.

Marketing (Jewell, *An Integrated Approach to Business Studies: Student's Book*, Part III)

C3.1a

Discussions on:

- trends in the marketplace;
- the ethics of advertising;
- the extent to which firms respond to or create demand;
- the value of the product lifecycle;
- market research techniques.

C3.1b

Presentation on:

- marketing strategies;
- new product development;
- distribution strategies;
- appropriate pricing policies;
- product elimination;
- sampling error.

C3.2

Synthesize information:

- reports on market trends;
- comparison of the marketing strategy of a specific firm with a textbook account;
- conflicting views of marketing strategies (such as globalization versus adaptation for the local market);
- asset-led marketing;
- marketing myopia.

C3.2

Write:

- an essay from the selection in the textbook or a past paper;
- a report on market trends;

- report on a firm's marketing strategy;
- a report on a firm's product range;
- a report on trends in advertising.

N3.1
Obtaining information:

- desk research using secondary sources;
- a market research data collection exercise.

The stress must be placed on obtaining and interpreting data and, in the case of one of the pieces of work, using a large data set.

N3.2
Multistage calculations, which could include:

- pricing policies (when combined with cost accounting);
- time series analysis;
- setting a complicated marketing budget;
- sampling analysis;
- complicated calculations involving price/income elasticity of demand.

N3.3
Present results – quantitative data relevant to marketing (sales, market share, market trends, marketing budget, time series analysis).

IT3.1
Utilizing sources of information by collecting data from IT-based sources, such as CD-ROMs and the Internet, on:

- market trends;
- business strategies;
- competition.

IT3.2
Explore, develop and exchange information. Market research assignments provide opportunities to do this and derive new information by generating charts, graphs and spreadsheets. Secondary data should be used in this exercise.

IT3.3
Word-processed reports on:

- marketing strategies;
- marketing research techniques;
- problems of international marketing;
- a firm's product range;
- segmentation policy.

Accounting and finance (Jewell, *An Integrated Approach to Business Studies: Student's Book*, Part IV)

C3.1a
Discussions on the:

- limitations of financial accounting;
- window dressing accounts;
- value of investment appraisal techniques;
- problem of uncertainty in budgeting.

C3.1b
A presentation on:

- a set of published financial accounts;

- the value of management accounting;
- the use of break-even analysis;
- methods of depreciation;
- FIFO versus LIFO;
- sources of finance;
- share issues;
- gearing;
- dividends policies.

C3.2

Synthesize information by identifying the limitations of financial data in an annual report and using financial commentaries in newspapers to present a brief report. Produce a report comparing a published set of accounts with the simplified accounts in textbooks.

C3.3

Write two documents, that could include:

- an essay chosen from the textbook or a past paper;
- a report on accounting policies adopted by a named company;
- report on the performance of a named company.

N3.1

Obtain and interpret information. The final accounts of public limited companies are available to everyone and could be used as the basis for this element. It is important to interpret the data rather than merely present it. Final reports obtained from the Internet also provide evidence for IT3.1.

N3.2

Multistage calculations, including:

- budget exercises;
- complicated break-even exercises;
- complicated investment appraisal exercises;
- costings;
- ratio analysis.

N3.3

Interpret results, giving a full report on:

- the performance of a company or variance against budget or investment appraisal.

Calculations, one graph, one chart and one diagram need to be provided, together with a justification of methods (why net present value was preferred over payback, for example).

IT3.1

Plan and search for information, using IT-based resources, relating to:

- company accounts;
- sources of finance;
- movements in share prices.

IT3.2

Develop and exchange information by:

- creating a database on company performance;
- using spreadsheets in budgeted accounts;
- developing spreadsheets for cash flow forecasting;
- producing a report from a database.

IT3.3

Present information by word-processing reports on a finance topic, such as:

- sources of finance;
- ratio analysis;

- techniques of investment appraisal;
- window dressing accounts.

Production and operations management (Jewell, *An Integrated Approach to Business Studies: Student's Book*, Part V)

C3.1a
Discussion on:

- lean production methods;
- work study;
- efficiency and working conditions;
- time-based competition;
- product standardization versus production variation.

C3.1b
A presentation on:

- the benefits of just-in-time methods;
- the adoption of lean production methods;
- CAD/CAM;
- the role of network analysis;
- the rise (and fall) of mass-production methods.

C3.2
Synthesize information by comparing:

- two reports on manufacturing in the UK;
- newspaper accounts of lean production with the models presented in textbooks;
- company public relations statements and textbook accounts;
- company statements and those of trade unions.

C3.3
Write two documents:

- essays chosen from the textbook or past papers;
- a report on batch production;
- a report on factory layouts;
- a report on a lean production technique;
- a report on waste.

N3.1
Plan and interpret data:

- on output and productivity;
- on stock levels;
- on the input of resources over time;
- on capacity utilization.

N3.2
Multistage calculations, such as:

- network analysis involving calculations of critical path, duration, float, resource constraints and Gantt charts to plan the use of resources;
- calculations involving economic order quantity and re-order levels.

N3.3
Interpret results of data:

- on output and production;
- on stock levels;
- relating to cost of production using a variety of methods.

IT3.1

Plan and search for information using IT-based resources to collect data on:

* output;
* productivity;
* new product development;
* labour force.

IT3.2

Exchange information:

* using IT-generated charts and graphs on a production topic;
* by developing a database on local industries;
* by creating a spreadsheet to analyse stock movements.

Human resources management (Jewell, *An Integrated Approach to Business Studies: Student's Book*, Part VI)

C3.1a

A discussion on:

* HRM versus personnel management;
* flexible workforce;
* motivation and leadership;
* the role of trade unions;
* the need for regulation and protection in the labour market;
* flatter organizational structures;
* Broadbanding of pay.

C3.1b

Presentation on:

* the ideas of a major writer on motivation;
* recruitment and selection methods at a named firm;
* the benefits of telecommuting;
* the role of employment tribunals;
* employment protection law;
* trends in trade unionism;
* the EU Social Chapter.

C3.2

Synthesize information by comparing:

* two or more accounts of the work of a major authority on motivation;
* accounts of scientific management;
* newspaper accounts of employee relations with textbook accounts.

C3.3

Write two documents:

* essays chosen from the textbook or from past papers:
* a report on the development of motivational theories;
* a report on recruitment and selection methods;
* a report on the nature and benefits of induction procedures;
* a report on training methods.

N3.1

Obtain data on:

* labour turnover;
* absenteeism;
* changes in the workforce.

N3.2
Multistage calculation, such as:

- an analysis of the workforce in terms of age and pay levels, involving calculations of central tendency, dispersion and skewness;
- a detailed analysis of turnover and/or absenteeism.

N3.3
Interpret results by:

- presenting data on a human resources topic – it must include at least one graph, one chart, one diagram and a justification of the method used.

IT3.1
Plan and search different IT-based sources to collect information on:

- recruitment and selection;
- training opportunities;
- trends in the labour market.

IT3.2
Explore and exchange information by:

- generating charts and graphs relating to statistics about the workforce;
- preparing reports from a database.

IT3.3
Present information by:

- word-processing reports on an HRM topic, such as employment legislation, human resource planning, equal opportunities or a flexible workforce – the report must include images and numbers.

The wider key skills
Working with others

Evidence requirements:

- identify collective goals and responsibilities;
- work to collective goals and responsibilities.

Opportunities for group activities include:

- a group presentation;
- a group market research exercise;
- group data collection;
- planning a conference;
- a mini-business enterprise.

The specification requires the group to work over an extended period and to review collaborative work.

Problem solving

Recognize, explore and describe two problems and agree the standards for their solution. Evidence requirements:

- recognize that a problem exists and has no immediate solution;
- select and use appropriate methods for exploring the problem;
- describe the main features of the problem and agree the standards that have to be met to show the problem has been solved.

Generate and compare at least three options that could be used to solve each of two problems, then select the best options to take forward. Evidence requirements:

- select and use appropriate methods for generating different options for tackling the problem;

- compare the main features of each option, including resource needs, time scales and its impact on others;
- select the option that is realistic and most likely to solve the problem.

Plan and implement at least one option for solving each of two problems, and review progress towards their solution. Evidence requirements:

- plan how to carry out your chosen option and obtain agreement to go ahead from an appropriate person;
- implement your plan, effectively using support and feedback from others to assist this process;
- review progress towards solving the problem and revise your approach as necessary.

Agree and apply methods for checking whether or not two problems have been solved, describe the results and review the approaches taken. Evidence requirements:

- agree with an appropriate person methods for testing whether or not standards have been met for solving the problem;
- apply these methods accurately and fully describe the results;
- review your approach to tackling the problem, including whether or not alternative methods and options might have proved more effective.

A Business Studies project or research assignment provides an ideal opportunity to demonstrate problem-solving skills. As recommended in the textbook and by the awarding bodies, the project must:

- be based on a problem to be solved or decision to be made;
- involve the collection of numerical and other data;
- analyse and evaluate data;
- produce a clear recommendation;
- devise a plan for implementation;
- implement and review the solution.

Improving own learning

- Identify targets.
- Follow a schedule to meet those targets.

Business Studies can contribute to this key skill if students:

- set themselves SMART objectives;
- take responsibility for their own learning;
- produce action plans with honest evaluation of progress;
- become self-starters in seeking information and understanding by exploring resources in libraries and on the Internet.

Conclusion

This chapter has offered many suggestions for a key skills portfolio, but the list is not intended to be exhaustive. By developing key skills assignments that develop understanding of the subject and key skills, the addition of these skills can enrich a course of study rather than become a burden.

Answers to data questions

Chapter 5

1 (a)

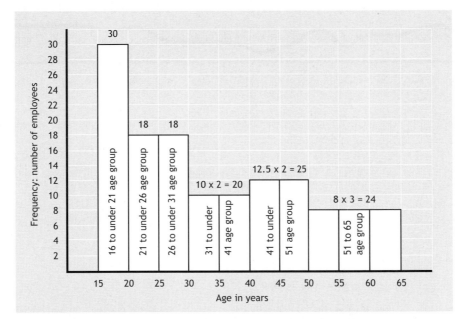

(b)

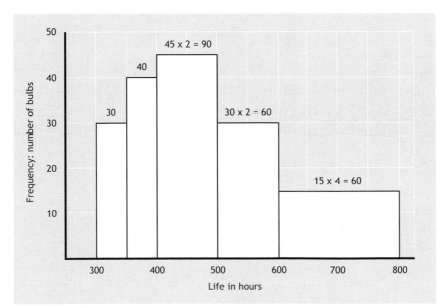

2

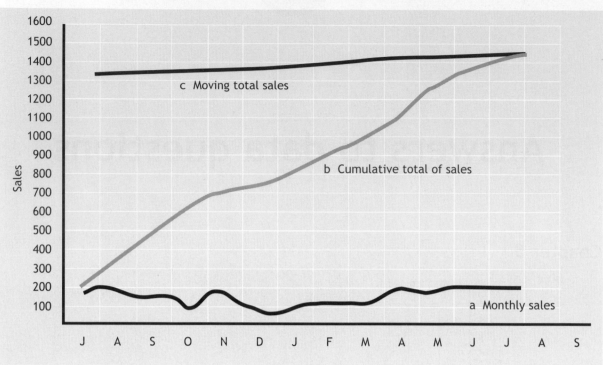

c Moving total sales

b Cumulative total of sales

a Monthly sales

(y-axis labelled Sales: 100, 200, 300, 400, 500, 600, 700, 800, 900, 1000, 1100, 1200, 1300, 1400, 1500, 1600)

(x-axis: J A S O N D J F M A M J J A S)

3

Peas		Pods		
3	×	10	30	
4	×	10	40	
5	×	30	150	
6	×	38	228	Mean = 5.62 peas
7	×	25	175	
8	×	5	40	
		118	663	

4 (a) 85 out of 125 arrived late. This is 68%.

	Mid-point	×	Buses	
(b) Lateness				
0 to under 15	7.5		30	225
15 to under 30	22.5		45	1012.5
30 to under 60	45		10	450
			85	1687.5

Mean number of minutes late $= \dfrac{1687.5}{85} = 19.9$

5 (a) 20% rise in output between Years 1 and 2

(b) $\dfrac{5}{120} \times 100 = 4.2\%$ rise between Years 2 and 3

(c) $\dfrac{15}{120} \times 100 = 12.5\%$ rise between years 2 and 4

6 **Index of output**

Year 1 = 100
Year 2 = 112.5*
Year 3 = 137.5
Year 4 = 162.5
Year 5 = 181.25

$$\frac{*180}{160} \times 100 = 112.5$$

7 **Index of output**

Year 1 = 88.8
Year 2 = 100
Year 3 = 122.2
Year 4 = 144.4
Year 5 = 161.1

8

Year	Index of output	Index of labour force
1	100	100
2	105	106.7
3	105	113.3
4	120	113.3
5	140	120

In Years 2 and 3, the workforce rose by a higher percentage than did output. From this we can conclude that productivity fell.

However, in Years 4 and 5 the rise in output outstripped the rise in the workforce – thus productivity rose. Over the whole period a 40% rise in output was achieved with a 20% rise in the workforce. This exercise was designed to illustrate the value of index numbers in comparing unlike variables.

9

		Weight × Price rise
a	(i)	150
	(ii)	400
	(iii)	75
	(iv)	50

675 divided by total weight (100) = 6.75%

b	(i)	160
	(ii)	120
	(iii)	160
	(iv)	90
	(v)	150

680 divided by total weight (200) = 3.4%

In both cases, the weighted average price rise differs from the crude average price rise.

10 Year 1 = 100
Year 2 = 110
Year 3 = 120
Year 4 = 126

The last number is 126 rather than 125 because there is a 5% rise over the Year 3 figure of 120.

11

Delivery time	Frequency	Cumulative frequency
5	10	10
6	12	22
7	20	42
8	30	72
9	20	92
10	8	100

IQR covers 25.5th to 75.5th delivery
25.5th delivery made in 6 days + 4 hours
75.5th delivery made in 8 days + 3 hours
IQR = 8 days 3 hours – 6 days 4 hours = 1 day 23 hours

12

£000 From to below		Mid-point £000	Frequency	M × F £000	Cumulative frequency	
6	8	7	5	35	5	← Q2
8	10	9	6	54	11	
10	12	11	6	66	17	← Median
12	14	13	7	91	24	← Q4
14	16	15	8	120	32	
16	18	17	3	51	35	
18	20	19	4	76	39	
20	30	25	1	25	40	
			40	518		

(a) Mean $= \dfrac{£518,000}{40} = £12,950$

Modal class £14,000 to under £16,000
Median: salary of 20.5th person = £10,000 plus £1000 = £11,000

(b) IQR covers the salary range of the 10.25th to the 307.5th person

$$\text{IQR} = £12,000 + \frac{6.75}{8} \times 2000$$

$$\text{minus } £6,000 + \frac{5.25}{6} \times 2000$$

$$= £13,687 - £7,750 = £5,937$$

13 (a)

Value	Frequency	V × F
6	6	36
7	8	56
8	12	96
9	14	126
10	10	100
11	4	44
	54	458

Mean $= \dfrac{458}{54} = 8.5$

(b)

Value	Mean	Deviation (d)	d^2	$\times$	f	=	fd^2
6	8.5	−2.5	6.25		6		37.5
7	8.5	−1.5	2.25		8		18
8	8.5	−0.5	0.25		12		3
9	8.5	0.5	0.25		14		3.5
10	8.5	1.5	2.25		10		22.5
11	8.5	2.5	6.25		4		25
					$\Sigma f = 54$		$\Sigma fd^2 = 109.5$

$$\text{Variance} = \frac{\Sigma f}{\Sigma fd^2} = \frac{109.5}{54}$$

$$= 2.03$$

(c) Standard deviation is the square root of the variance = 1.42.

14 (a)

Mid-point (m)	Frequency (f)	fm
1.5	40	60
4.5	69	310.5
7.5	38	285
10.5	31	325.5
13.5	15	202.5
16.5	8	132
	$\Sigma f = 201$	$\Sigma fm = 1315.5$

$$\text{Mean} = \frac{fm}{f} = \frac{1315.5}{201} = 6.54$$

(b)

Mid-point	Mean	Deviation (d)	d^2	$\times$	frequency (f)	=	fd^2
1.5	6.5	−5	25		40		1000
4.5	6.5	−2	4		69		276
7.5	6.5	1	1		38		38
10.5	6.5	4	16		31		496
13.5	6.5	7	49		15		735
16.5	6.5	10	100		8		800
					$\Sigma f = 201$		$\Sigma fd^2 = 3345$

$$\text{Variance} = \frac{3345}{201} = 16.64$$

(c) Standard deviation is the square root of the variance = 4.08.

15 (a) (b) **Speedy Service Limited**

Days	Frequency	D × F	Cumulative frequency	% Cumulative frequency
5	10	50	10	7.75
6	30	180	40	31
7	55	385	95	73
8	20	160	115	89
9	12	108	127	98
10	2	20	129	100
	129	903	129	100

(c) Mean $= \dfrac{903}{129} = 7$ days

(d) Range 10 − 5 = 5 days

(e) IQR 7.1 − 5.7 = 1.4

(a) (b) **High Speed Carriers Limited**

Days	Frequency	D × F	Cumulative frequency	% Cumulative frequency
2	6	12	6	3
3	8	24	14	7
4	5	20	19	10
5	19	95	38	20
6	45	270	83	44
7	40	280	123	65
8	29	232	152	80
9	12	108	164	87
10	10	100	174	92
11	5	55	179	95
12	5	60	184	98
14	2	28	186	99
15	2	30	188	100
	188	1314		100

(c) Mean $= \dfrac{1314}{188} = 6.99$ days

(d) Range $15 - 2 = 13$ days

(e) IQR $7.6 - 5.2 = 2.4$ days

16 Range £159.99 − £90 = £69.99

IQR: Lower quartile $= \dfrac{n+1}{4} = 25.25$

Upper quartile $= \dfrac{3(n+1)}{4} = 75.75$

Lower quartile covers pay up to
$£100 + \dfrac{(5.25 \times £10)}{25} = £102.1$

Upper quartile covers pay greater than
$£130 + \dfrac{(0.75 \times £10)}{10} = £130.75$

IQR   = £130.75 − £102.1
        = £28.65

This is the range of pay for the middle 50% of employees.

17 (a)

No. of items	Mid-points	Frequency	M × F
1–20	10.5	6	63
21–30	25.5	20	510
31–35	33	40	1320
36–40	38	35	1330
41–50	45.5	3	136.5
		104	3359.5

Mean $= \dfrac{3359.5}{104} = 32.3$ items

Modal group = 31 − 35 items
Median = 52.5th week

This is in the 31 – 35 class and lies $\dfrac{26.5}{40}$ in the class

$$31 + \left(\dfrac{26.5}{40} \times 5\right) = 34.3$$

(b)   This distribution is fairly symmetrical and, therefore, the mean, mode and median are close together. The mean is the most useful measure for further analysis and in this particular case there is no distortion by extreme values. The mode has limited use, except to indicate what is typical.

(c)

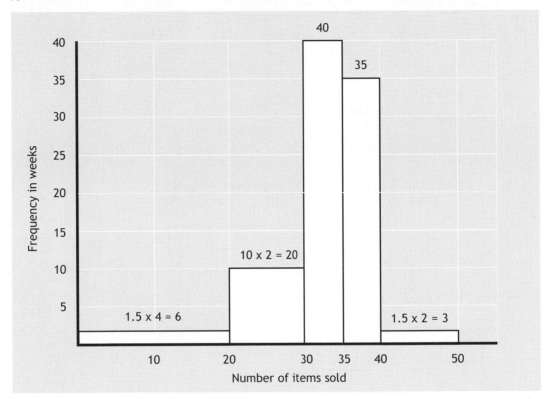

(d)   Assuming that distribution is even within each class.

Hence:

1   36 – 40 class
    1 out of 5 weeks ($\dfrac{1}{5} \times 35$), demand would be 39 and, as a result, 1 sale was lost per week 7 × 1.

2   1 out of every 5 weeks, demand would be 40 and as a result 2 sales lost in those weeks 7 × 2.

3   41 – 50 class
    1 week   3   sales lost
    1 week   4   sales lost
    1 week   5   sales lost

Total lost sales = 33

Total contribution lost = £33 × 30 = £990.

18   (a)   (i)

Year 2

Mid-point in pay band (m) (£)	No. of employees (f)	M × F (£m)
22,500	400	9
27,500	100	2.75
32,500	50	1.625
37,500	40	1.5
45,000	40	1.8
55,000	8	0.44
70,000	2	0.14
90,000	1	0.09
	641	17.345

$$\text{Mean pay} = \frac{£17,345,000}{641} = £27,059$$

Year 1

Mid-point in pay band (m) (£)	No. of employees (f)	M × F (£m)
22,500	350	7.875
27,500	80	2.2
32,500	48	1.56
37,500	30	1.125
45,000	20	0.9
55,000	7	0.385
	535	14.045

$$\text{Mean pay} = \frac{£14,045,000}{535} = £26,252$$

(ii)

Year 1 – with 535 employees, the middle person is the 267.5th person. He or she is in the £20,001 to £25,000 band and lies 267.5th out of 350 employees in the band.

$$\text{Median pay is } £20,001 \text{ plus } \frac{267.5}{350} \times 5000$$

$$= £23,822$$

Year 2 – with 641 employees, the middle person is the 320.5th person. He or she is in the £20,001 to £25,000 and lies 320.5th out of 400 employees in this band.

$$\text{Median pay is } £20,001 \text{ plus } \frac{320.5}{400} \times £5000$$

$$= £24,007$$

(b)   If we assume that pay is evenly distributed over the various pay bands and that distribution did not alter between the two years, then we can estimate the rise in the pay bill by using data from (a).

The pay bill rose from £14.045m in Year 1 to £17.345m in Year 2, giving a rise of £3.3m.

(c) (d)

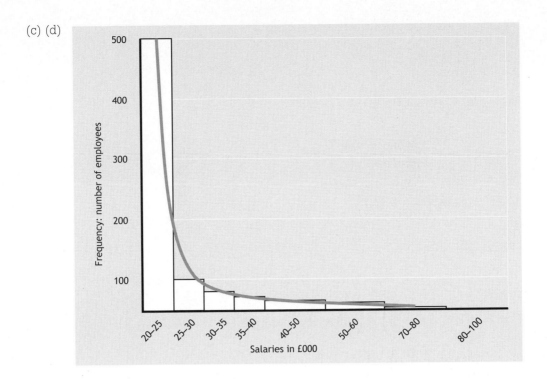

19   (a)   Bell-shaped curves for A and B, but A shows less dispersion. C is skewed to the right, whereas D is skewed to the left.

      (b)   Total number of employees 1000
Hence median is the 500.5th person

$$500\text{th person has a salary of } \pounds12,000 + \left(\frac{200}{500} \times 1000\right) = \pounds12,400$$

$$501\text{st person has a salary of } \pounds12,000 + \left(\frac{201}{501} \times 1000\right) = \pounds12,402$$

The median is £12,401

      (c)

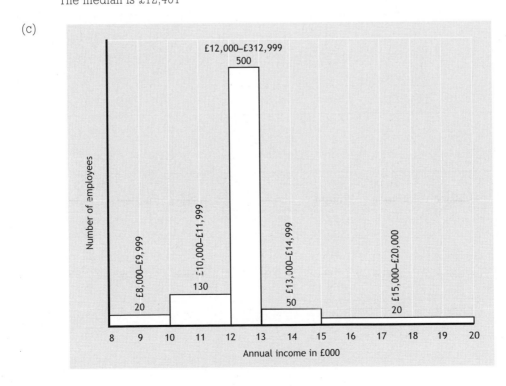

If X is the mean salary in the earlier year, then:

$$X \times \frac{110}{100} = £12,300$$

Therefore, $X = £12,300 \times \frac{100}{110} = £11,182$

20   (a)   Price relative $= \dfrac{\text{cost of pay, year X}}{\text{cost of pay, year 1}} \times 100$

Year 1   100

Year 2   106.25 $\left(\dfrac{8.50}{8.00} \times 100 \right)$

Year 3   112.5

Year 4   137.375

Cost index

(b)   Year 1   100

Year 2 $\left(106.25 \times \dfrac{60}{100} \right) + \left(110 \times \dfrac{40}{100} \right) = 63.75 + 44.0 = 107.75$

Year 3 $\left(112.5 \times \dfrac{60}{100} \right) + \left(120 \times \dfrac{40}{100} \right) = 67.50 + 48.0 = 115.5$

Year 4 $\left(137.375 \times \dfrac{60}{100} \right) + \left(125 \times \dfrac{40}{100} \right) = 82.425 + 50.0 = 132.425$

21   1   Calculate price relatives $\dfrac{(\text{year } x \text{ price})}{(\text{year 1 price})}$

     2   Multiply price relatives by weightings

     3   Calculate the average of the resulting figures

(a)

	Year 2 Price relative	Weight		Year 3 Price relative		Weight	
A	110	100	11,000	130	100	13,000
B	118	50	5,900	127	50	6,350
C	108	20	2;160	121	20	2,420
D	104	20	2,080	115	20	2,300
E	104	10	1,040	107	10	1,070

$$\frac{22,180}{200} = 110.9 \qquad \frac{25,140}{200} = 125.7$$

(b)

	Year 2 Price relative	Weight		Year 3 Price relative		Weight	
A	110	120	13,200	130	130	16,900
B	118	60	7,080	127	50	6,350
C	108	20	2,160	121	20	2,420
D	104	20	2,080	115	20	2,300
E	104	20	2,080	107	10	1,070

$$\frac{26,600}{240} = 110.8 \qquad \frac{29,040}{230} = 126.2$$

22　(a)　This exercise requires students to produce:
　　　　(i)　time series graphs with time in years on the horizontal axis and advertising expenditure and sales revenue (in £m) on the vertical axis;
　　　　(ii)　a scatter diagram with advertising revenue (the independent variable) on the horizontal axis and sales revenue (the dependent variable) on the vertical axis.

　　(b)　The line of best fit can be inserted by close inspection of the plot points. It should be a straight line, close to the bulk of plot points and rise from left to right. Students might like to comment on the strength of the correlation between the two variables. The closer the line of best fit to plot points, the stronger the correlation.

23　(a)　$50 \times .3 = 15$　　(b)　$10 \times .1 = 1$　　(c)　$24 \times .2 = 4.8$　　(d)　$100 \times .1 = 10$
　　　　$60 \times .5 = 30$　　　　　$12 \times .5 = 6$　　　　　$26 \times .2 = 5.2$　　　　　$120 \times .8 = 96$
　　　　$\underline{55 \times .2 = 11}$　　　　$14 \times .3 = 4.2$　　　　$28 \times .4 = 11.2$　　　　$\underline{130 \times .1 = 13}$
　　　　　　　　$\overline{56}$　　　　　$\underline{16 \times .1 = 1.6}$　　　$\underline{30 \times .2 = 6}$　　　　　　　$\overline{119}$
　　　　　　　　　　　　　　　　$\overline{12.8}$　　　　　　$\overline{27.2}$

24　(a)　The probability of one of the two occurring is equal to the probability of either occurring minus the probability of both occurring:

$$P (A\ or\ B) = P (A) + P (A) - P (A\ and\ B)$$

where P is the probability of an event, A successful marketing strategy and B is success in keeping within the budget.

$$P (A\ or\ B) = 0.8 + 0.7 - (0.8 \times 0.7)$$
$$= 0.94$$

　　(b)　The probability that both will succeed is shown as:

$$P (A\ and\ B) = P (A) \times P (B)$$
$$= 0.8 \times 0.7 = 0.56$$

25　To answer questions relating to Z scores, it is always advisable to draw a sketch graph in order to work it out logically.

　　(a)　2000 hours represents 500 from the mean, which in turn is 1.66 standard deviations below the mean. 50% plus 45% of all values are above this point, leaving approximately 5% below.

　　(b)　2300 is .66 standard deviations below the mean. This will cover approximately 24% of all values.

26　(a)　7 minutes is 2 minutes below the mean and this is equal to 1.33 standard deviations. 50% will be above the mean and approximately 40% will be within 1.33 standard deviations below the mean, leaving just under 10% more than 1.33 below the mean.

　　(b)　13 minutes is 4 minutes or 2.66 standard deviations above the mean. A negligible 0.4% of tyre changes will exceed 13 minutes.

27　(a)　32 is .5 standard deviations above the mean. Approximately 31% will exceed this weight.

　　(b)　25 is 1.25 standard deviations below the mean. Approximately 10.6% will be less than 25 grams.

　　(c)　28 is .5 standard deviations below and 33 is .75 standard deviations above the mean. This weight range will cover 19% plus 27% equals 46% of all packets.

28　(a)　Probability of no sale on either visit is .75. The probability of no sale on both visits is $.75 \times .75 = .56$

　　(b)　The probability of achieving just one sale is:
　　　　1 – (the probability of achieving no sales plus the probability of achieving two sales)
　　　　$1 - (.56 + .0625) = .3775$

　　(c)　The probability of succeeding on both occasions is $.25 \times .25 = .0625$

29   This question involves the binomial expansion where probabilities are expressed by expanding the
      equation $(f + e)^4 = 1$, where f is the probability of the pump being free and e is the probability of it
      being engaged.

      (a)   The probability of all in use is e^4
             $e = 0.3 \times 0.3 \times 0.3 \times 0.3 = 0.0081$

      (b)   The probability of 3 being in use is $4fe^3$
             $4fe^3 = 4 \times 0.7 \times 0.3 \times 0.3 \times 0.3 = 0.0756$

      (c)   The probability of none being in use is f^4
             $f^4 = 0.7 \times 0.7 \times 0.7 \times 0.7 = 0.2401$

30   This question involves the use of tables of areas under a curve of normal distribution. Although it does
      not involve a substantial amount of calculation, it does require logical thinking and students are advised
      to draw a sketch graph to aid their analysis and determine which part of the graph is relevant.

      (a)   30 is 2 standard deviations below the mean. A table of normal distribution curve areas tells us
             that the probability of being less than 2 standard deviations from the mean is 2% (or 0.0228 to be
             exact).

      (b)   60 is 1 standard deviation above the mean. The table informs us that around 16% will be above
             this point. That is 50% will be below the mean and 34% will be within 1 standard deviation above
             the mean. The exact answer is 0.1587.

      (c)   40 is 1 standard deviation below the mean and 60 is 1 standard deviation above. We know that
             68.26% of all values are within 1 standard deviation of the mean.

31   This question involves the binomial expansion of $(f + s)^5 = 1$, where f is the probability that the goods
      are faulty and s is the probability that the goods are satisfactory.

      (a)   The probability that all 5 are faulty is f^5, which is $(0.01)^5$.

      (b)   The probability that 3 items are faulty is $10 f^3s^2$, or $10 \times 0.01^3 \times 0.99^2$.

      (c)   The probability (P) that at least 2 items are not faulty is
             1 – (probability of three items being faulty)
             $P = 1 - (5 \times f \times s^4) = 1 - (5 \times 0.01 \times 0.99^4)$

32   (a)   900 is 46 hours or $\frac{46}{57} = 0.81$ standards deviations below the mean.

             Referring to the table of normal distribution, we find that this covers 29.1% of values.

             1000 is 54 hours or $\frac{54}{57} = 0.95$ standard deviations above the mean.

             The table of normal distribution informs us that this covers 32.9% of all values.
             Adding the two together, we conclude that 62% of all bulbs have a life of between 900 and 1000
             hours.

      (b)   What percentage of bulbs will have a life of less than 800 hours?

             800 is 146 hours or $\frac{146}{57} = 2.56$ standard deviations below the mean. The table of normal

             distribution informs us that 0.52% of bulbs will have a life of less than 800 hours.

      (c)   1000 is 154 hours or $\frac{154}{57} = 2.7$ standard deviations above the mean.

             0.35% of all values exceed this figure.

33   (a)   (i)   3 hours is 1.4 hours above the mean. This is equal to $\frac{1.4}{0.4}$ or 3.5 standard deviations

                    above the mean. Most tables do not go beyond 3 standard deviations, but it is clear that
                    the answer will be a negligible 0.1% or less.

(ii)   0.5 hours is 1.1 below the mean. This is $\dfrac{1.1}{0.4} = 2.75$ standard deviations.

0.3% of values lie beyond this point.

(b)   (i)   75% of all calls cover the 50% below the mean, plus 0.68 standard deviations above the mean (this figure is derived from looking up 25% or 0.25 in the normal distribution table and then reading across to discover the relevant Z value). From this we can conclude that 75% of all jobs are completed in 1.6 + (0.4 × 0.68 hours) = 1.872 hours. The maximum labour cost involved in 75% of all jobs is 1.872 hours × £20 equals £37.44.

(ii)   95% of jobs covers the 50% below mean plus 45% above. Again, reading 'backwards' from a table of normal distribution, we find that this goes up to a Z score of 1.65. In terms of hours, this is 1.6 hours + 0.66 hours = 2.26 hours. The labour cost involved in these jobs is up to 2.26 hours × £20 = £45.2.

(c)   (i)   £30 represents one hour of labour, which in turn is 0.6 hours or 1.5 standard deviations below the mean. 6.7% of all values are greater than 1.5 standard deviations below the mean.

(ii)   The call-out charge is £30 and there is a further charge of £20 per hour. A charge of £60 implies a job that took in excess of 2 hours (assuming that the £20 is per hour or any part thereof). This is 0.4 hours or 1 standard deviation above the mean and it covers 15.87% of jobs.

If the £20 per hour was charged on a pro rata basis, then we are referring to 2.25 standard deviations from the mean and this covers 1.22% of all jobs.

34   (a)   18,000 is 7000 or 2.33 standard deviations below the mean.
50% of all values are above the mean and 49.01% of values are within one standard deviation below the mean.
Hence 99% of concerts break even or make a profit.

(b)   22,000 is 3000 or 1 standard deviation below the mean.
50% of concerts attract an audience in excess of the mean and a further 34% attract an audience of between 22,000 and the mean.

(c)   29,000 is 1.33 standard deviations above the mean. 9.18% of values are beyond this point.

35   (a)   510 is 10 above the mean and has a Z score of 0.5.
30.85% of values are above this point

(b)   485 is 15 below the mean and has a Z score of 0.75.
22.66% of values are below this level leaving 77.34% above.

(c)   475 is 25 below the mean and has a Z score of 1.25.
10.57% of values will be below this point.

(d)   535 is 35 above the mean and has a Z score of 1.75.
45.99% of values are between the mean and 1.75 standard deviations above. To this we should add the 50% of values below the mean to conclude that 95.99% of values will be below 535.

(e)   490 is 0.5 standard deviation below the mean and covers 19.15% of values.
520 is 1 standard deviation above the mean and covers 34.13% of values.
This gives an answer of 53.28%.

(f)   470 is 1.5 standard deviations below the mean and covers 43.32% of values.
505 is 0.25 standard deviations above the mean and covers 9.87% of values.
This gives an answer of 53.19%.

36   (a)   (i)   £280 is £24 or 1.33 standard deviations above the mean. 9.18% of values are above this point.

(ii)   £250 is £6 or 0.33 standard deviations below the mean. 50% plus 12.93% of all values are above this point giving an answer of 62.93%.

(b)   (i)   £240 is £16 or 0.89 standard deviations below the mean. 18.67% of all values are amounts below £240.

       (ii)   £220 is £36 or 2 standard deviations below the mean. 2.28% of invoices will be for lower amounts.

(c)   (i)   £245 is 0.611 standard deviations below the mean and this covers 22.91% of values. £260 is 0.22 standard deviations above the mean and this covers 8.71% of values. The answer is 31.62% of all invoices.

       (ii)   £230 is 1.44 standard deviations below the mean and covers 42.51% of values. £290 is 1.89 standard deviations above the mean and covers 47.02% of values. The answer is 89.53% of all invoices.

37   (a)   (i)   200 goods are expected to be defective in a batch of 2000.

            (ii)   500 are expected to be defective in a batch of 5000.

      (b)   (i)   13 is 1 standard deviation above the mean and therefore 15.87% of batches will contain more than 13 defective goods.

            (ii)   16 is 2 standard deviations above the mean and therefore 2.28% of batches will contain more than 16 defective goods.

            (iii)   19 is 3 standard deviations above the mean and therefore 0.14% of batches will contain more than 19 defective goods.

38   (a)   30 is 0.2 standard deviations above the mean. 42.07% of values are above this point.

      (b)   35 is 0.4 standard deviations above the mean. 34.46% of values are above this point.

39   (a)   The probability of all components failing:
$P(X) \times P(Y) \times P(Z)$
$= 0.2 \times 0.1 \times 0.05 = 0.001$

      (b)   The probability of any 1 of the 3 failing is:
$P(X) + P(Y) + P(Z)$
$= 0.2 + 0.1 + 0.05 = 0.35$

40   This question involves the binomial expansion.

      (a)   The probability of no defective products is equal to $(0.98)^5 = 0.9039$

      (b)   The probability of just 1 defective product is $5 \times (0.98)^4 \times 0.02 = 0.0922$

      (c)   The probability of just 2 defective products is $10 \times (0.98)^3 \times (0.02)^2 = 0.00376$

      (d)   The probability of 5 defective products $(0.02)^5 = 0.000\ 000\ 0032$

Chapter 9

1   (a)   As the price rises, the quantity demanded falls.
As the price falls, the quantity demanded rises.

      (b)   (i)

Price (£)	QuD (million units)	Revenue (£m)
15	8	120
14	9	126
13	10	130
12	11	132
11	12	132
10	13	130
9	14	126

Revenue is maximized at prices of £12 and £11.

(ii)   Price elasticity of demand as price falls from £10 to £9 is:

$$\frac{+\frac{1}{13}}{-\frac{\cdot 1}{10}} = -\left(\frac{1}{13} \times \frac{10}{1}\right) = -\frac{10}{13} \text{ or } -0.77$$

PED as price falls from £15 to £14 is:

$$\frac{+\frac{1}{8}}{-\frac{1}{15}} = -\left(\frac{1}{8} \times \frac{15}{1}\right) = -1.88$$

PED varies from −0.77 through −1 (at prices of £11 and £12) to −1.88.

(c)   Demand is elastic at high prices, but inelastic at low ones.

2   (a)   (i)

Price (£)	QuD
£1.6	12.0
£1.5	12.5

$$\text{PED} = \frac{\frac{-0.5}{12.5}}{0.1/1.5} = -5/125 \times 15/1 = -0.6$$

(ii)

Price (£)	QuD
£2.5	7.5
£2.4	8.0

$$\text{PED} = \frac{-\frac{0.5}{8.0}}{\frac{-0.1}{2.4}} = \frac{-5}{80} \times \frac{24}{1} = \frac{-15}{10}$$

$$= -1.5$$

(b)   Starting at a price of £1.5, revenue rises from £18.75m to £19.2m, £19.55m, £19.8m, £19.95m, £20m, £19.95m, £19.8m, £19.55m, £19.2m, to £18.75m at price £2.5.

     (i)   Up to a price of £2, price rise increases revenue, but beyond this point a rise in price is followed by a fall in revenue.

     (ii)   Demand is elastic between the prices of £2.5 and £2.0, but inelastic at the lower prices.

(c)   Income elasticity of demand is +2. Therefore, a 5% rise in income leads to a 10% increase in demand at all prices. Demand is now 12.5m × 1.1 = 13.75m units at a price of £1.5. At other prices it is: 13.2m, 12.65m, 12.1m, 11.55m, 11m, 10.45m, 9.9m, 9.35m, 8.8m and 8.25m (at a price of £2.5).

(d)   (i)   Cross-elasticity of demand =

$$\frac{\text{Proportionate change in the demand for good A}}{\text{Proportionate change in price of good B}}$$

$$\frac{-2.5\%}{10\%} = -0.25$$

     (ii)   Cross-elasticity is negative and therefore the goods are complements.

3 (a)

Price	TR (£000)	Quantity (000 units)
6	840	140
7	910	130
8	960	120
9	990	110
10	1000	100
11	990	90
12	960	80
13	910	70
14	840	60

(b) (i) Price is elastic from £11 to £14.
   (ii) Price is inelastic below £10.

   Explanation: when demand is inelastic, a price rise leads to a rise in revenue.

(c) (i) A rise in quantity from 110,000 to 120,000 results in a fall in total revenue of £30,000. The MR of the

$$120,000\text{th unit is } \frac{-£30,000}{10,000} = -£3$$

   (ii) $$100,000\text{th unit} = \frac{£10,000}{10,000} = +£1$$

   (iii) $$80,000\text{th unit} = \frac{50,000}{10,000} = +£5$$

(d) Zero.

(e) No. Revenue refers to receipts from sales. To calculate profit, references should be made to the costs of production. The revenue maximizing output is likely to be different from the profit maximizing output.

4 (a) $$PED = \frac{-1/12}{1/16} = -1/12 \times 16/1 = -1.33$$

(b) $$PES = \frac{3/8}{2/21} = 3/8 \times 21/2 = +3.94$$

(c) $$YED = \frac{1/21}{1/13} = 1/21 \times 13/1 = +0.62$$

(d) $$XED = \frac{-1/50}{2/30} = -1/50 \times 30/2 = -0.3$$

(e) $$XED = \frac{+4/20}{+3/60} = 4/20 \times 60/3 = +4$$

5 (a) (b)

Price (£)	Qu (000)	TR (£000)	MR* (£)	TC (£000)	MC* (£)	Profits (£000)
20	10	200	–	200	–	0
19	11	209	9	201	1	8
18	12	216	7	204	3	12
17	13	221	5	206	2	15
16	14	224	3	210	4	14
15	15	225	1	220	10	5
14	16	224	–1	240	20	–16
13	17	221	–3	270	30	–49
12	18	216	–5	300	30	–84

*MR is the additional revenue from the sale of an additional unit. Quantity rises by 1000 at each price and, therefore, to calculate the MR of 1 more unit it is necessary to calculate the MR of 1000 units and then divide the resulting number by 1000.

(c)   Revenue is maximized at a price of £15 and an output of 15,000.

(d)   Profits are maximized at a price of £17 and an output 13,000 units. Notice that at the profit maximizing level of output, MC cuts MR.

(e)   £15,000 and £5000 respectively.

Part II (end of Chapter 13, page 184)

1   (a)   Boom: The phase in the business cycle in which output is high and unemployment is low.

Disposable income: Technically, it is national income, plus transfer payments, less compulsory deduction and retained profit. It can be regarded as take-home pay to dispose of as we please.

Real capital investment: Investment in capital equipment.

Monetary policy: Government policy relating to the supply of money (bank lending) and the price of loans (interest rates).

Real output: The level of national income (output) after adjusting for price changes.

(b)   There is a high level of demand and problems with satisfying it. This will result in demand pull inflation.

(c)   Although 88% suggests some spare capacity, there might be problems in acquiring complementary resources (such as labour). As the economy approaches full capacity, shortages begin to occur.

(d)   Tax reductions raise disposable income levels, thereby adding to aggregate demand. An inability to satisfy that demand will lead to demand pull inflation.

(e)   A high level of consumer demand will increase the profitability of investment.

(f)   Inflation will reduce the competitiveness. High levels of domestic demand will divert goods from the export market to the 'soft' domestic market.

2   (a)   In 1979, the UK had the highest marginal rate of personal taxation, but:

- this does not prove that the UK had the highest average rate;
- one country had a higher marginal rate of corporate taxation;
- the table tells us nothing about taxation on spending.

(b)   The trend towards lower taxation can be explained by the move in the 1980s towards market solutions to economic problems and the belief in low taxation to provide incentives for effort and enterprise.

(c)   Lower taxation (i) raises levels of disposable income and, therefore, demand and (ii) reduces disincentives.

(d)   Business enterprise sells goods and services to the government sector. A cut in government spending will reduce the availability of government contracts and have a detrimental impact on firms that rely on government contracts. In addition, lower government spending could mean less investment in the infrastructure and will have a downward multiplier impact on the economy.

(e)   Those who favour lower taxation often point to the economic success of lower taxation countries (such as former West Germany and Japan) and yet evidence suggests that some high taxation countries have also enjoyed economic success.

(f)   'Footloose' multinational corporations will move to lower taxation countries.

3   (a)   Rise in national income (y) = Injection × Multiplier, where the multiplier = $\dfrac{1}{\text{Marginal rate of withdrawal}}$

(i)   Rise in y = £600m × $\dfrac{1}{0.4}$ = £1500m

(ii)   Rise in y = £600m × $\dfrac{1}{0.6}$ = £1000m

(iii)   Rise in y = £600m × $\dfrac{1}{0.7}$ = £857.14m

(b)   (i)   Rise in y = £400m × $\dfrac{1}{0.6}$ = £666.7m

(ii)   Rise in y = £300m × $\dfrac{1}{0.8}$ = £375m

(iii)   Rise in y = £1b × $\dfrac{1}{0.75}$ = £1.33b

Note: the greater the marginal leakage, the smaller the multiplier.

(c)   Change in y = Change in injection × Multiplier

$$\text{Multiplier} = \dfrac{\text{Change in y}}{\text{Change in injection}}$$

$$= \dfrac{£750m}{£500m}$$

$$= 1.5$$

$$1.5 = \dfrac{1}{\text{MRW}}$$

$$\text{MRW} = \dfrac{1}{1.5} = 0.667$$

Check: £500 × $\dfrac{1}{0.667}$ = £750m

(d)   Change in y = Injection × $\dfrac{1}{\text{MRW}}$

£800m = Injection × $\dfrac{1}{0.65}$

Injection = £800m × 0.65 = £520m

Check: £520m × $\dfrac{1}{0.65}$ = £800m

4   Country A is an affluent country that is experiencing only modest economic growth. Its small population and growth limits its potential as a market. Nevertheless, it is a possible target for high-tech, engineering and consumer goods exports. As an affluent and stable country it is a possible destination for overseas investment, but the high inflation rate and the green movement place a question mark by its suitability.

    Country B is a low-income country. Its population and economic growth will increase its market potential, but social tension and IMF-imposed deflation will make it less attractive, both as an export market and a destination for investment. Of the three types of exports, engineering goods have the greatest potential.

    Country C is a large, middle-income country with great potential as a market, but chronic inflation, corruption and inequality are negative factors. Inequality means that a large proportion of the population lives in poverty and is unlikely to buy UK consumer goods. On the other hand, the existence of wealthy capitalist entrepreneurs increases its suitability as a market for capital goods. Market liberalization policies will increase trade in the long run, but could worsen the position in the short run. It is not a secure destination for overseas investment.

5 (a) Foreign ownership of British industry does not matter because:
- it contributes to national output (GDP);
- it provides employment;
- it provides investment in the UK;
- we benefit from the transfer of technology, expertise and organizational skills;
- it is part of the internationalization of capital;

but:
- profits are remitted abroad;
- decision making occurs abroad;
- footloose firms have low commitment to the UK;
- UK operations are reduced to screwdriver plants with high-value activities located elsewhere.

(b) Outward overseas investment:
- diverts capital away from UK industry;
- assists the build-up of foreign rivals;
- causes capital outflow on the balance of payments;
- diverts investment, production and employment abroad;

but:
- generates inflow of profit, interest and dividends in the long run;
- capital should be invested where it can be most profitably employed.

(c) The flows are the outcome of countless decisions made by thousands of firms and individuals. Foreign investors have seen the potential benefits of investment in the UK whereas UK investors have seen the benefits of different types of investment overseas.

(d) Since 1979, there have been no controls on the movement of capital in to and out of the UK, a move since followed by our EU partners. This enables UK residents to invest freely abroad while at the same time providing residents of foreign countries with greater confidence about investing in the UK.

6 (a) The government of Barbados is keen to attract multinational companies for the following reasons:
- to encourage investment in the country;
- as a source of employment;
- to increase national output;
- as a source of possible export earnings;
- to increase tax base.

(b) (i) Cooperative government: pro-business government that will not impose excessive or unnecessary burdens and will not threaten nationalization.
(ii) Basic infrastructure: essential services necessary in a modern economy, such as roads, communication links.
(iii) Tariff concession: favourable treatment in terms of import duties.

(c) Each of the above is encouraging for a multinational.
A cooperative government will not threaten nationalization, thus removing what is a common fear that deters inward investment from some countries.
Multinational companies will only invest in those countries possessing at least a minimum standard of services essential in a modern economy.
Tariff concessions are encouraging as, by reducing the tax burden, they increase potential profits.

(d) No. If low pay is accompanied by low productivity, then labour can turn out very expensive. In assessing the cost or labour per unit of output, account has to be taken of productivity as well as rates of pay.

(e) A multinational company setting up in Barbados will need to hire local labour and want to ensure that it is literate, trained or trainable and hardworking. The language is an additional attraction for American or British multinationals, whose staff will need to communicate with the workforce. Japanese multinationals also like to operate in an English-speaking environment.

7   (a)   It is unlawful to discriminate against people on grounds of ethnic origin. If Jerome was rejected because he was black, then the firm acted unlawfully.

    (b)   Jerome should seek advice from a lawyer, a law centre or the Commission for Racial Equality. If the latter body is satisfied with his case, it will take it up in employment tribunals and courts. It will be necessary to demonstrate that the prospective employer acted unlawfully. If he is successful, then he is entitled to compensation.

    (c)   Jerome has to demonstrate that he failed to get the job because of his ethnic origin rather than some other reason. He will have to show that he was as good as the successful candidate in terms of qualifications, personal qualities and experience. To demonstrate this he should refer to the job description and person specification. If Jerome possesses all the essential requirements set out in the person specification and yet the successful candidate lacked one or more essential requirement, then Jerome has a very strong case.

8   There was a legally binding contract between the builder and Mr Shah, even if it was not written down. There was:

- an offer to perform the work;
- acceptance of the offer;
- consideration – that is, payment promised for work to be carried out;
- capacity;
- an intention to be legally bound.

The builder did not complete the job – at best performance was only partial and, under English law, partial performance is no performance. However, in the case of a job such as Mr Shah's drive and patio, the courts are likely to treat it as two separate jobs under the one contract. As work on the drive was completed, the builder is entitled to demand payment for this part of the work. Equally, Mr Shah is entitled to regard the builder's failure to complete the patio within an agreed time as evidence of breach of contract by the builder. Therefore, the patio contract is brought to an end.

9   (a)   Product design
        The most important areas of law for product design relate to product safety and the liability of manufacturers in the case of injury to consumers and others. The producer has strict liability where a consumer sustains injury or ill health caused by the product. Producers should also ensure that, in designing a product, subsequent production processes do not endanger employees or contravene environmental protection laws.

    (b)   The keeping of records on computer
        The relevant legislation is the Data Protection Act 1984, which imposes restrictions on computer records. Such records should be:

- used only for the registered purpose;
- sufficient but not excessive for that purpose;
- be open to inspection by the individuals referred to;
- kept securely;
- accurate and up to date;
- be kept no longer than required.

    (c)   Production processes
        The relevant areas of law are the:

- Health and Safety at Work Act 1974, which imposes an obligation on employers to create a safe working environment;
- Environmental Protection Act, which controls emissions of specified substances.

    (d)   Selection and recruitment
        Relevant legislation includes the Sex Discrimination Act and the Race Relations Act (which prohibit discrimination on grounds of gender or race), Equal Pay Act (equal pay for the same or broadly similar work), Data Protection Act (relating to computer records) and the Employment Protection Acts (on the rights of employees). Mention could also be made of the law relating to spent (criminal) convictions and the employment of disabled people.

10   The question is, was the college lecturer unfairly dismissed or did she breach her contract of employment by engaging in outside activities? The statement in the contract leads one to conclude that she breached her contract and, as such, made the contract of employment void. However, was the clause that lecturers undertake no outside work fair and reasonable?

If not, then the main consideration should be whether or not these outside activities interfered with her college duties – for instance by engaging in activities that competed with her employer or took up such time that it reduced her effectiveness as a teacher.

11   Vicarious liability is liability for the actions of others. Employers are vicariously liable for the actions of employees who are in their normal course of duties.

(a)   The accident was caused by the lorry driver. We are not told whether he was driving a Speedy Carriers' lorry or his own car. If he was driving the lorry and was therefore engaged in his duties for Speedy Carriers Limited, then the employer is vicariously liable for damage sustained to the car.

(b)   Employers are vicariously liable for actions of employees, but, in this case, Jim was a subcontractor rather than an employee.

12   (a)   Population forecasts are based on past trends extrapolated into the future and projections of age structure into the future.

(b)   An ageing population presents:
- increased demand for products bought by older people;
- reduced demand for products bought by the young.

In addition, there will be a deterioration in the dependency ratio (ratio of dependants to workers) and a possible shortage of labour.

(c)   There will be an increase in the demand for healthcare, such that the NHS will be required to increase the level of, and expenditure on, healthcare merely to maintain the present position. This will necessitate higher taxes.

The consequences for private-sector firms could be:

- increased tax burden;
- NHS contracts for supply firms;
- increase of opportunities to provide healthcare.

(d)   In the 1980s, there was concern about the 'demographic time bomb' – the expected shortage of labour caused by a fall in the number of new entrants into the market. In reality, this did not prove to be a problem because of the recession of the early 1990s, but the long-term problem remains. Solutions take the form of:

- substitution of labour by capital;
- flexible working practices to retain the services of married women (flexitime, job share, prolonged maternity leave with periodic updating of training);
- concentration on core activities
- multiskilling.

13   (a)   The rise of the motor car.
Increase in leisure.
Changes in family life.
Rise in real disposable income.
Lower rents out of town.
Development of purpose-built retail units on greenfield sites.

(b)   Local authorities benefit from the business rates paid on industrial and commercial premises in their area. In an increasingly mobile society, authorities compete with one another to attract business into their areas.

(c)   Capital cost is allowed against tax, thus reducing the tax liability of developers.

(d)   The big names (Marks & Spencer, BHS, C&A) act as a magnet that attracts the smaller retailers. By attracting the 'big names' the smaller retailers will follow.

(e)   Concessions on rent.
        Purpose-built facilities.

(f)   Sited in the North East, the Metro Centre attracts visitors from Scandinavian countries. The latter enjoy high living standards even though living costs are high. A weak pound makes British goods cheaper to residents of foreign countries, thus making it attractive to Scandinavians to travel to the Metro Centre on a shopping trip.

14   This is intended as an investigative exercise. Inevitably students will be heavily dependent on material produced by the firm itself and/or material produced by an environmental pressure group. In each case, there is an opportunity to assess the material and separate out facts from PR statements (something that many students fail to do in project work).

(a)   Reference should be made to the Environmental Protection Act 1990, the Water Act 1990 and, of increasing importance, EU legislation on packaging, recycling, disposal of waste, disclosure of information and environmental management practices.

(b)   In identifying environmentally friendly activities, students should distinguish between claims and reality. It is likely that these activities will relate to the use of renewable resources, waste management, recycling and packaging.

(c)   Students should identify environmentally harmful activities, such as emissions, excessive waste, use of non-renewable materials and inefficiency in energy use. They should avoid libelling firms.

(d)   At this point, students should describe the environmental policies adopted by their firm, including its environmental review and audit arrangements.

15   Once again, students should avoid an uncritical acceptance of PR statements, while at the same time taking care not to libel the firm concerned.

16   The cases mentioned in this question are designed to encourage students to think clearly about the issues involved, including the hard business ones. In the student text, various ethical stances are identified:

•   the absolutist approach that certain practices are wrong;
•   the 'we play by the rules of the jungle' approach;
•   the 'unethical behaviour is not in the firm's or society's long-term interest' approach.

(a)   Foregoing this contract could jeopardize sales, output, jobs and profits and, in any case, if it is approved by the Ministry of Defence, then why should it bother a private-sector firm? However, military equipment sold to such a regime could add to human misery and harm the long-term prospects of the firm.

(b)   Once again, business profits are pitted against the immoral treatment of the workers concerned. Firms do have a moral responsibility for their actions.

(c)   Bio-diversity is important for the environmental health of our world, which is infinitely poorer as species become extinct. Business enterprises should be concerned about the future – if only for reasons of self-interest.

(d)   The use of non-sustainable/non-renewable resources is a form of short termism that will eventually backfire on the firm concerned.

Chapter 16

1 (a)

Quarter	Sales (£000)	Moving average (£000)
2002/1	235	
2	202	
3	203	208
4	192	207
		206.25
2003/1	231	204.25
2	199	201.25
3	195	198.50
4	180	197
2004/1	220	195.75
2	193	193.25
3	190	190.75
4	170	190
2005/1	210	
2	190	

Note: The position of the moving average between quarters.

(b) (c)

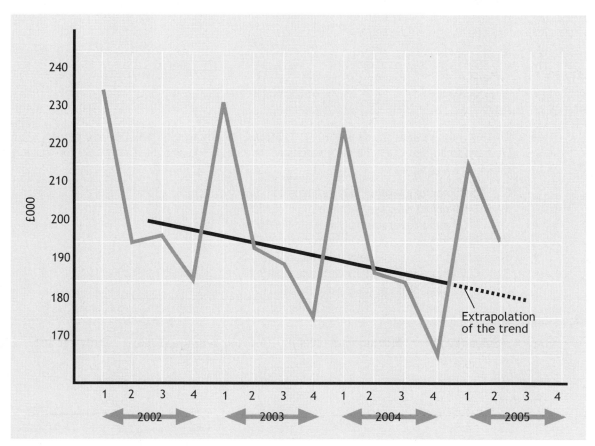

2   (a) (b)

Day	Sales	Moving average	Variation
S	300		
M	400		
T	400		
W	400	450	−50
Th	500	451	+49
F	550	451	+99
S	600	451	+149
S	310	453	−143
M	400	456	−56
T	400	456	−56
W	410	456	−46
Th	520	459	+61
F	550	460	+90
S	600	463	+137
S	330	461	−131
M	410	466	−56
T	420	469	−49
W	400	471	−71
Th	550	474	+76
F	570	474	+96
S	620	473	+147
S	350	476	−126
M	410	476	−66
T	410	480	−70
W	420	481	−61
Th	550		
F	600		
S	630		

(c)   The moving average shows a slowly rising trend that, by week 5, will be £490 per day. To this we have to add/subtract the daily variations that (on the basis of the four weeks for which data is given) are as follows:

S: £490 minus average daily variation of £133
M: £490 minus average daily variation of £58
Tu: £490 minus average daily variation of £58
W: £490 minus average daily variation of £57
Th: £490 plus average daily variation of £62
F: £490 plus average daily variation of £95
S: £490 plus average daily variation of £145.

3   (a) (b)

Day	Sales (£000)	Moving total (£000)	Moving average (£000)	Daily variation (£000)
S	5.0			
M	3.1			
Tu	3.6			
W	4.0	33.7	4.81	−0.81
Th	4.8	33.8	4.83	−0.03
F	6.6	33.9	4.84	+1.76
S	6.6	33.8	4.83	+1.77
S	5.1	34.2	4.89	+0.21
M	3.2	34.3	4.9	−1.7
Tu	3.5	34.5	4.93	−1.43

W	4.4	34.7	4.96	−0.56
Th	4.9	34.9	4.99	−0.09
F	6.8	35.2	5.03	+1.77
S	6.8	35.5	5.07	+1.73
S	5.3	35.6	5.09	+0.21
M	3.5	35.8	5.11	−1.61
Tu	3.8	35.9	5.13	−1.33
W	4.5	36.0	5.14	−0.64
Th	5.1	36.1	5.16	−0.06
F	6.9	36.2	5.17	+1.73
S	6.9	36.3	5.18	+1.72
S	5.4	36.4	5.20	+0.20
M	3.6	36.5	5.21	−1.61
Tu	3.9	36.6	5.23	−1.33
W	4.6	36.9	5.27	−0.67
Th	5.2			
F	7.0			
S	7.2			

Daily variation	Average
Sunday: 0.21, 0.21, 0.2,	0.21
Monday: −1.7, −1.61, −1.61	−1.64
Tuesday: 1.43, −1.33, −1.33	−1.36
Wednesday: −0.81, −0.56, −0.64, −0.67	−0.67
Thursday: −0.03, −0.09, −0.06	−0.06
Friday: 1.76, 1.77, 1.73	1.75
Saturday: 1.77, 1.73, 1.72	1.74

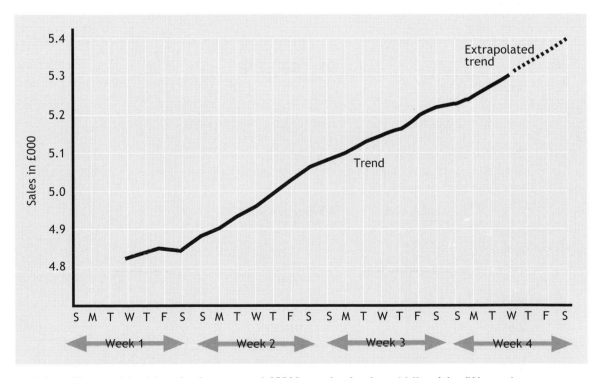

(c)   The trend is rising slowly to around £5500 per day by the middle of the fifth week.
From the extrapolated trend, we should add £210 for Sunday, £1750 for Friday and £1740 for Saturday. We should subtract £1640 for Monday, £1360 for Tuesday, £670 for Wednesday and £60 for Thursday.

(d)   The moving average technique enables you to smooth out the fluctuations in time series data and therefore separate out the trend from random, seasonal and cyclical fluctuations. By extrapolating the trend and adjusting for fluctuations, we can make forecasts for the future. The value of the technique depends on the trend continuing into the future with fairly regular fluctuations around the trend. If fluctuations are not regular and if there are unforeseen random factors at work, the forecasting value of the technique is limited.

4   (a) (b)

Quarter	Index	Moving total	Moving average	Centred average	Deviation
3	118				
4	101				
		418	104.5		
1	100			105	−5
		422	105.5		
2	99			106	−7
		426	106.5		
3	122			108	+14
		438	109		
4	105			110	−5
		442	110.5		
1	112			113	−1
		462	115.5		
2	103			115	−12
		458	114.5		
3	142			117	+25
		478	119.5		
4	101			120	−19
		482	120.5		
1	132				
2	107				

(c)

	Q1	Q2	Q3	Q4
Seasonal variation	−5	−7	+14	−5
	−1	−12	+25	−19
Average seasonal variations	−3	−9.5	+19.5	−12

5   (a)   The data shows cyclical fluctuations related to the state of the economy. Although the cycle is not completely regular, it does show a cycle over four to five years. Hence a 5-point moving average should be used.

	Sales (£m)	Moving average
1982	10	
1983	12	
1984	15	12.4
1985	13	13.6
1986	12	15.4
1987	16	17.2
1988	21	18.8
1989	24	20.2
1990	21	22
1991	19	22.8
1992	25	23.0
1993	28	23.6
1994	22	24.8
1995	24	25

1996	25	25.4
1997	26	26.2
1998	30	26.2
1999	26	25.8
2000	24	25.4
2001	23	25.6
2002	24	
2003	31	

(b) (c)

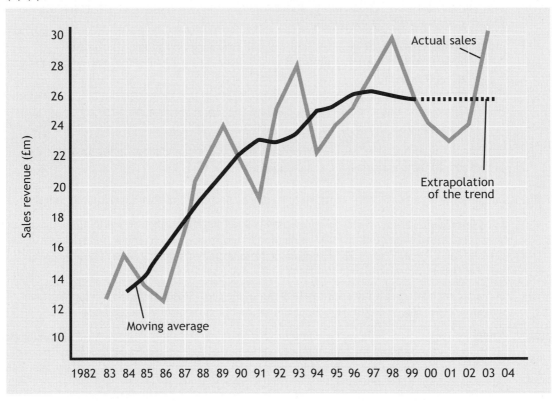

(d)   The report should draw attention to the following points.

- The data shows a rising tend to 1999, but a plateau seems to have been reached in early 2000. There are fluctuations around the trend in a four- to five-year cycle and, for this reason, a five-year moving average was used.

- Based on past experience, a downturn is highly probable in 2004 or 2005, but the cycle is not entirely predictable.

- If the downturn occurs in 2004 or 2005, the forecast sales for these years will be the trend minus the average seasonal variation.

- Limitations of the moving average method of forecasting:

    - it is based on the assumption that the past provides an insight into the future;
    - it assumes that fluctuations occur in a regular seasonal or cyclical manner;
    - it is unable to take account of random factors.

- Limitations of the additive method:
    - forecasting by this method involves the extrapolated trend plus or minus the average seasonal or cyclical variation from the trend;
    - it assumes that there is a constant cycle around the trend whereas it is more probable that the fluctuations will intensify in the case of a rising trend and diminish in the case of a falling trend.

Part III (end of Chapter 23, page 282)

1   This should be written in report form to cover the elements specified in the question and at the same time be consistent with the data given.

   (a)   Current state of the market
         Rather than merely restating the points given in the question, students should explain the significance of the reference to recovery, market share and consumer profile.

   (b)   Marketing strategies
         Students should outline possible strategies in relation to new markets, new segments and product development. For instance, the alternatives to concentrating on the popular end of the young market should be explored.

   (c)   Recommendations should be consistent with the evidence and should be realistic.
         (i)   In deciding on a pricing strategy, account should be taken of the market and the position of the firm within it.
         (ii)   Promotional strategies have to be feasible and within the constraint of a £1m budget.
         (iii) Channel strategy could either be a continuation of the existing strategy or an alternative (such as 'own shops', contract production, mail order).

         In all cases, students should attempt to justify their recommendations in terms of the data provided and their understanding of the market.

2   This is intended as an investigative exercise to explore and try out marketing research techniques.

   (a)   The report on secondary sources should be judged in terms of reference to specialist sources in your local library. It should go beyond national publications such as the *Annual Abstract of Statistics* and *Social Trends*. Local census material together with specialist market research reports should be quoted.

   (b)   The account should specify a survey technique, the most likely of which is a face-to-face questionnaire. This should be evaluated in terms of time, cost and reliability of data.

   (c)   Sampling methods include quota, random, systematic and cluster. In project work, many students claim to use the random method, but in the absence of a sampling frame this is not possible. Standing on the corner asking passers-by is *not* random sampling. A more appropriate method is quota sampling, but students must first calculate the size of quotas.

         The justification should be in terms of time, cost and reliability.

   (d)   The questionnaire should be judged in terms of:
         • coverage;
         • clarity of questions;
         • choice of language;
         • how realistic the questions are;
         • the avoidance of leading questions;
         • the use of structured, unstructured and scaling questions.

   (e)   Appropriate methods should be used in presenting the data. These should include tables, pie charts, bar charts and, where appropriate, histograms. Students should be encouraged to avoid endless repetition of pie charts in student projects and should appreciate that the method of presenting data should be clear and complete, have visual appeal and be efficient in terms of time and space.

   (f) (g) The final parts of this exercise require students to draw conclusions and make recommendations. The conclusion should be drawn from the data collected and presented and, following the conclusion, the report should make recommendations as to action. It is worth while reminding students that recommending no action is valid in the context of this assignment.

3   (a)   Plans detail the action to be taken. Inevitably plans are based on a forecast of the future course of events in the external environment. The forecasts are, in turn, based on assumptions, for example:

- real incomes;
- the level of employment;
- the pattern of a family life;
- exchange rates;
- competition in the marketplace.

       (b)   The overall objectives relate to profits, sales revenue, market share and their rate of growth. Marketing objectives are set for the marketing department and relate to its contribution to securing overall objectives. Examples include the volume and value of sales, not just overall but also for specific products.

       (c)   Marketing objectives for a new premium brand of ice-cream could include:

- 10% market share;
- 80% level of consumer awareness;
- £10m of sales;
- Sales of 20m units of ice-cream.

In each case, the objective should be time-specific – for example, the 10% market share to be achieved within 2 years.

       (d)   Objectives are statements of what the business seeks to achieve. Objectives should be quantified, verifiable and time-specific.
Strategies are statements of the broad campaign as to how the objectives are to be achieved – such as the marketing strategies to be used to achieve the objectives.
Tactics are more detailed statements of how the objectives are to be achieved.

       (e)   Budgets are plans expressed in financial terms. A sales budget is a forecast of sales revenue broken down by time and region. An appropriation budget will relate to planned expenditure on marketing activities, such as advertising, promotion, selling. Budget holders have discretion within the budget, but are required to keep within the budget total. Budgets play an essential role in the control process as actual results are compared with planned or budgeted results.

       (f)   Appendices should be used for detailed data or support material. By including it in the appendix, the material is available for the interested reader, but does not disrupt the flow of the report.

Possible appendix material includes:

- detailed market research findings;
- trends in sales of rivals or in similar countries;
- trends in leisure activities.

4 and 5   These exercises require students to adopt an imaginative approach to devising an appropriate plan. This should be judged by means of the following criteria:

- appropriateness of objectives and strategies;
- how realistic the plan is;
- the internal consistency of the plan;
- the extent to which it keeps within the constraints that have been identified;
- quality of language;
- the use of quantitative data.

6   (a)   The product is launched at the start of Year 1. Its sales grow over the next ten years, when it reaches a plateau of sales. This is either temporary or it has reached saturation.
The product generates a negative cash flow until Year 5, when it produces a sharply rising positive cash flow.
The explanation for earlier negative flow is:

- continuing development costs;

- high promotional expenditure in the early years;
- low volume of production means costly production.

In the later years, production costs fall as sales and output grow. Moreover, it is likely that promotional expenditure will be reduced.

(b) (i) Marketing objectives:

- Y% customer awareness by year 3;
- X% growth in sales per year over 6 years;
- £50,000 sales revenue by year 6;
- 10% market share by year 3.

Objectives should be set for each year.

(ii) Promotional strategies relate to the use of advertising, personal selling and sales promotion. It is likely that advertising will feature significantly in the early years, but will be reduced later. The nature of the promotion and the message will change over the years – for example, from information to persuasion to reminders.

(c) The product has reached the saturation or even the decline phase in Year 10. Sales have peaked and are likely to fall unless an extension strategy is used such as:

- product improvement;
- price reduction;
- repackaging;
- new promotional strategy;
- repositioning.

7 (a) The rise in profits follows the rise in sales revenue after a time lag. In the early years, the product is unprofitable because of inadequate sales volume, high costs of production and high promotional expenditure. It becomes increasingly profitable in the middle years in line with rising sales revenue. Profits level off as sales revenue reaches a plateau.

(b) Alternative extension strategies include:

- changes in packaging;
- a new pricing policy;
- a new promotional policy;
- changes in distribution.

(c) In the Boston Matrix, a cash cow is defined in terms of low sales growth and low market share. The graph does not provide data on market share, but the levelling off of sales suggests that little further growth is possible.

(d) (i) The pre-launch development phase was four years.

(ii) Products with an R&D phase of more than four years include:

- pharmaceutical products;
- motor vehicles;
- aircraft.

In the case of pharmaceutical products, the prolonged R&D time is the result of the necessity for prolonged testing to ensure product safety. Complicated, assembled products require extensive design work, although it should be pointed out that computer-aided design is reducing the design time required.

(iii) Products are aborted before launch for the following reasons:

- inadequate demand;
- changes in the external environment that reduce sales potential;
- problems with design and performance;
- actions of competitors;
- technological changes that make the product obsolete;
- high costs of production that reduce the profitability of the product.

Chapter 24

1

	FIFO	LIFO	Weighted average
Sales	500	500	500
Less Costs of sales			
Opening stock	50	50	50
plus purchases	400	400	400
minus closing stock	70	55	57
	380	395	393

(a) Gross profit   120   105   107

(b) Gross profit as percentage of sales revenue
(i) 24% (ii) 21% (iii) 21.4%

This exercise was designed to emphasize that, in calculating cost of sales, accountants add the cost of stock inherited from the past (opening stock), but do not charge up to the year's sales the cost of stock bequeathed to subsequent years (closing stock). Hence cost of sales equals opening stock, plus purchases, minus closing stock. The exercise also illustrates the point that the choice of method for evaluating stock affects the cost of sales and therefore the declared profits of the business.

2 (a) Under FIFO, stock is assumed to be used in the order in which it is purchased and therefore the closing stock is valued at the most recent price.

$70 \times £22 = £1540$

(b) Under LIFO, the most recent stock is assumed to be used first, resulting in the oldest stock remaining. At the end of April, 20 units were left from the January batch. To this was added a further 50 from the May batch.

$$20 \times £20 = £400$$
$$\text{plus } 50 \times £21 = £1050$$
$$£1450$$

(c) We first have to calculate the weighted average value.

$$100 \times £20 = £2,000$$
$$100 \times £21 = £2,100$$
$$300 \times £22 = £6,600$$
$$500 \qquad £10,700$$

Weighted average = £21.4

Value of stock $70 \times £21.4 = £1,498$

3 (a) FIFO and LIFO are two methods of valuing stock issues and closing stock. As such, the choice of method affects the value of cost of sales in a profit and loss account and therefore the declared profits.
Under FIFO it is assumed that the oldest stock is used first and therefore the closing stock is valued at the price paid for recent purchases.
Under LIFO it is assumed that the most recent stock is used first and therefore the remaining stock is derived from earlier purchases.

(b) FIFO The earlier stock is all used up and therefore the closing stock of 200 units come from the March batch.

$200 \times £8.75 = £1750$

LIFO The August batch was used up in September and so the 400 units left at the end of March consist of 200 from September and 200 from March. Under LIFO, the latter batch is used in May, leaving the residue of September batch as closing stock.

$200 \times £8.25 = £1650$

4

	£000
Sales revenue	300
Less Cost of sales	
Labour	100
Materials	75
Gross profit	125
Less Overheads	20
Trading profit	105
Less Interest	60
Profit before tax	45
Less Tax (33.3%)	15
Profit after tax	30
Less dividend	22.5
Retained profit	7.5

5

	£m
Sales revenue	6
Less Cost of sales	
Stock	2.4
Labour	1
Gross profit	2.6
Less Overheads	1.5
Less Interest	0.2
Profit before tax	0.9
Less Tax	0.27
Profit before tax	0.63
Distributed profit	0.315
Retained profits	0.315

6

	£000
Sales revenue	420
Less Cost of sales	
Labour	180
Materials	120
Gross profit	120
Less Overheads	30
Less Interest	20
Profit before tax	70
Less Tax	23.3
Profit after tax	46.66
Less dividend	35
Retained profits	11.66

7

	£000
Sales revenue	15,000
Less Cost of sales	7,500 (i)
Gross profit	7,500
Less Labour	600
Less Overheads	250
Less Costs associated with van	2,700
Net profit	3,950
Less Drawings	1,800
Retained profit	2,150

Note: Even though Barry had purchased £800 of stock on credit, this is still charged against the three months' trading. As the goods were sold during the period, so the costs associated with the sales are charged against the period's sales.

8

	A £000	B £000	C £000	D £000	E £000
Sales revenue	500	800	900	2,000	5,000
Cost of sales	400	400	700	1,000	3,000
Gross profit	100	400	200	1,000	2,000
Overheads	80	200	300	700	1,000
Operating profit	20	200	(100)	300	1,000
Non-operating profit	100	0	500	0	1,000
Profit before interest and tax	120	200	400	300	2,000
Interest	50	100	100	150	500
Profit before tax	70	100	300	150	1,500
Tax	30	30	200	50	500
Profit after tax	40	70	100	100	1,000
Dividend	30	50	40	50	500
Retained profit	10	20	60	50	500

9   Turnover rises 10% to £4562 × 1.1 = £5018
Gross profit rises to 35% of £5018 = £1756
Hence cost of sales is £5018 – £1756 = £3262
Distribution costs have to be disaggregated into fixed (40%) and variable (60%)

Fixed: £872 × 40% × .9 = £314
Variable: £872 × 60% × 1.1 = £575

Administrative costs fall to £624 × .9 = £562

	£000	£000
Turnover		5018
Less Cost of sales		3262
Gross profit		1756
Less Distribution costs	889	
Administrative costs	562	
		1451
Profit		305

10

	£000	£000
Sales (10% up)		2,200
Less Cost of sales (10% up)		1,430
Gross profit		770
Less Administrative costs (5% up)	315	
Selling costs (5% up)	210	525
Profit before tax		245
Less Corporation tax (25%)		61.25
Profit after tax		183.75
Less Dividend (50%)		91.875
Retained profit (50%)		91.875

Chapter 25

1 (a) Clearly this question is based on the reducing balance method as annual depreciation becomes smaller each year. The percentage rate used was:

Asset 1 $\dfrac{6,315}{20,000} \times 100 = 31.575\%$

Asset 2 $\dfrac{1,295}{10,000} \times 100 = 12.95\%$

(b) First, calculate the net book value at the end of the Year 4.
Asset 1 £20,000 less £15,616 = £4384
Less depreciation for Year 5 at 31.575% = 1384
Asset 2 £10,000 less £4258 = £5742
Less depreciation for Year 5 at 12.95% = £744

(c) Net book value at the end of Year 5 is NBV for end of year 4 less depreciation in Year 5.
Asset 1 £4384 – £1384 = £3000
Asset 2 £5742 – £744 = £4998

2 (a) (i) and (ii)

	£m
Historic cost	2
Less Depreciation (Year 1)	0.8
Balance	1.2
Less Depreciation (Year 2)	0.48
Balance	0.72
Less Depreciation (Year 3)	0.288
Balance	0.432

(b) £2m to £0.432m in 3 years:

Annual depreciation $= \dfrac{£2m - £0.432}{3} = £522,667$

(c) Depreciation is a negative item on a profit and loss account. As a result, profit figures would have been lower than the £10m by the extent of the annual depreciation.

	Straight line	Reducing balance
Year 1	£9,477,333	£9,200,000
Year 2	£9,477,333	£9,520,000
Year 3	£9,477,333	£9,712,000

The purpose of this last question is to demonstrate that declared profits are affected by the choice of depreciation method.

3 (a) Annual depreciation $= \dfrac{\text{Historic cost} - \text{Residual value}}{\text{Expected life}}$

(i) $\dfrac{£1.5m - £0.3m}{5} = \dfrac{£1.2}{5} = £0.24m$ per year

(ii)
End of Year 1	£1.26m
End of Year 2	£1.02m
End of Year 3	£0.78m
End of Year 4	£0.54m
End of Year 5	£0.3m

(b)

			£m
(i)(ii)	Balance	£20m	20
	Less Depreciation	(Year 1)	5
	Balance		15
	Less Depreciation	(Year 2)	3.75
	Balance		11.25
	Less Depreciation	(Year 3)	2.8125
	Balance		8.4375
	Less Depreciation	(Year 4)	2.109374
	Balance		6.328125
	Less Depreciation	(Year 5)	1.5820312
	Balance		4.7460937

The net book value at the end of Year 5 = £4,746,094

(c) (i)

Historic cost	£600,000
Less Depreciation (4 × £80,000)	£320,000
NBV after 4 years	£280,000

(ii)

Historic cost	£600,000
Residual value	£200,000
Total depreciation	£400,000

at £80,000 per year, this represents 5 years

(iii) £600,000 to zero at £80,000 per year:

$$\frac{£600,000}{£80,000} = 7.5 \text{ years}$$

4 (a) (i) and (ii)

	£m
Historic cost	40
Less Depreciation (Year 1)	20
Balance	20
Less Depreciation (Year 2)	10
Balance	10
Less Depreciation (Year 3)	5
Balance	5
Less Depreciation (Year 4)	2.5
Balance	2.5
Less Depreciation (Year 5)	1.25
Balance	1.25

(b) £40m to £1.25m in 5 years:

$$\text{Annual depreciation} = \frac{£40m - £1.25m}{5} = £7.75m$$

(c)

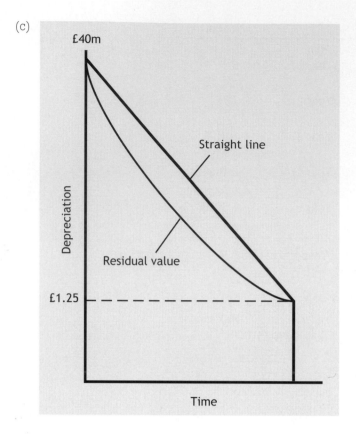

5

		£000	£000
Fixed assets	Land	210	
	Machinery	180	
	Fixtures	53	443
Current assets	Stock	62	
	Debtors	19	
	Cash	11	
Current liabilities	Creditors	34	58
Net assets			501
Financed by:			
	Loans		125.25
	Owners' equity		375.75

Source of funds			Use of funds	
	£000			£000
Owners' equity	375.75		Land	210
Loans	125.25		Machinery	180
Current liabilities	34		Fixtures	53
			Current assets	92
	535			535

6

	£000	£000
Fixed assets	60	
Depreciation	(20)	40
Current assets		
Stock	11	
Debtors	8	
Balance at bank	3	
	22	
Current liabilities	(14)	
Working capital (net current assets)		8
Net assets		48
Liabilities		5
		43
Shares issued and paid up		35
Reserves		8

7

	£000	£000
Fixed assets	1,700	
Less Depreciation	400 (i)	1,300
Current assets		
Stock	300	
Debtors	130	
Current liabilities		
Creditors	150	
Tax payable	70 (ii)	
Bank overdraft	80	
Working capital (net current assets)		130
Less Long-term liabilities		600
Shareholders' equity		830
Share capital		500
Reserves		330

Notes: (i) This is the cumulative figure.
      (ii) The £50,000 tax bill should have been paid in the year to 31 March 2005. This is a new tax bill.
      (iii) If current assets amount to £430,000 and working capital is £130,000, then current liabilities amount to £300,000. The 'missing' £80,000 can be attributed to a bank overdraft.

8

	£000	£000
Fixed assets *Less* Depreciation		25
Stock	3	
Debtors	16	
Cash	9	
Creditors	10	
Provisions	2.1	
Net current assets/working capital		15.9
Total assets *Less* Current liabilities		40
Financed by:		
Loan capital		10
Share capital		20
Reserves		10.9

Chapter 26

1 (a) (i) Working capital = Current assets – Current liabilities.

   Year 1   £51m – £35m   =   £16m
   Year 2   £61m – £68m   =   –£7m

   (ii) Current asset ratio $= \dfrac{\text{Current assets}}{\text{Current liabilities}}$

   Year 1 $\dfrac{£51m}{£35m}$ =   1.46

   Year 2 $\dfrac{£61m}{£68m}$ =   0.90

   (iii) Acid test ratio $= \dfrac{\text{Current assets – Stock}}{\text{Current liabilities}}$

   Year 1 $\dfrac{£27m}{£35m}$ =   0.77

   Year 2 $\dfrac{£26m}{£68m}$ =   0.38

(b) Explanations for deteriorating liquidity:

- increase in stockholding financed by trade credit and/or bank overdraft;
- the increase in stockholding might be the result of expansion plans or reflect problems in selling goods;
- the bank overdraft might reflect problems in selling goods or loss-making operations;
- the rise in debtors suggests either an increase in sale (with debtors rising in proportion) or difficulties in converting debtors into cash.

Although the Year 2 position looks precarious, much depends on the timing of the four payments and the bank's confidence in the business.

(c) Suggested improvements:

- reduce stockholdings, thereby reducing trade creditors and/or bank overdraft;
- provide incentives for prompt payment by customers, stricter credit control;
- unless the prepayments are particularly advantageous, it would have been better to retain the cash.

2 (a) (i) Current asset ratio

   Year 1 $= \dfrac{£1.5m}{£0.5m}$ =   3

   Year 2 $= \dfrac{£2m}{£1m}$ =   2

   (ii) Working capital   1   £1.5m – 0.5m = £1m
                          2   £2m – £1m = £1m

   (iii) If the acid test ratio is 1 in each year, then current assets less stock equals current liabilities.

   Year 1   Current assets   =   £1.5m
            CA *less* Stock   =   £0.5m
            Stock   =   £1m
   Year 2   Current assets   =   £2m
            CA *less* Stock   =   £1m
            Stock   =   £1m

(iv) If the debtor figure is the same as cash (and assuming no other current assets), then:

Year 1 cash = £0.25m
Year 2 cash = £0.5m

(b)

	CAR	Acid test
Year 1	3	1
Year 2	2	1

The acid test ratio remained unchanged but the current asset ratio (CAR) worsened (although still remaining very safe). Along with the 100% increase in current liabilities, there was a 100% rise in current assets other than stock. This suggests that either the firm did not invest in stock in line with an overall expansion or stock moved rapidly.

3 (a)

		A	B	C	D	E	F
(i)	Working capital (£000)	90	50	0	30	60	90
(ii)	CAR	2.12	1.62	1	1.25	2	2.8
(iii)	Acid test	0.87	1.5	0.09	0.83	1.67	2.4

(b) The starting point for this question is the textbook 'ideal' ratios of 1.5 to 2 for the current asset ratio and 1 to 1.5 for the acid test ratio.

With the exception of C and D, the current asset ratios can be regarded as safe and cautious. The acid test for C appears on the dangerously low side.

However, much depends on the nature of the business and the date of the balance sheet. For instance, in the run up to a seasonal peak in sales, C might be regarded as highly satisfactory. On the other hand, it would be unsatisfactory if the balance sheet was dated after the seasonal peak in sales.

4 (a) $\text{Debtor days ratio} = \dfrac{\text{Debtors}}{\text{Credit sales}} \times 365$

	Year 1	Year 2
Firm A	$\dfrac{500}{2500} \times 365 = 73$	$\dfrac{700}{2800} \times 365 = 91.25$
Firm B	$\dfrac{25}{950} \times 365 = 9.6$	$\dfrac{20}{920} \times 365 = 7.9$

(b) Company A is not only waiting longer than Company B for receipt of cash from debtors, but the waiting time is lengthening. This might be a sign of future problems as customers are finding it more difficult to pay their debts.

(c)

	Year 1	Year 2
Firm A	$\dfrac{40}{280} \times 365 = 52.1$	$\dfrac{50}{290} \times 365 = 62.9$
Firm B	$\dfrac{30}{300} \times 365 = 36.5$	$\dfrac{50}{340} \times 365 = 53.7$

(d) In both cases, the period before creditors are paid is lengthening. Although extended credit is helpful to a business, it might be the result of an inability to pay creditors.

(e) For company A, the longer time involved in receiving cash from debtors exceeds the extension of time in settling its own debts. Company B is in the more fortunate position of earlier payment by debtors, but increased length of time for paying its own debt.

(f) (i) This question focuses on credit sales and purchases, but no reference is made to the proportion of these transactions to cash sales and purchases.

(ii)   Comparison of the firms is only valid if they are similar in terms of product mix.

(iii)   The ratios do not inform us whether delays in payment or receipt are willingly agreed to or reflect an inability to settle.

5   (a)   'Debtors' means money that a firm expects to receive from its credit sales to individuals or organizations. Bad debt refers to money owed to a firm but which it has little or no prospect of receiving.

(b)   Contribution = Revenue – Variable costs
Contribution per unit = Price – Unit variable costs
Contribution = $10,000 \times (£10 – £8)$
$\qquad\qquad\quad$ = £20,000 per year

(c)   Sales revenue = £10 × 10,000 units
Credits sales are 50% of sales revenue
Bad debt is 10% of credit sales
$= £10 \times 10,000 \times .5 \times .1$
$= £5,000$ per year

(d)   Credit sales = £50,000 per year
Cost of financing credit sales for an average of 40 days

$$= £50,000 \times \frac{15}{100} \times \frac{40}{365} = £821.92$$

6   (a)   Stock turnover $= \dfrac{\text{Cost of sales}}{\text{Average stock level}}$

Average stock is taken as the average of opening and closing stock.

A $\quad \dfrac{£12,400}{£1200} \;=\; 10.3$

B $\quad \dfrac{£20,000}{£2600} \;=\; 7.7$

C $\quad \dfrac{£72,000}{£5500} \;=\; 13.1$

D $\quad \dfrac{£42,000}{£6000} \;=\; 7$

E $\quad \dfrac{£198,000}{£11,000} \;=\; 18$

F $\quad \dfrac{£42,000}{£1300} \;=\; 32.2$

(b)   A high turnover figure is expected in fast-moving goods (bread, newspapers, food, petrol). Hence, the stock turnover in company F would be usual for supermarket items but unusual in the case of furniture. The turnover figure in company D might be regarded as usual and satisfactory in the case of clothes retailing, but would be unusual and unsatisfactory in the case of a sweet shop.

7 (a)   Missing numbers

Company A	Depreciation	200
	Net current assets	90
	Long-term loans	330
Company B	Fixed assets	60
	Net current assets	10
	Reserves	20
Company C	Net fixed assets	80
	Creditors	50
	Share capital	20

(b) (i)   Working capital = Net current assets = Current assets – Current liabilities

Company A   £90,000
Company B   £10,000
Company C   £50,000

(ii) Current asset ratio = $\dfrac{\text{Current assets}}{\text{Current liabilities}}$

(iii) Acid test ratio = $\dfrac{\text{Current assets – Stock}}{\text{Current liabilities}}$

	A	**B**	**C**
Current asset ratio	$\dfrac{210}{120}$	$\dfrac{60}{50}$	$\dfrac{110}{60}$
	= 1.75	= 1.2	= 1.83
Acid test ratio	$\dfrac{110}{120}$	$\dfrac{40}{50}$	$\dfrac{60}{60}$
	= 0.92	= 0.8	= 1

(c)   Company A $\dfrac{330}{890} \times 100 = 37.1\%$

Company B $\dfrac{20}{60} \times 100 = 33.3\%$

Company C $\dfrac{100}{130} \times 100 = 76.9\%$

8 (a) (i)   Current asset ratio = $\dfrac{\text{Current assets}}{\text{Current liabilities}} = \dfrac{750}{600} = 1.25$

(ii)   Acid test = $\dfrac{\text{Current assets – Stock}}{\text{Current liabilities}} = \dfrac{250}{600} = .42$

(iii)   Working capital = Current assets – Current liabilities = £150,000

(b)   This question is designed to illustrate the impact on the above values of various transactions. It shows the ways in which the ratios can be affected by transactions.
(i)   Stock is up, but cash is down. This leaves the CAR and working capital unchanged, but the acid test is now $\dfrac{210}{600} = .35$

(ii)   Stock is up, but so too are current liabilities.
Working capital is unchanged.

CAR is now $\dfrac{790}{640} = 1.23$

Acid test is $\dfrac{250}{640} = .39$

(iii)   Cash is up, but other items are unchanged.

CAR $= \dfrac{850}{600} = 1.4$

Acid test $= \dfrac{350}{600} = .58$

Working capital is £850,000 – £600,000 = £250,000

(iv)   Debtors are down, but cash is up.
CAR, acid test and working capital are unchanged.

Chapter 27

1   (a)   If price–earnings ratio $= \dfrac{\text{Market price per share}}{\text{Earnings per share}}$

then market price $=$ Price–earnings ratio × Earnings per share
$= 14 \times 35\text{p} = 490\text{p}.$

(b)   Dividend yield $= \dfrac{\text{Dividends per share} \times 100}{\text{Market price}}$

$= \dfrac{11}{490} \times 100 \qquad = 2.24\%$

(c)   Profit margin $= \dfrac{\text{Operation profits}}{\text{Sales revenue}}$

$= \dfrac{80}{700} \times 100 \qquad = 11.43\%$

(d)   Interest cover $= \dfrac{\text{Operating profits}}{\text{Interest charges}}$

then interest charges $= \dfrac{\text{Operating profits}}{\text{Interest cover}}$

$= \dfrac{£80\text{m}}{3.8} \qquad = £21.05\text{m}$

2   **Profitability ratios**

(i)   Gross profit % $= \dfrac{£350}{£800} \times 100 = 43.75\%$

(ii)   Net profit % $= \dfrac{£300}{£800} \times 100 = 37.5\%*$

*Including non-operating income.
Excluding non-operating income, NP% = 31.25%

(iii)   Mark-up $= \dfrac{£350}{£450} \times 100 = 77.8\%$

(iv)   Return on capital employed (ROCE) $= \dfrac{£300}{£2020} \times 100 = 14.85\%$

Liquidity ratios

(i) Current asset ratio $= \dfrac{£150}{130} = 1.15$

(ii) Acid test ratio $= \dfrac{£150 - 50}{£130} = 0.77$

Investment ratios

(i) Dividend cover $= \dfrac{£150}{50} = 3$

(ii) Earnings per share $= \dfrac{£150}{£1000} = 15p$

(iii) Dividend per share $= \dfrac{£50}{£1000} = 5p$

(iv) Interest cover $= \dfrac{£300}{£100} = 3$

(v) Gearing $= \dfrac{£420}{£2020} = 20.8\%$

Efficiency ratios

In general, opening and closing figures are required for efficacy ratios, but, if we assume that values in the two accounts are also the average for the year, we can conclude that:

(i) Stock turnonver $= \dfrac{£50}{£200} \times 365 = 91.25$ days

(ii) Debtor days $= \dfrac{£50}{800} \times 365 = 22.8$ days

(iii) Creditors days $= \dfrac{£70}{£200} \times 365 = 127.75$ days

3 This exercise gives and opportunity for an historical comparison of performance. In addition to calculating appropriate ratios, students should draw conclusions about the performance of the company in the two years. It is this latter task that students find difficult and often neglect. A few general comments to make:

- the change in ratios might reflect a change in the firm's product mix;
- the identified movements in ratios might be short term rather than part of a longer-term trend;
- an inter-firm comparison with an enterprise possessing a similar product mix is essential for a full analysis.

Among the ratios that can be calculated are:

- ROCE: a rise from 9% to 10% on investment in the business – a move in the right direction;
- ROCE: a rise from 12.9% to 13.6% on shareholder's equity – again, a move in the right direction, although a proper evaluation should involve a comparison with the return on other investment (that is, opportunity costs);
- gross profit margin is down from 30% to 24%, illustrating the fact that growth of sales was not accompanied by an equivalent growth in profit;
- net profit margin also down from 11% to 8.9% for the same reason;
- mark-up on cost of sales fell from 42% to 31.5%, suggesting price cutting to increase the volume of sales and/or a change in the product mix;
- fixed asset turnover rose from 0.97 to 1.18, suggesting that an increase in sales was achieved with a less than proportionate rise in fixed assets;

- dividend cover fell from 2.4 to 2.3, reflecting the fact that dividends rose by more than profits;
- earnings per share rose from 7.6 pence to 8 pence.

Overall, this appears to be a company that is increasing its sales, but the benefits are not (yet) coming through in substantially increased profits.

4

		X	Y	Z
	Profit before interest and tax (£m)	10	10	10
(a)	Interest at 12% (£m)	0	2.4	6
	Profit before tax (£m)	10	7.6	4
(b)	Tax liability (£m)	3.3	2.5	1.3
(c)	Earnings available for distribution (£m)	6.7	5.1	2.7
(d)	Earnings per share (pence)	19	17	27

Note: Although Z recorded the lowest earnings available for distribution, the low number of shares issued raised the earnings per share.

5   (a)   Sales revenue = Average stock × Stock turnover
Net profit = Sales revenue × Net profit %

$$\text{ROCE} = \frac{\text{Net profit}}{\text{Capital employed}} \times 100$$

Total expenses (indirect costs) as % of sales revenue = $\dfrac{\text{Sales revenue} \times (\text{Gross profit \%} - \text{Net profit \%})}{\text{Sales revenue}}$

		A	B
(i)	Sales revenue	£480,000	£300,000
(ii)	Net profit	£24,000	£15,000
(iii)	ROCE	6%	10%
(iv)	Expenses as % of sales	15%	5%

(b)   The superior ROCE in the case of business B reflect its lower indirect costs (as well as its smaller capital figure). Hence, despite its slower turnover and lower gross profit percentage, it is able to achieve a net profit percentage in line with business A. It has indirect costs under greater control.

(c)   The interest that can be gained on deposit represents the opportunity cost of running a business enterprise. Business A is less profitable than the return on a bank deposit. Business B is no more profitable than the return on a bank deposit.

Chapter 28

1   (a)

	1 £000	2 £000	3 £000	4 £000	5 £000	6 £000
Inflow:						
Cash sales	100	125	150	200	225	250
Cash from credit sales	–	100	125	150	200	225
Total inflow (A)	100	225	275	350	425	475
Outflow:						
Stock	100	100	100	100	100	100
Pay	100	100	100	100	100	100
Electricity	–	–	50	–	–	50

	1 £000	2 £000	3 £000	4 £000	5 £000	6 £000
Advertising	20	10	10	10	10	10
Rates	–	–	30	–	–	–
Miscellaneous	10	10	10	10	10	10
Total outflow (B)	230	220	300	220	220	270
Net flow (A–B)	–130	+5	–25	+130	+205	+205
Opening balance	–45					
Closing balance	–175	–170	–195	–65	140	345

(b) The answer to this question will be similar to the above, but with one crucial difference – there will be no payment for stock in Month 1. Consequently, cash flow will improve by £100,000, giving a closing balance as follows:

			£
Month	1	–	75,000
	2	–	70,000
	3	–	95,000
	4	+	35,000
	5	+	240,000
	6	+	445,000

(c)

Stock:	from data available we have to conclude that stock was zero.
Debtors:	£225,000 owed to the firm from credit sales in Month 6.
Cash:	£445,000 – the closing balance in Month 6.
Less creditors:	£100,000 owed for stock purchases in Month 6.
Working capital	= £670,000 – £100,000
	= £570,000

2

							£000					
	J	F	M	A	M	J	J	A	S	O	N	D
Inflow:												
Cash sales	7	9	9	13	25	31	35	25	17.5	15	12.5	10
Cash from credit sales	0	7	9	9	13	25	31	35	25	17.5	15	12.5
Total inflow (A)	7	16	18	22	38	56	66	60	42.5	32.5	27.5	22.5
Outflow:												
Expenses	24	24	24	24	24	24	24	24	24	24	24	24
Rates	–	–	–	1.5	–	–	–	–	–	1.5	–	–
Electricity	.25	–	–	.25	–	–	.25	–	–	.25	–	–
Telephone	.2	–	–	.2	–	–	.2	–	–	.2	–	–
Total outflow (B)	24.45	24	24	25.95	24	24	24.45	24	24	25.92	24	24
Net cash flow (A – B)	–17.45	–8	–6	–3.95	14	32	41.55	36	18.5	6.55	3.5	–1.5
Opening balance	30											
Closing balance	12.55	4.55	–1.45	–5.4	8.6	40.6	82.15	118.15	136.65	143.2	146.7	145.2

3 (a)

£000

	J	F	M	A	M	J	J	A	S	O	N	D
Inflow:												
Cash sales	0	0	.9	1.8	2.7	3.6	4.5	4.5	2.7	1.8	.9	.9
Cash from credit sales	0	0	0	.1	.2	.3	.4	.5	.5	.3	.2	.1
Total inflow	0	0	.9	1.9	2.9	3.9	4.9	5	3.2	2.1	1.1	1
Outflow:												
Purchases of stock	0	.5	.5	.5	.5	1	1.5	1.5	1	.5	.5	.5
Labour	0	0	.2	.2	.2	.4	.4	.4	.4	.2	.2	.2
Rent	4	0	0	0	0	0	4	0	0	0	0	0
Equipment	1	1	1	1	1	0	0	0	0	0	0	0
Electricity	0	0	.1	0	0	.15	0	0	.2	0	0	.15
Advertisements	0	.05	.05	.05	.05	.05	.05	.05	.05	.05	.05	.05
Drawings	1	1	1	1	1	1	1	1	1	1	1	1
Total outflow	6	2.55	2.85	2.75	2.75	2.6	6.95	2.95	2.65	1.75	1.75	1.9
Net flow	(6)	(2.55)	(1.95)	(.85)	(.15)	1.3	(2.05)	2.05	.55	.35	(.65)	(.9)
Closing balance	1*	(1.55)	(3.5)	(4.35)	(4.2)	(2.9)	(4.95)	(2.9)	(2.35)	(2)	(2.65)	(3.55)

*Note: He started the year with savings of £7000.

(b) Dave will need an overdraft throughout the year, rising to £3400 by December.

(c) Dave faces the problems of:
- high start-up costs;
- seasonality.

Even allowing for these problems, the performance of the business is unsatisfactory. Not only does Dave end the year with an overdraft, it is unlikely that by the end of year 2 he will have restored his bank balance to the £7000 he started with. If he had phased the purchased of equipment over a longer period, his cash position would have been healthier, but, unless he reduces running costs or increases sales revenue, the café will provide only a modest return.

4 (a)

£000

	J	F	M	A	M	J
Inflow:						
Cash sales	500	500	500	500	500	1,000
Cash from credit sales	200	500	500	500	500	500
Total inflow	700	1,000	1,000	1,000	1,000	1,500
Outflow:						
Stock	300	200	200	200	200	200
Rent	250	0	0	250	0	0
Electricity	0	150	0	0	150	0
Labour	0	0	0	0	0	500
Drawings	700	700	700	700	700	700
Total outflow	1,250	1,050	900	1,150	1,050	1,400
Net flow	(550)	(50)	100	(150)	(50)	100
*Closing balance	(50)	(100)	0	(150)	(200)	(100)

*Note: They started the year with a balance of £500.

	J	A	S	O	N	D
Inflow:						
Cash sales	1,000	1,000	1,000	500	500	500
Cash from credit sales	1,000	1,000	1,000	1,000	500	500
Total inflow	2,000	2,000	2,000	1,500	1,000	1,000
Outflow:						
Stock	200	200	200	200	200	200
Rent	250	0	0	250	0	0
Electricity	0	150	0	0	150	0
Labour	500	500	0	0	0	0
Drawings	700	700	700	700	700	700
Total outflow	1,650	1,550	900	1,150	1,050	900
Net flow	350	450	1,100	350	(50)	100
Closing balance	250	700	1,800	2,150	2,100	2,200

(b)   The cost of stock will rise by £20 per month from April, although the one month's credit means that the first outflow of the higher amount will be in May. Hence, £20 per month should be added to total outflow and the same amount should be deducted from both new flow and the closing balance. They will now finish the year with a balance of £2200 – (8 × £20) = £2040.

(c)   A one-off payment of £700 in September will increase total outflow in the month by £700. This will reduce net flow in September and will reduce the closing balance figure by £700. The end of the year balance will now be £2040 – £700 = £1340.

5   (a)   (i)   A cash statement (whether a budget or an after-the-event cash flow statement) only includes those items in which cash flows in to and out of the firm. A profit and loss account includes items in which there is no cash flow or no cash flow during the time period concerned. Non-cash items include:

  - depreciation;
  - credit sales;
  - purchases of input on credit.

   (ii)   Gross profit   =   Sales revenue – Direct costs
         Net profit   =   Gross profit – Indirect costs

(b)

	Year 1 £000	Year 2 £000	Year 3 £000
Cash from sales	876	1,238	1,890
Cash outflow – direct costs	(682)	(812)	(1176)
– indirect costs	(192)	(231)	(235)
Net cash flow	2	195	479

As depreciation does not involve a cash outflow, it is not included in the calculation. Hence, the net cash flow is £61,000, £71,000 and £71,000 (respectively) higher than the net profit figure.

(c)

	Year 1 £000	Year 2 £000	Year 3 £000
Inflow:			
Cash sales	788.4	1,114.2	1,701
Cash from credit sales	0	87.6	123.8
Total inflow	788.4	1,201.8	1,824.8
Outflow:			
Cash outflow			
Direct costs	(682)	(812)	(1,176)
Indirect costs	(192)	(231)	(235)
Total outflow	(874)	(1,043)	1,411
Net cash flow	85.6	158.8	413.8

6   This question concerns the first item on a cash flow statement. The starting point is operating profit, from which we subtract items leading to cash outflow, but add back in terms where there was no cash outflow.

	(a) (£m)	(b) (£m)	(c) (£m)
Operating profit	2	10	15
Depreciation	0.3	2	3
Reduction (increase) in stocks	(0.2)	1	2
Reduction (increase) in debtors	(0.3)	2	(3)
(Reduction) increase in creditors	0.1	(3)	(1)
	1.9	12	17

7   **Company A**

	£000	£000
Net cash inflow from operations		155
Tax paid		(80)
Return on investment and servicing of finance:		
Interest paid	(105)	
Interest received	25	
Dividends paid	(75)	(155)
Investing activities:		
Purchase of fixed assets	(400)	
Proceeds from disposals	48	(352)
Net cash flow before financing		(432)
Financed by:		
Share issue	250	
Debenture issue	200	
Loan	100	550
Increase in cash		118

Company B

	£000	£000
Net cash inflow from operations		950
Tax paid		(300)
Return on investment and servicing of finance:		
Interest paid	(50)	
Interest received	30	
Dividends paid	(200)	(220)
Investing activities:		
Purchase of fixed assets	(1,700)	
Proceeds from disposals	(50)	(1,650)
Net cash flow before financing		(1,220)
Financed by:		
Share issue	200	
Debenture issue	(100)	
Loan	200	300
Decrease in cash		920

Company C

	£000	£000
Net cash inflow from operations		1,020
Tax paid		(200)
Return on investment and servicing of finance:		
Interest paid	(40)	
Dividends paid	(300)	(340)
Investing activities:		
Purchase of fixed assets	(600)	
Proceeds from disposals	20	(580)
Net cash flow before financing		(100)
Financed by:		
Debenture issues	(200)	
Loan	500	300
Increase in cash		200

Chapter 29

1   (a)   Shares offered to the public as against shares being placed with a large institutional investor.

     (b)   These merchant banks guarantee to buy up unsold shares, thus ensuring the success of a share issue.

     (c)   115p is the issue price of these shares, which had a nominal (or face) value of 10p. The difference between the two values is recorded as the share premium in the balance sheet.

     (d)   Value of the company in terms of the current market value of shares.

     (e)   The attractiveness of a share offer is linked to the prospects for profit.

        •   Refurbishment and the development of out-of-town superstores is crucial to the success of a retail chain.
        •   The enhanced and expanded product range will enable the chain to increase sales in the future.
        •   Vertical integration will increase profitability via economies of scale and elimination of the middleman.
        •   Cost control is essential in securing profits. Without cost control, profits will be eroded. Controlling working capital could take the form of stock reductions (just-in-time techniques) or credit control.

2   (a)   Nominal value = 40m × 10p = £4m
           Market value = 40m × £1 = 40m

     (b)   Underwriting a share issue is essential to guarantee its success. Merchant banks charge commission for underwriting an issue.

     (c)   Companies are allowed to issue shares up to their authorized issue. This can only be raised if approved by shareholders. Issued share capital refers to the amount of shares actually issued.

     (d)   Shareholders should be interested in the extent of loan capital for two reasons:

        •   inability to meet interest payments could lead to closure of the business;
        •   the greater the commitment to meet interest charges, the lower the profits available for distribution.

     (e)   Value of shares to be issued is £40m and yet the net proceeds are only £38.4m. Public issue of shares is very expensive and is only available to the very largest of companies.

     (f)   Net asset value per shares: 96.05p
           Number of shares   40m
           Net asset value of trust   =   £38.42

3   (a)   The company has not issued shares up to its authorized share capital figure. Consequently, it can raise more finance by a share issue without seeking the approval of the sharesholders.

       (b)   Preference shares carry a fixed percentage rate of interest and holders have a prior claim on profits and proceeds from the sale of assets in the event of liquidation. The fact that they are cumulative means that any shortfall in dividends will be made up in subsequent years.
The dividends on ordinary shares are not fixed and holders only receive dividends after all prior claims have been met.

       (c)   The prior claim reduces the dividends available to ordinary (equity) shareholders, especially as shortfalls in dividends on preference shares are carried forward.

       (d)   (i)   110,932 shares: £28,000.

             (ii)   Preference shares have declined in popularity as a result of inflation (at times dividends were negative in real terms), the availability of other forms of investment and the lower rights of participation conferred on preference shareholders.

       (e)   The authorized capital is stated in the memorandum of association. This can only be altered by a 75% majority of votes in an extraordinary general meeting of shareholders.

4   (a)

	1	2	3	4	5
Profit	500	400	300	250	210
Interest	20	20	20	20	20
Profit after interest	480	380	280	230	190
Tax	168	133	98	80.5	66.5
Profit after tax	312	247	182	149.5	123.3
Preference dividend	10	10	10	10	10
Profits for distribution	302	237	172	139.5	113.5
Retained profit	151	118.5	86	69.75	56.75
Dividend	151	118.5	86	69.75	56.75 (£000)

       (b)   The dividend on ordinary shares ranges from $\dfrac{£151,000}{1,000,000} \times 100 = 15\%$

             to $\dfrac{£56,750}{£1,000,000} \times 100 = 5.7\%$

             This compares with the fixed 10% on preference shares. Hence, the dividends on ordinary shares are higher in the years of high profit but lower in the years of low profit.

       (c)   The amount of retained profit depends on the profitability of the business in the year in question and the dividend. Although the latter can be reduced in order to retain profits for reinvestment, shareholders will insist on satisfactory dividends. Hence, retained profit cannot be relied on as a source of finance.

5   (a)   (i)   Dividends received by the company from its shareholdings in other companies.

             (ii)   The equity of shareholders in a subsidiary company.

             (iii)   Profits available for distribution.

       (b)   By the board of directors to shareholders in the annual meeting of shareholders.

       (c)   Dividends are determined by:
- profits;
- investment plans of the company.

             Despite the fall in profits, the amount paid out in dividends remained unchanged.
It is necessary to provide shareholders with a satisfactory level of dividends.

       (d)   Shareholders' fund equals the value of a company after all prior claims against its assets have been met. It is equal to share capital plus reserves.

$$\text{Shareholders' fund per share} = \frac{\text{Share capital + Reserves}}{\text{Number of shares issued}}$$

(e) Dividends paid in Year 2 = £154m
Dividends per share in Year 2 = £5.38

$$\text{Share capital} = \frac{£154m}{£5.38} = £28,624,535$$

6 (a)
Personal	–	individuals who own shares.
Charities	–	charitable bodies that invest in shares. It should be appreciated that many organizations in the not-for-profit sector seek charitable status for tax reasons.
Public	–	this refers not to the general public but to public-sector bodies.
Financial institutions	–	collect savings from people and firms and invest the money in shares and other stock exchange securities.
Companies	–	companies buying shares in other companies.
Overseas	–	ownership of shares in UK companies by overseas individuals, companies and governments.

(b) The table shows the:

- long-term decline in private shareholders;
- continuing rise of institutional shareholders;
- rapid growth in pension fund and insurance company ownership of shares;
- relative decline of investment trusts;
- rise of foreign ownership of shares in UK companies.

(c) Popular capitalism was a declared policy of the Thatcher government and it was continued under Major. The objectives were to increase share ownership in order to secure funds for industry, encourage individuals to share in capital gains and alter the culture of the UK. The mechanisms to achieve this change were:

- privatization issues, which were weighted in favour of small investors;
- development of share shops;
- the unlisted securities market (now resurrected as the Alternative Investment Market) and the Business Expansion Scheme;
- employee share ownership schemes, encouraged by tax concessions;
- deregulation of markets, such as the changes in the building society sector.

The evidence suggests that they were not successful because:

- new shareholders own small quantities of shares;
- many of the new class of shareholders sold their shares (usually to institutions) soon after buying them; some of the big privatization issues resulted in short-term capital gain.

(d) Overseas ownership grew in the 1980s because of:

- investment in the UK was seen as attractive and profitable, especially during the period of rapid growth during the Lawson boom;
- low taxation in the UK;
- investors liking the deregulation policy of the then Conservative government;
- the abolition of exchange controls in 1979, which facilitated the transfer of capital;
- membership of the EU.

Implications:

- increases in the supply of funds for UK companies;
- capital inflow to improve the balance of payments;
- dividends remitted abroad become debit items on the balance of payments.

7 (a) High Gee: $\dfrac{\pounds 7}{\pounds 10m} \times 100 = 70\%$

Low Gee: $\dfrac{\pounds 2.5m}{\pounds 10m} \times 100 = 25\%$

(b)

High Gee	Year 1	2	3	4
Dividend: (£m)	0.5	0.3	0.1	0
% dividend = $\dfrac{\text{Dividend}}{\text{Share capital}} \times 100$	16.7	10	3.3	0

Low Gee	Year 1	2	3	4
Divdend (£m)	0.95	0.75	0.55	0.45
% dividend	12.7	10	7.3	6

This question was designed to illustrate the impact of gearing on profits available for distribution.

8 (a) Gearing ratio = $\dfrac{\text{Loan stock}}{\text{Shareholders' equity + Loan}} \times 100$

A: $\dfrac{\pounds 8m}{\pounds 10m} \times 100 = 80\%$

B: $\dfrac{\pounds 2m}{\pounds 10m} \times 100 = 20\%$

(b) Earnings per share = $\dfrac{\text{Profit after interest and tax}}{\text{Number of shares}}$

For this question, ignore taxation.

	Company A Interest charge: £800,000 Number of shares: 2m			**Company B** Interest charge: £200,000 Number of shares: 8m		
	Profits (£m)	PAI (£m)	EPS (p)	Profits	PAI	EPS (p)
1	0.8	0	0	0.8	0.6	7.5
2	1.0	0.2	10	1.0	0.8	10
3	1.2	0.4	20	1.2	1.0	12.5
4	1.4	0.6	30	1.4	1.2	15
5	1.6	0.8	40	1.6	1.4	17.5
6	1.8	1.0	50	1.8	1.6	20

(c) Where a high proportion of long-term finance comes from fixed interest capital (debentures or preference shares), the profits available for distribution to equity shareholders is subject to greater fluctuation than when a low proportion of finance is fixed interest.

(d) Gearing is also significant in terms of:

- the degree of dilution of ownership;
- vulnerability to business failure.

9 (a) (i) Dividends paid = £100m – £40m = £60m

(ii) Number of shares = $\dfrac{\text{Dividends paid}}{\text{Dividends per share}} = \dfrac{\pounds 60m}{\pounds 0.3} = 200m$

(iii) Earnings per share = $\dfrac{\text{Profits available for distribution}}{\text{Number of shares}}$

$\qquad = \dfrac{£100\text{m}}{200\text{m}} = 50\text{p}$

(b) Earnings per shares is the amount of earnings available for distribution per share whereas dividends per share is the amount actually distributed per share.

(c) Price–earnings ratio = $\dfrac{\text{Market price per share}}{\text{Earnings per share}}$

$\qquad = \dfrac{£1.50}{£0.50} = 3$

The price–earnings ratio reflects investor confidence. The higher the ratio, the more confident the market is that the level of earnings will be maintained or improved.

10 (a) ROCE = $\dfrac{\text{Profit after tax}}{\text{Capital employed}} \times 100$

$\qquad = \dfrac{£150,000}{£1,000,000} \times 100 = 15\%$

(b) Dividend yield = $\dfrac{\text{Dividends per share}}{\text{Market price}} \times 100$

$\qquad = \dfrac{12\text{p}}{250\text{p}} \times 100 = 4.8\%$

(c) Dividend cover = $\dfrac{\text{Earnings per share}}{\text{Dividends per share}}$

Earnings per share = $\dfrac{\text{Profits available for distribution}}{\text{Number of shares}}$

$\qquad = \dfrac{£150,000}{1\text{m}} = 15\text{p}$

Dividend cover = $\dfrac{15\text{p}}{12\text{p}} = 1.25$

(d) 15p

(e) Price–earnings ratio = $\dfrac{\text{Market price per share}}{\text{Earnings per share}}$

$\qquad = \dfrac{250\text{p}}{15\text{p}} = 16.67$

11 (a) (i) Instead of retained profits being added to reserves, this represents losses, which are subtracted from reserves.
(ii) Accumulated losses of £36m.

(b) Should dividends be paid at all? With no positive reserves and a loss on current activities, the financing of dividends will lead to a further rise in liabilities.

(c) The negative reserve means that shareholders' equity is substantially less than the share capital in the company.

12 (a) (i) Extraordinary items arise from abnormal events lying outside the ordinary ranges of business activity and are not expected to recur.
(ii) Generated internally means generated from sales less outgoings.
(iii) Revaluation involves placing a different valuation on an asset from the current recorded value.
(iv) Book value is the value of an asset as recorded in the accounts.

(b)   The value of property owned by the company is 366% of the nominal value of shares.

(c)   £87.863 million divided by 3.66 = 24,006,284 shares.

(d)   When a company is sold, it is important to revalue assets in line with current market values. A rise in the value of fixed assets must be accompanied by a corresponding rise in shareholders' equity in the form of a revaluation of reserves.

(e)   The three adjustments are extraordinary items (which raise profits), taxaton (which reduces profits available for distribution) and retained profits (which are retained at the expense of dividends).

(f)   The dividend as a percentage of the value of shares.

Chapter 30

1   Initial outlay £20,000
Annual savings £8000 less (£1500 + £500)
Residual value £5000

Year	Cash flow (£000)	Discount factor	Present value (£000)
0	−20	1	−20
1	6	0.91	5.46
2	6	0.82	4.92
3	6	0.74	4.44
4	6	0.67	4.02
5	6+5	0.61	6.71
		NPV+	5.55

NPV = £5550

2

Year	Discount factor	A (£000)	B (£000)	C (£000)
0	1	−100	−100	−100
1	0.91	91	9.1	0
2	0.86	86	8.6	8.6
3	0.79	0	79	79
4	0.73	0	73	73
5	0.68	0	0	102
	NPV	+77	+69.7	+162.6

Rank order of profitability: C, A, B.

3   (a)   (i)

Year	Cash flow (£000)	Cumulative cash flow (£000)
0	−750	−750
1	200	−550
2	250	−300
3	250	−50
4	200	+150
5 + RV	200	+350

Answer: 3.25 years

(ii)   Total return   =   £1,100,000
Total profit   =   £1,100,000 − £750,000
                 =   £350,000 over 5 years
Profit per year = £70,000

$$ARR = \frac{£70,000 \times 100}{£750,000} = 9.33\%$$

(b) (i)

Year	Cash flow (£000)	DF (8%)	PV
0	−750	−1	−750
1	200	0.93	186
2	250	0.86	215
3	250	0.79	197.5
4	200	0.74	148
5 + RV	200	0.68	136
			NPV = £132,500

(ii)

Year	Cash flow (£000)	DF (10%)	PV
0	−750	1	−750
1	200	0.91	182
2	250	0.83	207.5
3	250	0.75	187.5
4	200	0.68	136
5 + RV	200	0.62	124
			NPV = £87,000

(iii)

Year	Cash flow (£000)	DF (12%)	PV
0	−750	−1	−750
1	200	0.89	178
2	250	0.80	200
3	250	0.71	177.5
4	200	0.64	128
5 + RV	200	0.57	114
			NPV = £47,500

In all three cases, the NPV figure is positive, suggesting that at each rate of discount the project is worth while.

(c) The internal rate of return (IRR) is in excess of 12%. Applying a rate of 14%, we find that the NPV is +£2,400.

Therefore IRR is a fraction above 14%. The exact figure can be interpolated from a graph.

4 The three-year payback rule as a screening device rules out project B.

Year	Discount factor	Present value Project A (£m)	Project C (£m)
0	1	−10	−10
1	0.91	3.64	7.28
2	0.83	3.32	4.98
3	0.75	6.00	3.00
4	0.68	5.44	2.72
5	0.62	6.20	2.79
	NPV =	£14.6	£10.77

Note: The return in Year 5 includes residual values.

Project A has a higher NPV and therefore should be chosen.

5 (a) (i) Project A, payback in 4 years.
Project B, payback in 4.5 years.

(ii)　　Project A　　Total return = £300,000
　　　　　　　　　　Net return = £100,000 or £20,000 p.a.

$$ARR = \frac{£20,000 \times 100}{£200,000} = 10\%$$

Project B　　Total return = £350,000
　　　　　　　Net return = £100,000 or £20,000 p.a.

$$ARR = \frac{£20,000 \times 100}{£250,000} = 8\%$$

(iii)

Year	DF	Project A Cash flow	PV	Project B Cash flow	PV
0	1	−200	−200	−250	−250
1	0.91	50	45.5	40	36.4
2	0.83	50	41.5	40	33.2
3	0.75	50	37.5	60	45
4	0.68	50	34	60	40.8
5 + RV	0.62	100	62	150	93
			NPV = +20.5		NPV = −1.6

(b)　Project A pays back in a shorter time and has a higher ARR. More importantly, only project A has a positive NPV. Therefore Project A should be recommended.

6　(a)　Cumulative discount rates can be used as the return is the same in each year.
PV of £500,000 p.a. for 5 years:
− at 8% = £500,000 × 4.0 = £2,000,000
− at 10% = £500,000 × 3.79 = £1,895,000
− at 12% = £500,000 × 3.61 = £1,805,000

(b)　NPV at 8% = +£110,000
NPV at 10% = +£5,000
NPV at 12% = −£85,000
Answer 10%

(c)　The IRR is the rate of discount at which the NPV is zero. This will be a fraction in excess of 10% – say 10.1%.

(d)　If the rate of interest is 12%, then the firm should use a 12% rate of discount in the investment appraisal exercise. The 12% rate gives a negative NPV. The IRR is less than 12% and therefore the project is not profitable.

7　In each case, the initial cost of investment has been deducted.

$$\text{Profits per year for Project X} = \frac{£160,000}{4} = £40,000$$

$$ARR = \frac{£40,000}{£300,000} \times 100 = 13.3\%$$

$$\text{Profits per year for Project Y} = \frac{£160,000}{4} = £40,000$$

$$ARR = \frac{£40,000}{£300,000} \times 100 = 13.3\%$$

$$\text{Profits per year for Project Z} = \frac{£200,000}{4} = £50,000$$

$$ARR = \frac{£50,000}{£300,000} \times 100 = 16.7\%$$

Recommendation:
On the basis of the ARR, project Z is recommended, despite the slow return.
It should also be noted that the ARR fails to discriminate between project X and project Y, despite the difference in the timing of the return.

8   (a)   (i)   Payback $= \dfrac{£370,000}{£90,000} = 4.11$ years

        (ii)

Year	Cash flow (£000)	DF	PV (£000)
0	−370	1	−370
1–6	90	3.889	350.1
RV	20	0.456	9.2
		NPV =	−10.7

        (iii)   The IRR is less than 14%
                13% rate of discount gives an NPV of −£580
                12% rate of discount gives an NPV of +£10,300
                Therefore, the IRR is between 12 and 13%, but closer to the latter – say 12.9%.

    (b)   Other factors to consider:

        • availability of funds;
        • liquidity;
        • alternative uses of the funds;
        • target return;
        • external environment;
        • impact on gearing.

    (c)   The payback methods is easy to understand and discriminates in favour of projects with an early return. However, it ignores the time value of money and leads to neglect of profitable, long-term projects. NPV takes total return and timing into account, but its validity depends on the choice of discount rate. The IRR overcomes the problem of choosing a rate of discount, but is more complicated than other methods.

9   In each case, the cash inflow is the same in each year and therefore cumulative discount factors can be used. The IRR is the rate of discount at which NPV is zero.

    (i)   (£100,000 × cumulative discount factor) – £375,000 = 0

        Cumulative discount factor $= \dfrac{375,000}{100,000} = 3.75$

        Consult a table of cumulative discount factors to identify the rate of discount in which factors total 3.75 over 5 years.
        Answer, between 10 and 11%

        10% rate of discount will result in an NPV of £100,000 × 3.791 = 379,000   375,000 = +£4100

        11% rate of discount will result in an NPV of £100,000 × 3.696 = 369,600 – 375,000 = −£5400

    (ii)   (£50,000 × CDF) – 190,000 = 0

        CDF $= \dfrac{£190,000}{£50,000} = 3.8$

        Consult a cumulative discount factor table to discover the rate of discount that totals 3.8 over 6 years.
        Answer, between 14 and 15%, but closer to the latter.

117

(iii) $(£40,000 \times \text{CDF}) - £250,000 = 0$

$$\text{CDF} = \frac{£350,000}{£40,000} = 6.25$$

Over 8 years, the CDF for 6% is 6.21, for 5% it is 6.463.
Answer, between 5 and 6%, but closer to the latter.

(iv) $(£100,000 \times \text{CDF}) = \dfrac{£410,000}{100,000} = 4.1$

Over 5 years, the discount factors sum to 4.1
Answer, 7% exactly.

For all previous questions, the exact IRR can be obtained by interpolating a graph.

10   (i)

Cash flow (£000)	Cumulative discount factor		Present value (£000)
−600	1		−600
+250	3.17		+792.5
		NPV =	+192.5

(ii)

−1,500	1		−1,500
+400	4.623		+1,849.2
		NPV =	349.2

11   (i) $(£200,000 \times \text{CDF}) - £600,000 = 0$

$$\text{CDF} = \frac{600,000}{200,000} = 3.0$$

19% rate of discount gives a CDF of 3.58
20% rate of discount gives a CDF of 2.99
Answers, close to 20% – say 19.9%

(ii) $(£100,000 \times \text{CDF}) - £500,000 = 0$
CDF = 5

10% rate of discount gives a CDF of 4.868
9% rate of discount givs a CDF of 5.033
Answer, between 9% and 10%, but closer to the former.

12   For these questions we can use a table of cumulative discount factors.

(i)

Cash flow		Discount factor		Present value
−£700,000	×	1		£700,000
£200,000	×	3.791		£758,200
			NPV =	+£58,200

(ii)

−£1,500,000	×	1		−£1,500,000
£500,000	×	3.312		£1,656,000
			NPV =	+£156,000

13   (i) The IRR when the net present value is 0 – that is, when the present value of the return = initial cost

£100,000 × Discount factor = £400,000

Consult a table of cumulative discount factors to find the rate of discount that gives a cumulative factor of 4 over 5 years.

Test rates
7% gives a factor of 4.1
8% gives a factor of 3.993

−£400,000	×	1	=	−£400,000
+£100,000	×	4.1	=	+£410,000
			NPV =	+£10,000
−£400,000	×	1	=	−£400,000
−£100,000	×	3.993	=	+£399,300
			NPV =	−£700

Answer, the IRR is between 7 and 8%, but closer to the latter. The exact figure can be obtained by reading a value off a graph.

(ii) £150,000 × Cumulative discount factor = £600,000

Consult a table of cumulative discount factors to find the rate of discount that gives a cumulative factor of 4 over 7 years.

16% gives a factor of 4.039
17% gives a factor of 3.992

−£600,000	×	1	=	−£600,000
+£150,000	×	4.039	=	+£605,850
			NPV =	+£5,850
−£600,000	×	1	=	−£600,000
+£150,000	×	3.922	=	+£588,300
			NPV =	−£11,700

Answer, the IRR is between 16 and 17%, but closer to 16%.

14

		Project A	Project B
(i)	Payback	3.66 years	3 years
(ii)	ARR	£560,000 − £250,000	£470,000 − £200,000
		= £310,000 or £51,667 p.a.	= £270,000 or £45,000 p.a.
		$\dfrac{51,667}{250,000} \times 100$	$\dfrac{45,000}{200,000} \times 100$
		= 20.7%	= 22.5%

		£000	£000
(iii)	NPV	−250 × 1 = −250	−200 × 1 = −200
		150 × .75 = 112.5	60 × .91 = 54.6
		150 × .68 = 102	50 × .82 = 41
		160 × .62 = 99.2	90 × .75 = 67.5
		100 × .56 = 56	90 × .68 = 61.2
		+119.7	90 × .62 = 55.8
			90 × .56 = 50.4
			130.5

Chapter 31

1

Number of sales		Probability	
800	×	.1	80
810	×	.4	324
820	×	.3	246
830	×	.2	166
			816

Expected sales revenue = 816 sales × £6000 = £4,896,000

2

Number of sales		Probability	
1100	×	.2	220
1110	×	.3	333
1120	×	.4	448
1130	×	.1	113
			1114

Expected sales revenue = 1114 × £5000 = £5,570,000

3

Option A		Option B	
0.4 × 50 =	20	0.3 × −30	−9
0.6 × 80 =	48	0.5 × 50	25
	68	0.2 × 80	16
			32

Option C		Option D	
0.4 × 30	12	0.3 × 50	15
0.5 × 60	30	0.3 × 60	18
0.1 × 100	10	0.4 × 90	36
	52		69

Other things being equal, Option D should be accepted as it produces the highest expected value.

4   **Option** (i)   Large-scale investment

Expected value of return   500 × .4   =   200

                            50 × .6   =   30

                                         230

                  less   400

                                   −170

Option (ii)   Small-scale investment

Expected value of return   250 × .3   =   75

                            50 × .7   =   35

                                        110

                  less   50

                                         60

Option (iii)   No change

Expected return   0

Advice to owner: opt for the small-scale investment.

5   (a)

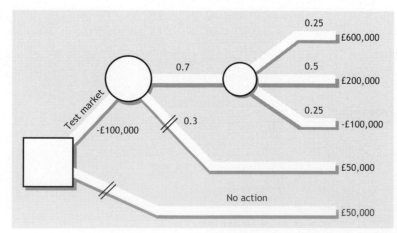

(b)   Expected value of the test market:

$0.25 \times £600,000$	=	£150,000	
$0.5 \times £200,000$	=	£100,000	
$0.25 \times -£100,000$	=	-£25,000	
		£225,000	

0.7	×	£225,000	=	£157,500
0.3	×	£50,000	=	£15,000
				£172,500
		less		£100,000
				£72,500

(c)   The firm should go ahead with the test market on the basis that the expected value of the return net of the test market costs exceed the £50,000 available if the project is abandoned.

Chapter 32

		Café	Motorcycle	Hotel
1	Fixed costs	Rent	Insurance	Rent
		Rates	Tax	Rates
		Interest	Interest	Interest
	Variable costs	Food	Petrol	Food
		Fuel	Repairs	Laundry

2   Direct costs $=$ $£7.5 \times 500,000 = £3,750,000$
Overheads $=$ £170,000
(a)   Total costs $=$ 3,920,000

(b)   Unit costs $= \dfrac{£3,920,000}{500,000} = £7.84$

3   (a)   Direct costs = $£7.5 \times 600,000$ $=$ £4,500,000
Overheads $=$ £170,000
Total costs $=$ £4,670,000
Unit costs $= \dfrac{£4,670,000}{600,000}$ $=$ £7.78

(b)   Direct costs = $£7.5 \times 700,000 = £5,250,000$
Overheads $=$ £170,000
Total costs $=$ £5,420,000
Unit costs $= \dfrac{£5,420,000}{700,000} = £7.74$

This question was designed to illustrate the principle of 'spreading overheads'. As output rises, average fixed costs fall. Direct costs are £7.5, irrespective of output. To these costs are added average fixed costs which are:

- at 500,000, 34 pence;
- at 600,000, 28 pence;
- at 700,000, 24 pence.

4 (a) (i)

	Total (£000)	A (£000)	B (£000)	C (£000)
Sales	1,300	300	400	600
Direct costs	860	190	290	380
Variable overheads	240	40	100	100
Fixed costs	90	30	30	30
Profit	110	40	(20)	90

(ii)

	Total (£000)	A (£000)	B (£000)	C (£000)
Sales	1,300	300	400	600
Variable costs	1,100	230	390	480
Contribution	20	70	10	120
Fixed costs	90			
Profits	110			

(b) On both the original allocation of fixed costs and the equal allocation, product B appears to be unprofitable and, therefore, is a candidate for elimination. However, any method of allocating fixed costs is arbitrary. Moreover, the elimination of B will not necessarily reduce fixed costs. The same level of fixed costs might have to be allocated to the remaining two products, thus reducing their profitability.

5 A cost centre is a definable area of activity within a business enterprise for which costs can be attributed. The advantages of organizing things in terms of cost centres are as follows:

- responsibility can be attributed;
- the costs of the activity are made transparent rather than hidden;
- performance can be compared with expected performance;
- it aids decision making.

(a) (i) Pressing   £600 × 140%   = £840
Plating   £100 × 140%   = £140
Assembly   £50 × 140%   = £170

(ii) Pressing   £100 + £600 + £840 = £1540
Plating   £40 + £100 + £140   = £280
Assembly   £200 + £50 + £70   = £320

(b) If overheads were allocated in relation to direct labour costs, then pressing would be allocated £309, plating would be allocated £120 and assembly would be allocated £618.
This results in total costs being as follows: pressing £1009, plating £264 and assembly £868. (All figures are in thousands.)

(c) Often used interchangeably, there is, in fact, a distinction between full and absorption costing. In the former, overheads are treated as a whole, whereas in the latter the absorption would vary with the nature of the overhead. Full costing was used in this question.

6 (a) (i) Model A   £300 − (£150 + £50) = £100
Model B   £200 − (£100 + £40) = £60
Model C   £80 − (£40 + £20) = £20

(ii) Model A   £100 × 500 = £50,000
Model B   £60 × 500 = £30,000
Model C   £20 × 1000 = £20,000

(iii) Profit = total contrbution – fixed costs
            = £50,000 + £30,000 + £20,000 – £70,000
            = £30,000

(b)

	A (£000)	B (£000)	C (£000)	Total (£000)
Sales revenue	150	100	80	330
Direct costs	100	70	60	230
Contribution	50	30	20	100
Fixed costs				70
Profit				30

7 (a) Profits equal sales revenue less all costs.
        Contribution equals sales revenue less variable costs.

   (b) Contribution – Fixed costs = Profit
        Contribution – Profit + Fixed costs

        Each department had £75,000 of fixed costs allocated to their activities.

        Department A: £50,000 + £75,000 = £125,000
        Department B: (£50,000) + £75,000 = £25,000
        Department C: £40,000 + £75,000 + £115,000
        Department D: £20,000 + £75,000 = £95,000

   (c)

	A (£000)	B (£000)	C (£000)	D (£000)	Total (£000)
Sales	300	400	150	100	950
Direct costs	175	375	35	5	590
Contribution	125	25	115	95	360
Fixed costs					300
Profit					60

   (d) On the basis of equal allocations of overheads, department B is making a loss and, therefore, should be closed. As the department is responsible for a disproportionate amount of sales and direct costs, it should carry more than an equal share of fixed costs.
        However, unless closure can reduce fixed costs, it is not worth while closing it down. This department does make a contribution, albeit a small one, to fixed costs.

8 (a) Contribution = selling price – variable costs per shirt
        (i)   £12 – £7 = £5
        (ii) £12 – £8 = £4

   (b) Lost contribution per unit = £5 – £4 = £1
        Lost contribution= £1 × 100,000 = £100,000

   (c) Saving amounts to £150,000 less lost contribution of £100,000, which is £50,000.
        On financial grounds, there is a strong case for subcontracting, but non-financial factors, such as quality and reliability of suppliers, should also be taken into consideration.

9 (a) (i) Variable cost = Materials + Labour + Variable overheads
             or
             Total costs – Fixed overheads

(ii)   Contribution = Sales revenue – Variable costs

	(i) Variable costs (£000)	(ii) Contribution (£000)
Bears	300	200
Rabbits	220	130
Penguins	560	90

(iii)   Profits = £100,000 + £50,000 + (£20,000)
          = £130,000

(iv)   Total fixed costs = £290,000

(b)   The discontinuation of the penguin will reduce the overall contribution by £90,000.
Assuming that fixed costs are unchanged, this will reduce profits to £130,000 – £90,000 = £40,000.

10 (a) (i)   Standard labour cost per unit
12 hours × £8.50 = £102

(ii)   Actual labour cost = $\frac{£308,000}{2800}$ = £110

(iii)   Labour variance per unit = £8 (adverse)

(b)   Variance can be attributed in almost equal measures to a rise in labour costs per hour and the need for the workers to work more hours to produce a given quantity of output.

Labour cost per hour was budgeted at £8.50 but was actually $\frac{308,000}{35,000}$ = £8.80

Labours hours per unit was budgeted at 12 (hours) but was actually $\frac{35,000}{2,800}$ = 12.5 (hours)
Extra half hour per unit = $\frac{£8.50}{2}$ + $\frac{30 p}{2}$ = £4.40
Rise in labour cost = 30p × 12 = £3.60
Together these two add up to the £8 variance.

(c)   Explanations for the variance include:
- rise in cost per hour, due to:
  - overtime rates of pay;
  - use of more expensive, higher-grade labour;
  - unexpected pay rise.
- rise in labour requirement, due to:
  - underestimating labour required;
  - using untrained labour;
  - unexpected high wastage;
  - delays caused by machines.

11 (a) (i)   Product X requires 300,000 × 3 = 900,000 hours of labour.
This leaves 300,000 hours left for product Y.
Output combination: 300,000 X and 150,000 Y

(ii)   Product Y requires 200,000 × 2 = 400,000 hours of labour.
This leaves 800,000 hours for product X.
Output combination: 200,000 Y and 266,666 X.

(iii)   600,000 hours available for each product.
This enables the firm to make 200,000 X and 300,000 Y.
In terms of the sales budget, this is an excess of Y.

(b) (i)   Product X: £12 – £8 = £4 contribution per unit
Product Y: £10 – £7 = £3 contribution per unit

(ii)   Total contribution = Contribution per unit × Quantity.

In the case of (a)(i), this is £1,200,000 X and £450,000 Y.
In the case of (a)(ii), this is £1,066,666 X and £600,000 Y.
In the case of (a)(iii), this would be £800,000 X – £900,000 if the excess quantity of Y could be sold.

(iii)   Product X: $\dfrac{£4}{3 \text{ hours}}$ = £1.33 per hour

Product Y: $\dfrac{£3}{2 \text{ hours}}$ = £1.50 per hour

(c)   Management should be advised to produce the output combination that maximizes contribution. Equal division of labour resources should be rejected as it results in excess production of Y. In terms of both total contribution and contribution per hour of the limiting factor (labour), the combination outlined in (a)(ii) is advisable.

12   (a)   Beyond a certain level of production, unit costs will rise. For instance, it might be necessary to employ labour at premium overtime rates, maintenance costs rise as machinery is operated for longer periods and supplies become more scarce.

(b)   (i)   Contribution per pair:
Selling price – variable costs = £10 – (£3.4 + £3.3 + £0.3) = £3

(ii)   Break-even output = $\dfrac{\text{Fixed costs}}{\text{Contribution per unit}}$

Fixed costs = £2 × 150,000 = £300,000

Therefore, the break even output = $\dfrac{300,000}{3}$ = 100,000

(c)   (i)   Total contribution = Contribution per unit × Quantity
= £3 × 100,000 = £300,000

(ii)   Contribution per unit
= £10 – (£3.8 + £3.7 + £0.5) = £2
Total contribution = £2 × 20,000 = £40,000

(iii)   £40,000. The fixed costs are covered by the first 100,000 units of output. Contribution beyond this point is profit.

13   (a)   Contribution = Sales revenue – Variable costs
A   £200,000 – (£60,000 + £40,000 + £10,000) = £90,000

B   £130,000 – (£40,000 + £30,000 + £10,000) = £50,000

C   £330,000 – (£100,000 + £50,000 + £20,000) = £160,000

The same answers can be obtained by adding fixed cost apportionment to profit.
Contribution – Fixed costs = Profit
Contribution = Profit + Fixed costs

(b)   The £150,000 limit on raw materials represents a constraint. The product mix in the budget is not feasible, so it is necessary to decide which combination of the three products should be made. The scarce resource should be used to make the goods with the greatest proportionate contribution.
Product A: Each £1 of sales revenue generates a 45p contribution.
Product B: Each £1 of sales revenue generates a 38p contribution.
Product C: Each £1 of sales revenue generates a 48p contribution.
Recommendation: Use the raw materials to produce the full amount of C, with the remainder (£50,000 worth) used for B.

(c) Contribution from C = £160,000

Costing for A:	£000
Sales	166.6
Less Variable costs:	
Raw materials	50
Direct labour	33.3
Variable overheads	8.3
Contribution	75

Total contribution = £160,000 + £75,000
Less fixed costs = £160,000
Profits = £75,000

14 (a) (i) Contribution = £25 – £14 = £11 per unit or £110,000 in total
(ii) Contribution when contracting out = £25 – £18 = £7 per unit, or £700,000 in total
(iii) Lost contribution = £11 – £7 = £4 per unit, or £400,000 in total

(b) Contribution lost = £400,000
Overheads saved = £500,000
Net saving from contracting out = £100,000

(c) When the lost contribution is equal to the saving on fixed costs, the manufacturer will be indifferent between the two options ($\frac{£500,000}{4}$ = 125,000 units, for example).

15 (a) Contribution lost = £18m – £15m = £3m

(b) Savings amount to £650,000.
Even on financial grounds, a subcontractor should not be used as the loss in contribution is greater than any savings on fixed costs.

(c) If subcontracting was justified on financial grounds, then other factors to consider are:

• the danger of dependence on a subcontractor;
• the quality and reliability of the product.

The other factor to consider when the financial logic was not to subcontract is opportunity cost – could the resources be put to more profitable use?

16 (a) Direct costs £2.5 × 4,000 = £100,000
Overheads = £200,000
Total costs = £300,000

(i) Unit costs = $\frac{£300,000}{40,000}$ = £7.5

(ii) Price = £7.5 × $\frac{150}{100}$ = £11.25

(b) Direct costs £8 × 160,000 = £1,280,000
Overheads = £700,000
Total costs = £1,980,000

(i) Unit costs = $\frac{1,980,000}{160,000}$ = £12.375

(ii) Price = £12.375 × $\frac{175}{100}$ = £21.66

17 (a)

Materials	X	200	× £1.4	=	£280
	Y	50	× £5.2	=	£260
Labour		10	× £8	=	£80
		5	× £6	=	£30
Overheads		15	× £200	=	£3000
Standard cost per 100 units				=	£3650

(b) Selling cost per unit $\qquad$ = £36.5

25% mark-up: $\dfrac{125}{100} \times £36.5$ = £45.625

18 (a)

	A £000	B £000	C £000	D £000	Total £000
Sales revenue	120	120	125	96	461
Less Direct costs	75	76	70	64	285
Less Indirect costs	40	40	40	40	160
Profit	5	4	15	(8)	16

(b)

	A £000	B £000	C £000	D £000	Total £000
Sales revenue	120	120	125	96	461
Less Direct costs	75	76	70	64	285
Contribution	45	44	55	32	176
Less Fixed costs					160
Profit					16

(c) On the basis of equal allocation of overheads, D is making a loss and, therefore, should be deleted. However, equal allocation is not a fair or rational basis for allocation, given the low selling price and direct costs. Moreover, if D was deleted, it is unlikely that fixed costs would fall by £40,000. However, deletion of D might reduce overall profits and make one or more of the products 'unprofitable'.

Chapter 33

1 (a) Contribution is equal to sales revenue less variable costs. Contribution per unit is equal to selling price less variable costs per unit. It represents each unit's contribution to fixed costs and profits.
In this case, it is £10 less £4, which is £6.

(b) Break even $= \dfrac{\text{Fixed costs}}{\text{Contribution per unit}} = \dfrac{£90,000}{6} = 15,000$ units

(c) Current output $= \dfrac{\text{Profits + Fixed costs}}{\text{Contribution per unit}} = \dfrac{£360,000}{£6} = 60,000$ units

(d) (i) Sales revenue = £10,000 × 60,000 = £600,000
(ii) Price falls by 10% to £9, but sales rise 25% to 75,000 units
Sales revenue will be £9 × 75,000 = £675,000

(e) (i) Sales revenue rose by £75,000
(ii) Costs rose by £4 × 15,000 = £60,000

(f) Yes, the price reduction will lead to a rise in revenue that exceeds the rise in costs.

2   For A, price £2.20, contribution = £2.20 – £1.25 = 95p

(a)   Break-even output = $\dfrac{£1.2m}{£0.95}$ = 1,263,158 units

(b)   Margin of safety at full capacity is 1,436,842.
Margin of safety at current output is 1,336,842.

(c)   To find the profit, multiply the margin of safety by the contribution.
Hence, 1,436,842 × £0.95 = £1,364,999.9 (full capacity output)
1,336,842 × £0.95 = £1,269,999.9 (current output)

(d)   (i)   Break-even output = $\dfrac{1,263,158}{2,700,000}$ × 100 = 46% of full capacity output

    (ii) $\dfrac{1,263,158}{2,600,000}$ × 100 = 48% of current output

For B, price £2.00, contribution = 75p

(a)   Break-even output = 1,600,000

(b)   Margin of safety at full capacity = 1.1m
Margin of safety at current output = 1m

(c)   Profit is 1.1m × £0.75 = £825,000 at full capacity
or 1m × £0.75 = £750,000 at current output

(d)   (i)   59.3% of full capacity output
    (ii)   61.5% of current output

For C, price £1.80, contribution = 55p

(a)   Break-even output = 2,181, 819

(b)   Margin of safety of full capacity = 518,181
Margin of safety of current output = 418,181

(c)   Profit at full capacity = 518,181 × £0.55 = £284,999.55
Profit at current output = 418,181 × £0.55 = £229,999.55

(d)   (i)   80.0% of full capacity output
    (ii)   83.9% of current output

For D, price £1.70, contribution = 45p

(a)   Break-even output = 2,666,667

(b)   Margin of safety at full capacity = 33,333
Margin of safety at current ouput = –66,667

(c)   Profit at full capacity = £14,999.85
Loss at current output = –£30,000.15

(d)   (i)   98.8% of full capacity output
    (ii)   102.6% of current output

3   (a)   (i)   Contribution per mug = 60p – 20p = 40p

    (ii)   Break-even output = $\dfrac{£20,000}{£0.4}$ = 50,000

    (iii)   Margin of safety at current output = 90,000 – 50,000 = 40,000

    (iv)   Margin of safety at full capacity output = 120,000 – 50,000 = 70,000
Profits at full capacity = 70,000 × £0.4 = £28,000

(b)   Target profit at full capacity output = £40,000

Contribution per unit to achieve target profit = $\dfrac{£40,000 + £20,000}{120,000}$ = 50p

Price required to achieve target profit = 50p + 20p = 70p

4   (a)

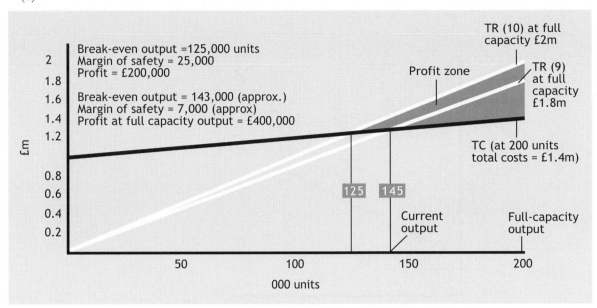

(b)   Verification of results from graphical analysis:

    (i)   break-even output = $\dfrac{£1m}{£8}$ = 125,000 units

    (ii)   margin of safety = 150,000 – 125,00 = 25,000 units

    (iii)   profits at current output = 25,000 × £8 = £200,000

(c)   See graph. Graphical analysis is unlikely to produce an exact answer to this question and this shows the inferiority of graphical over numerical techniques.

The break-even output is actually $\dfrac{£1m}{£7}$ = 142,858 units

At full capacity, the margin of safety is 57,142 and profits amount of £399,994. The margin of safety is therefore 7142 and profits amount to 7142 × £7 per unit contribution = £49,994 at 150,000 units

(d)   At the original price and quantity, profits amounted to £200,000.
The lower price of £9 will increase sales to 200,000 units.
The margin of safety will now be 7142 + 50,000.
The contribution per unit will be £7.
Profits will therefore be 57,142 × 7 = £399,994
Conclusion: provided variable costs remain constant at £2 per unit, the price reduction will raise overall profits. However, it might be pointed out that full-capacity production is difficult to achieve.

5   (a)   (i)   Total contribution at full capacity = £7 × 150,000 = £1,050,000
                 Less fixed costs   =   £800,000
                 Profits   £250,000

            (ii)   Break-even output = $\dfrac{£800,000}{£7}$ = 114,286 units

            Note: Always round upwards; break even is not reached at the lower level.

(b)   (i)   Target contribution = £800,000 + £200,000

Output to achieve target $= \dfrac{\text{£1m}}{\text{£7}} = 142{,}858$ units

    (ii)   Total contribution required is £1m.
Two thirds capacity output is 100,000.
Therefore, a contribution of £10 per unit is required.
Price = £14 + £10 = £24.

6   (a)

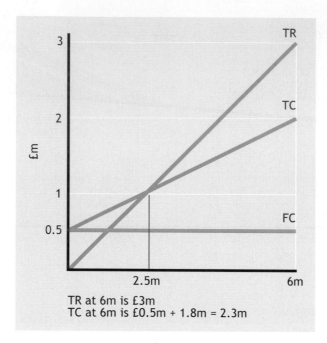

TR at 6m is £3m
TC at 6m is £0.5m + 1.8m = 2.3m

(b)   Contribution per unit = Selling price less variable cost per unit:
50p – 30p = 20p.

(c)   (i)   Break-even output $\dfrac{\text{£500,000}}{\text{£0.20}} = 2.5\text{m}$

    (ii)   Margin of safety = 5m – 2.5m = 2.5m

    (iii)   Contribution at full capacity

= 6m × 20p	=	1.2m
Less Fixed costs	=	0.5m
Profit		0.7m
OR 20p × 3.5m	=	0.7m

(d)

Contribution from special order 500,000 × 5p	=	25,000
Less Additional fixed costs		10,000
Additional profit		15,000

The order should be accepted provided there is no more profitable order available. Spare capacity exists.
The original fixed costs have to be covered whether or not the special order is accepted.

7   (a)   (i)   Contribution is equal to sales revenue less variable costs.
It is the contribution of the product (or each unit of the product) to fixed costs and profits.
    (ii)   Break-even output is the level of output at which all costs are covered, resulting in neither loss nor profit.
    (iii)   Margin of safety is the excess of actual output over break-even output.

(b) (i) 15 pence – 10 pence 5 pence

(ii) £1m divided by 5p = 20 million units

(iii) 32 million – 20 million = 12 million units

(iv) Profits = Margin of safety × Contribution per unit
= 12 million × 5 pence = £600,000

(c) Yes. Each unit makes a 1 pence contribution, adding £50,000 to overall profits. Provided there is spare capacity and no more profitable offer available, it is worth while accepting any contract that makes a positive contribution.

(d) The Goodprice contract offers a higher contribution and is therefore even more worth while. However, there is a danger of being 'locked-in' to this contract for a second year when the problem of excess capacity might not be present.

8 (a) (i) Price = £500
Variable costs = £300
Contribution = £200 per unit

(ii) Break-even ouput $= \dfrac{£110,000}{£200} = 550$ tables

(iii) Margin of safety = 2000 – 550 = 1450
Profit = 1450 × £200 = £290,000

(b) Target contribution = £110,000 + £150,000 = £260,000

Target contribution per unit $\dfrac{£260,000}{2000} = £130$

Price to be charged = £130 + £300 = £430

9 (a) (i) Break-even ouput = 100,000
Sales revenue at this output = £250,000

(ii) At break-even output, total revenue = total costs
Total revenue = £250,000
Total costs = £40,000 + variable costs
Variable costs = £250,000 – £40,000 = £210,000

(iii) Fixed costs = £40,000 (the costs when output is zero)

Break-even output $= \dfrac{\text{Fixed costs}}{\text{Contribution per unit}}$

Contribution per unit $= \dfrac{\text{Fixed costs}}{\text{Break-even output}}$

$= \dfrac{£40,000}{100,000} = £0.4$

or Total contribution = £40,000
Output = 100,000 units
Contribution per unit is £0.4

(b) Contribution required = £66,000 + £40,000 = £106,000

Required level of output $= \dfrac{£106,000}{£0.4} = 265,000$ units

(c) Total contribution = 90,000 × £0.4 = £36,000
Less Fixed costs = £40,000
Loss = £4,000
or
at 90,000 units, output is 10,000 less than break-even output
Deficiency of contribution = 10,000 × £0.4 = £4,000

(d)   Fixed costs rise by 25% to £50,000

New break-even output $= \dfrac{£50,000}{£0.4} = 125,000$

10   (a)   (i)   Capacity utilization $= \dfrac{12}{15} \times 100 = 80\%$

(ii)   Contribution per unit = £1.40 − 70p = 70p

Break-even ouput $= \dfrac{£5m}{£0.70} = 7,142,858$ units

(iii)   Margin of safety = 12m − 7,142,858 = 4,857,142

(iv)   Total contribution = 12m × 70p =   £8,400,000
       Less overheads   £5,000,000
       Profit   £3,400,000

(v)   Unit costs $= 70p + \dfrac{£5m}{12m}$
                   = 70p + 41.7p = 111.7p

(b)   Accept the contract provided no more profitable work is available.
      Reasoning:

   • overheads are fixed and are incurred whether or not the special order contract is accepted;
   • spare capacity exists;
   • each unit makes a 10p contribution, thus adding to profits by 10p × 1m = £100,000.

Chapter 34

1   (a)

Month	Sales	Stock at end of month	Less stock at beginning of month	Ouput
April	1,000	600	0	1,600
May	1,200	700	600	1,300
June	1,400	700	700	1,400
July	1,400	700	700	1,400
August	1,400	600	700	1,300
September	1,200	600	600	1,200
October	1,200	?	600	?

In the absence of knowlede of likely sales in November it is not possible to produce figures for production in October, but, in any case, the question only relates to the period up to the end of September.

(b)

	April	May	June	July	August	September
Output	1,600	1,300	1,400	1,400	1,300	1,200
	£000	£000	£000	£000	£000	£000
Direct costs						
Materials	24	19.5	21	21	19.5	18
Labour	16	13	14	14	13	12
Overheads	20	20	20	20	20	20
Total costs	60	52.5	55	55	52.5	50

2   (a)   It is first necessary to calculate the costs of Department D in order to allocate them between the other departments.

Labour costs 20 × £150 = £3,000
Fixed costs   £1,500
Interest (£4000 at 12%)   £96 (based on a working year of 50 weeks)
Total cost   £4,596
Allocation to A   £2,298
Allocation to B and C   £1,149

	Dept A £000	Dept B £000	Dept C £000
Labour costs	40	17.5	16
Other variable costs	1	0.8	1
Fixed costs	2.5	2	2
Interest charge per week	0.24	0.24	0.192
Allocation of admin. costs	4.60	2.325	2.325
Total costs	48.40	22.865	21.517

(b)   Unit costs   £48.40   £57.1625   £43.034

3   Total costs: Actual   −£1,567,000
    Budgeted   −£1,680,000
Profit   Actual   −£1,533,000
    Budgeted   −£1,315,000

Variance	**£000**
Direct materials	+11 (F)
Direct labour	+94 (F)
Variable production overheads	+8 (F)
Variable administrative overheads	−5 (A)
Fixed overheads	+5 (F)
Total costs	+113 (F)
Sales	+105 (F)
Profits	+218 (F)

4   (a)   (i)   Contribution
    Budgeted   £2.7 × 25,000 = £67,500
    Actual   £2.7 × 23,000 = £62,100
    (ii)   Sales revenue
    Budgeted   £5.2 × 25,000 = £130,000
    Actual   £5.3 × 23,000 = £121,900
    (iii)   Profits = Contribution − Fixed costs
    Budgeted   £67,500 − £31,500 = £36,000
    Actual   £62,100 − £30,500 = £31,600

(b)

	Budgeted £	Actual £	Variance £
Sales revenue	130,000	121,900	8,100 (A)
Direct costs	62,500	59,800	2,700 (F)
Contribution	67,500	62,100	5,400 (A)
Fixed costs	31,500	30,500	1,000 (F)
Profits	36,000	31,600	4,400 (A)

(c) The £4,400 fall in profits can be explained by a reduction in the volume of sales. Unit direct costs rose, although total direct costs fell as a result of the reduction in volume. Fixed costs also fell, thus reducing the shortfall in profits (£4,400 = £8,100 – £2,700 – £1,000).
The fall in the volume of sales can be explained by:

- recession;
- decline phase of the lifecycle;
- competition from lower-price and/or superior goods.

The fall in direct and fixed costs can be explained by greater efficiency and lower-priced inputs.

5 (a) (i) Contribution per unit
  Budgeted £5.4 – £2.9 = £2.5
  Actual   £5.5 – £3.1 = £2.4
(ii) Total contribution
  Budgeted £875,000
  Actual   £804,000
(iii) Total revenue
  Budgeted £5.4 × 350,000 = £1,890,000
  Actual   £5.5 × 335,000 = £1,842,500
(iv) Total costs
  Budgeted £2.9 × 350,000 = £1,015,000
              +   £451,560
                  £1,466,560

  Actual   £3.1 × 335,000 = £1,038,500
              +   £442,958
                  £1,481,458

(b)

	Budgeted £	Actual £	Variance £
Sales revenue	1,890,000	1,842,500	47,500 (A)
Direct costs	1,015,000	1,038,500	23,500 (A)
Contribution	875,000	804,000	71,000 (A)
Fixed costs	451,560	442,958	8,602 (F)
Profits	423,440	361,042	62,398 (A)

Profits fell by £62,398. This can be attributed to a £47,500 fall in sales revenue, plus at £23,500 rise in direct costs. These adverse variances were partly mitigated by a £8,602 favourable variance on fixed costs (£47,500 + £23,500 – £8,602 = £62,398).

6 (a) A cost that contains both a fixed and variable element. This might take the form of a fixed charge (unrelated to output), but with a variable element attached, such as telephone charges. Alternatively, it might be seen as a cost that is fixed over a narrow range of output.

(b)

	18,000 units	22,000 units
Prime costs	£36,000	£44,000
Production overheads	£19,000	£21,000
General overheads	£30,000	£30,000
	£85,000	£95,000

(c)

	Budgeted £	Actual £	Variance £
Prime costs	42,000	44,100	2,100 (A)
Production overheads	20,500	20,710	210 (A)
General overheads	30,000	30,000	0
	92,500	94,810	£2,310

7 (a)

	£000	£000
Sales		22,000
Direct materials	5,500	
Direct labour	8,640	
Variable overheads	2,000	
Fixed overheads	5,000	21,140
		860

(b) To retain profits at £3m, it is necessary to raise sales revenue to £21,140,000 plus £3,000,000. This is a rise of £2,140,000 or 9.73%.

8 (a)

Volume	250	240	260	300
Sales	500	480	520	600
Labour	200	192	208	240
Materials	100	96	104	120
Overheads	150	150	150	150
Profit	50	42	58	90

(All figures in £000)

Note: Overheads remained fixed at 150. The remaining values are multiplied by

(i) $\dfrac{240}{250}$ (ii) $\dfrac{260}{250}$ (iii) $\dfrac{300}{250}$

(b)

	Budget	Actual	Variance	
Sales	600	550	50	Adverse
Labour	240	250	10	Adverse
Materials	120	130	10	Adverse
Overheads	150	160	10	Adverse
Profit	90	10	80	Adverse

Possible explanations:

- price reductions were necessary because of increased competition or reducd demand;
- labour costs exceeded budgeted costs because of pay rises or the use of higher-grade labour or labour at premium rates, or greater than expected use of labour.
- materials either rose in price or more materials were used (for example, in wastage);
- overhead charges (such as interest, electricity) rose.

9

	Per unit (£)	Budget 20,000	22,000	24,000	Actual 24,000	Variance 0
Sales	15	300	330	360	376	+16
Materials	6	120	132	144	154	−10
Labour	4	80	88	96	100	−4
Variable overheads	2	40	44	48	50	−2
Contribution	3	60	66	72	72	0
Fixed costs	1	20	20	20	28	−8
Profit	2	40	46	52	44	−8

(All figures in £000)

10

	Per unit (£)	Budget 20,000	Budget 22,000	Budget 24,000	Actual 24,000	Variance 0
Sales	12	240	264	288	276	−12
Materials	3	60	66	72	75	−3
Labour	3	60	66	72	100	−28
Variable overheads	1	20	22	24	30	−6
Contribution	5	100	110	120	71	−49
Fixed costs	3	60	60	60	80	−20
Profit	2	40	50	60	(9)	−69

(All figures in £000)

Chapter 42

1

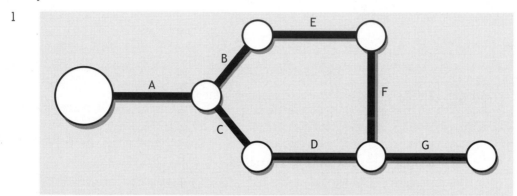

2

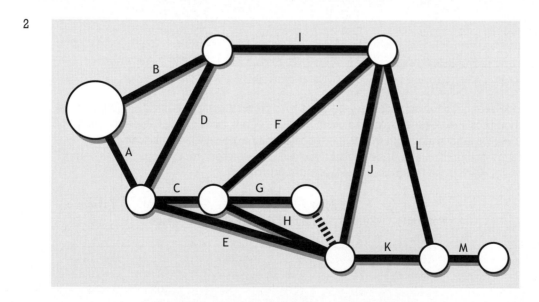

3   (a)

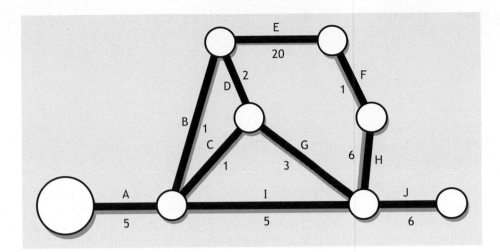

(b)   The critical path is A, C, D, E, F, H, J. The minimum time needed to complete this job is 41 days – the sum of the time needed to complete the critical activities

(c)   (i)   There is a 2-day float on activity B – critical activities C and D take 3 days whereas B only requires 1 day. The float is insufficient to cope with a 4-day delay and therefore this will delay the start of critical activity E.

       (ii)   On activity I there is a float of 30 – 5 days = 25 days. As a result, the delay in supplies will not endanger the prompt completion of the work.

       (iii) There is a 29 – 3 days = 26-day float on activity G. Consequently, even a 10-day delay will not delay the completion of the project.

(d)   The pressure points in terms of the labour constraints relate to activities A, E and J. A is a critical activity and must start on time, but the float on activity I means that it can be delayed until after the completion of both A and E. J presents no problem in that all other activities must be completed before J is started.
The float on activities G and I mean that they can be delayed until after E is finished. In fact, there is sufficient labour to complete activities H, G and I concurrently.
This assumes that labour is sufficiently flexible to move between these activities to ensure completion at the earliest possible time.

4   (a)   Critical path 1–7 to 13 to 19 to 25 to 30.

   (b)   Earliest finishing time = 57 days

Activities	EST	LFT	Float
1–7	1	4	0
7–13	4	16	0
13–19	16	23	0
19–25	23	38	0
25–30	38	57	0

Each of the above activities is critical – they must be started at the earliest time and finished in the scheduled number of days. There is no float on critical activities.

1–11	1	13	8
1–13	1	16	8
11–19	5	23	8
13–20	16	38	12
13–25	16	38	20

   (c)   The pressure points is 1 to 11, which requires 7 workers. If activities 1 to 11 are undertaken in the first 5 days, they will not impede the critical activities. Activities 1–13 can be delayed by 8 days, by which time the 7 workers are released from activity 1–11.

5

Activities	Total float	Free float	Independent float
C	0	0	0
D	7	7	7
E	3	3	0
F	0	0	0
G	0	0	0

Total float = c – (e + a)
Free float = d – (e + a)
Independent float = d – (e + b).

6   (a)   Seasonal fluctuations in sales result from changing patterns of consumption during the year. These reflect changes in the weather and patterns of behaviour. Superimposed on these seasonal factors are patterns of consumption dictated by religious and other holidays. Most products display a seasonal pattern to sales, although it is more noticeable in the case of certain products.

       (b)   The pattern of production in part reflects seasonality in sales. To avoid excessive stock levels, the firm will adjust production levels throughout the year. In addition, it might adjust output levels to cope with the pattern of holidays among employees.

       (c)   Possible explanations include building up stocks prior to staff holidays or to cope with declining stock levels. If the extra output involves the employment of workers on overtime, then premium rates of pay will raise unit costs.

       (d)   Changing production levels will have implications in terms of:

- human resources requirements;
- stock levels;
- capacity utilization.

7   (a)   Retailers sell own-brand goods for a variety of reasons, such as:

- to build up customer loyalty;
- to assert greater control over product design;
- closeness to customers means greater awareness of customers' needs;
- to offer unique products;
- to assert control over manufacturers.

Manufacturers produce retailer's own-brand goods under contract because:

- they can involve large numbers of products;
- they can concentrate on production and leave the marketing to retailers;
- it increases capacity utilization and makes a contribution to fixed costs and profits.

       (b)   (i)   Sales fluctuate because of seasonal impact. Although worn throughout the year, slippers are bought mainly in the weeks leading up to Christmas, for example.

            (ii)   Output fluctuates partly in response to the seasonal pattern of sales. In addition, versatile, machinery and labour will be used to produce other products at certain times during the year. Employees' holidays might also affect production at particular times.

       (c)   Problems associated with fluctuations in sales

Production problems with:

- stock levels;
- capacity planning;
- capacity utilization;
- production scheduling.

Personnel problems with:

- human resource requirements;

- varying manpower levels;
- costs associated with overtime pay.

Financial problems with:

- variations in cash flow;
- financing stock levels;
- need to seek short-term loans.

(d)   Seasonality in sales can be reduced by appropriate strategies in relation to product development (such as by developing products with complementary seasonal patterns), promotion, price (reduce prices off peak) and new markets.

(e)   Implications of diversifying include:

- need for new machinery;
- nature and level of stock;
- re-tooling;
- scheduling of production;
- training of production workers.

8   (a)   (i)   Economic order quantity is the optimum size of orders that minimizes the total cost incurred each year as a result of holding and ordering stock.

        (ii)   Buffer stock is the minimum level of stock held in reserve to avoid stockout.

        (iii)   Reorder level is the stock level that will instigate the reordering of stock. The reorder level should be distinguished from the reorder quantity, which is the quantity of goods that is reordered.

(b)   Economic order quantity $= \sqrt{\dfrac{2 \times \text{Buying costs} \times \text{Annual use}}{\text{Stockholding cost}}}$

Substance X

$$\sqrt{\frac{2 \times £10 \times 1000}{£2}} = \sqrt{\frac{£20,000}{£2}}$$

$$= \sqrt{10,000} \qquad = \quad 100 \text{ units}$$

Substance Y

$$\sqrt{\frac{2 \times £20 \times 500}{£4}} = \sqrt{\frac{£20,000}{£4}}$$

$$= \sqrt{5000} \quad = \qquad = \quad 71 \text{ units}$$

(c)   Substance X: with a lead time of 2 weeks, the firm will place an order when stock falls to:

$$\frac{1000 \text{ units} \times 2 \text{ weeks}}{50 \text{ weeks}} = 40 \text{ units}$$

Substance Y: with a lead time of 1 week, the firm will place an order when stock falls to:

$$\frac{500 \text{ units}}{50 \text{ weeks}} = 10 \text{ units}$$

(d)   Deliveries per year $= \dfrac{\text{Annual use}}{\text{Economic order quantity}}$

Substance X $= \dfrac{1000}{100} = 10$

Substance Y $= \dfrac{500}{71} = 7.04$

9   Economic order quantity $= \sqrt{\dfrac{2 \times \text{Order cost per order} \times \text{Annual use}}{\text{Stockholding per unit}}}$

(a) $\sqrt{\dfrac{2 \times 80,000 \times £20}{£.5}} \qquad = \sqrt{\dfrac{£3,200,000}{£.5}}$

    $= \sqrt{6,400,000} \qquad = \quad 2530 \text{ units}$

(b) $\sqrt{\dfrac{2 \times 150,000 \times £50}{£3}} \qquad = \sqrt{\dfrac{£15,000,000}{£3}}$

    $= \sqrt{5,000,000} \qquad = \quad 2236 \text{ units}$

(c) $\sqrt{\dfrac{2 \times 250,000 \times £70}{£10}} \qquad = \sqrt{\dfrac{£35,000,000}{£10}}$

    $= \sqrt{£3,500,000} \qquad = \quad 1871 \text{ units}$

10   (a)   Lead time is a week.

    (b)   Size of delivery is 150,000 – 50,000 = 100,000 units.

    (c)   The buffer stock is equal to one week's use of the goods. If suppliers fail to deliver, the firm has one week left before stockout occurs. The maximum stock level is fixed after considering the cost of stockholding and the economic order quantity.

    (d)   As the depletion rate is the same throughout, the explanation of the events of week 11 must lie with the ordering, supplying or delivering – for example:

- failure to order;
- failure to act on the order;
- shortage of inputs;
- strike at supply firm;
- transport problems.

    (e)   It lacks expertise in the production of plastic containers, does not have the resources, the supplier can produce them at lower cost and Davidson wishes to concentrate on its core activity.

    (f)   A group of related products sold under the same brand name, such as Fairy.

    (g)   The answer is not 4 months as the excess production in the early months provides a stock to be used up when sales exceed current production. Instead the answer is 8 months, when cumulative output is:

    $8 \times 20,000 = 160,000$ units and cumulative sales reach $\dfrac{8 \times 40,000}{2} = 160,000$ units.

    (h)   Factors to be considered include:

- expected contribution per unit;
- capital investment required;
- area of expertise;
- availability of resources, human and capital;
- cost;
- the extent to which the new product fits the firm's product portfolio.

    (i)   The rival might be willing to supply Davidson on a contract basis if there is spare capacity and the contract work generates a contribution to fixed costs.

    (j)   The failure of market research can be attributed to:

- sampling errors;

- non-sampling errors;
- unexpected changes in the external environment.

Part VI (end of Chapter 47, page 542)

1   This exercise requires a knowledge of the contents of the two documents, an understanding of the jobs in question and some imagination. The answer should be written in an appropriate form with subheadings and numbered points and, in the case of the person specification, the qualities should be identified as either essential or desirable.

   (a)   Content of a job description:

      1   job title;
      2   general description of the job;
      3   relationship with other postholders:
         - responsible to a superior;
         - responsible for subordinates;
      4   location within the organization – both physical and in terms of the organizational chart;
      5   main tasks;
      6   degree of authority;
      7   resources available;
      8   special circumstances.

   (b)   Content of a person specification:
      1   physical make-up – health, appearance;
      2   attainments – qualifications and experience;
      3   general level of intelligence required;
      4   special aptitudes;
      5   interests;
      6   disposition;
      7   special circumstances.

   In addition to positive factors, a person specification should list contraindications that would rule out some applications (although the provisions of anti-discrimination laws need to be borne in mind).

2   This requires an answer in report format, for which some marks should be given.
   Points to consider.

   (a)   The turnover rate is not exceptionally high, given the nature of the workforce and the competition for labour. Moreover, there is a solid core of loyal and experienced workers. Nevertheless, labour turnover involves a cost and the high turnover in particular departments is a matter of great concern and deserves special attention.

   (b)   In practice, it will be impossible to cost out the turnover and, as a result, most accounts will deal with disadvantages such as:

      - adminstrative costs of adding or subtracting from the workforce;
      - cost of recruitment and selection;
      - training costs;
      - loss of output;
      - increased waste and scrap;
      - use of other labour on overtime.

   Although exact costing is impossible, it is important for students to appreciate that labour turnover is not just a nuisance but involves a monetary cost.

   (c)   Before taking action, it is necessary to analyse the problem to identify reasons for high turnover. Recommended action will include:

      - pay rises;

- changes in the hours of work, such as greater flexibility;
- provision of transport;
- improvements in working conditions;
- changes in group working;
- greater autonomy;
- changes in the pattern of supervision.

Student should appreciate that some of these recommendations have cost implications.

3   The answer should be written in report style, as required by the question. Marks should be awarded for format.

(a)   Relevant points to be covered are that:

- redundancy is a fair reason for dismissal provided it is carried out fairly and according to procedures laid down in legislation and previous agreements;
- the law requires firms to consult with representatives of the workforce;
- a procedure to select people to be made redundant should be agreed and adhered to;
- compensation is determined by a formula linked to age and length of service.

(b)   Principles and procedures to be adopted are:

- full disclosure of the situation and the reasons for redundancy being necessary;
- consultation with recognized unions;
- choice of method, such as last in, first out (deemed as fair) or selection on skills, qualifications and value to the firm;
- generous notice or pay in lieu of notice;
- assistance with employees attempts to gain other employment.

(c)   Strategies to secure acceptance of change could include:

- full disclosure of reasons;
- consultation and participation in change;
- negotiations to secure a compromise agreement;
- retraining to ease the process of adjustment.

(d)   For training implications, reference could be made to:

- training needs analysis;
- appropriate methods of training the workforce;
- the cost of training.

4   This requires an imaginative approach, written in a report format. The benefits of training in general are not required, but, instead, practical suggestions about the nature and form of the training programme should be offered. Reference should be made to training needs analysis, which should precede all training, and to the expected benefits from particular programmes. Finally, students should understand budgetary limitations on training programmes and the need to obtain value for money.

(a)   Induction – reference should be made to the content of the induction programme and the most cost-effective method of delivering it.

(b)   Training within the company – reference should be made to training needs analysis, priorities in training, the training budget, the method of delivery and the method of evaluating training.

(c)   The staff college – reference could be made to the use of the staff college and programmes planned for the coming year.

(d)   External provision – students should avoid giving a list of courses (such as GNVQ) at the local college of further education and instead make reference to private-sector provision and facilities for customized short courses to suit the needs of the company.

5   (a)   The answer should be in report form, to include the following format points (which are normally given credit in an examination):

- a statement of who the audience is for the report;
- an identification of the author;
- date;
- asbtract;
- numbered points;
- subheadings where appropriate;
- conclusion.

An appropriate claim should be made. This might be in the region of 8–12%, but there are constraints that must be taken into account.

The claim should be justified in terms of:

- the rise in productivity, which permits non-inflationary pay rises;
- the current inflation rate and the need to maintain pay in real terms;
- the high labour turnover and the need to retain staff;
- the profitability of the business.

      (b)   This also requires a report, but this time to the union executive committee. The report should recommend action, but account must be taken of:

- moderation within the union;
- the constraints identified in the passage;
- trade union law.

Reference could be made to action that could be taken short of a strike and the possibility of third-party intervention by ACAS.

Comments on essays

Chapter 1

1   Assess the advantages of:

(a)   a partnership over a sole trader business;

(b)   company status over a partnership.

(a)   A partnership gives access to additional sources of finance not available to a sole trader and spreads the workload, although if the latter is a problem an alternative solution is to take on paid employeees. Partners remain fully liable for debts and a partnership is not a legal entity.

(b)   Company status confers the privilege of limited liability on shareholders (but the company remains fully liable for debts). A legal entity, distinct from the individuals within the company, is created and, as a result, legal action involves the company rather than individual shareholders and the company has continuing existence beyond the death of these shareholders. These advantages make it easier for companies to raise finance, although the benefits of limited liability are reduced if banks insist on founder members of a company accepting personal liability for repayment of loans.

2   (a)   **What are the advantages of converting to a public limited company?**

    (b)   **In the light of these advantages, why did well-known entrepreneurs such as Andrew Lloyd Webbber and Richard Branson opt 'to go private'?**

(a)   Public limited companies have access to a greater range of sources of finance than private companies. In particular, unlike private companies, they can appeal to the public to subscribe to a share issue.With additional finance they can:

- enjoy greater economies of scale;
- diversify into new markets;
- invest in R&D;
- spread the risks.

(b)   The downside of going public is loss of control and vulnerability to takeover. Both Lloyd Webber and Branson found that they had to spend a disproportionate amount of time keeping shareholders happy.

3   (a)   **Describe the processes involved in privatization**

    (b)   **Analyse the consequences for an organization when it is privatized.**

(a)   An Act of Parliament is required to convert a public corporation into a public limited company. In the case of smaller nationalized industries, shares are purchased *en bloc* by an existing firm, but in the case of larger privatizations a public flotation of shares is arranged by a merchant bank on behalf of the government.

144

(b) Consequences include:
  - the formulation of new objectives;
  - payment of dividends;
  - annual shareholders' meetings;
  - freedom from governmental control;
  - the ability to raise capital on the commercial markets;
  - increased competition;
  - possibility of mergers and takeovers.

In the case of privatized monopolies, regulators have been appointed to protect consumer interests.

4 (a) **Describe the contents of a memorandum and articles of association.**

  (b) **Assess the signifance of the objects clause.**

  (a) The memorandum establishes the business and it includes a company's:
  - name;
  - registered office;
  - objects clause;
  - statement of authorized share capital.

  The articles lay down the rules for the internal governance of the company:
  - powers of directors;
  - rights of shareholders.

  (b) The objects clause is a statement of the business/market that the company is in. Activities outside the objects clause are ultra vires.

5 (a) **Describe the roles of shareholders and directors in a large public company.**

  (b) **Evaluate the extent to which shareholders are able to control large companies.**

  (a) Shareholders provide the permanent capital of the company. They are the owners of the company and have voting rights at the annual shareholders' meeting. Collectively they vote directors in to and out of office.

  Directors provide leadership to a company. Collectively, they make strategic decisions and hold managers accountable. Directors are required to act in the interest of shareholders and are subject to election at meetings of shareholders. A distinction should be made between executive and non-executive directors.

  (b) In theory, shareholders exert control by means of voting at shareholders' meetings, but in practice:
  - share ownership is fragmented;
  - the individual private shareholder is in a weak position;
  - shareholders rarely unite against directors;
  - shareholder power is limited by unequal access to information;
  - a satisfactory return is always sufficient to win votes;
  - most shareholders do not attend annual meeetings.

  The other mechanism for shareholder power is via the stock market – poor performance will lead to the selling of shares, thus making the firm vulnerable to takeover.

Chapter 2

1   (a)   **Outline the main functional areas of management.**

        (b)   **Irrespective of function, there are activities that are common to all managers. Discuss.**

        (a)   This question merely requires a definition and description of management functions in relation to marketing, finance, personnel/human resources and production/operations.

        (b)   The activities common to all managers have been identified by writers from Fayol onwards. Depending on the classification used they are:

- setting objectives;
- planning;
- staffing;
- organizing;
- commanding/directing/leading;
- motivating
- controlling.

In all these activities, managers are involved in decision making.

2   (a)   **Outline the format of a functional plan in business.**

        (b)   **Planning is more important than a plan. Evaluate this statement.**

        (a)   Functional plans for marketing, production, human resources or finance consist of:

- a situational audit ('Where are we now?');
- objectives ('Where are we going?');
- strategies/tactics/programmes/budgets ('How are we to get there?');
- monitoring and control ('How are we doing?')

        (b)   Preparing the plan forces managers to:

- clarify objectives;
- consider resource implications;
- identify constraints;
- identify what is feasible;
- communicate with others in the organization;
- decide on programmes of action.

The final document merely records the process and decisions made.

3   (a)   **Explain the differences between strategic and operational management.**

        (b)   **How will the balance of managerial activities change as we move up the hierarchy towards top management.**

        (a)   Strategic management is concerned with:

- the direction in which the organization is going;
- the longer-term future;
- acquiring new resouces;
- corporate objectives.

Operational management (not operations management) is concerned with the effective and efficient use of existing resources.

        (b)   As we move towards the top of the hierarchy, we find that more time is spent on:

- setting objectives;
- strategic planning;

- leading and motivating;
- meetings;

and less time is spent on operational matters.

4   Assess the value of a business plan in the case of:
  (a)   a start-up business seeking external finance: and
  (b)   an existing business financing expansion from internal sources.

  There is a need for a plan in both cases, although clearly there is an extra need in the case of (a). Banks will only consider a loan if the application includes a full business plan.

  The planning process forces top management to:
  - consider the external environment;
  - be aware of constraints;
  - clarify objectives;
  - consider resource implications;
  - decide what is feasible;
  - schedule activities;
  - allocate responsibility;
  - devise means for evaluating performance.

5   (a)   Outline the principles of control.
  (b)   Describe the role and nature of budget control and quality control.

  (a)   Control involves:
  - the establishment of standards;
  - the collection of data to monitor performance;
  - an evaluation of performance in relation to standards;
  - feedback of results;
  - corrective action where necessary.

  Concurrent control occurs during the process, other controls occur after the event.

  (b)   Budgetary controls require the comparison of budget accounts with actual accounts. Variances need to be identified and analysed.

  Traditionally, quality control takes place at the end of the line, is undertaken by specialist staff and involves inspection of a sample of output. Defective goods are either rejected or reworked.

Chapter 3

1   (a)   What do you understand by delayering?
  (b)   Assess it consequences.

  (a)   The removal of a tier from the hierarchy to produce a flatter organization.
  (b)   Consequences are likely to include:
  - a flatter structure;
  - increased span of control;
  - less distance between senior management and the shop floor;
  - greater autonomy for the employees;
  - increase in horizontal communication.

2   **Explain why in classical organizational theory six was considered the ideal span of control and yet today the notion of an ideal span is dismissed.**

Classical theory was developed early in the twentieth century and based on the notion of:

- hierarchical structures;
- control of the workforce;
- what we would now regard as theory X assumptions.

    Fewer than six was seen as too costly and unnecessary whereas more than six threatened managerial control over the workforce.

Modern theory is based not on the idea of a single best solution, but what is appropriate in the circumstances. The following factors have widened the span of control:

- increased skill and education of the workforce;
- increase in communication technology;
- changes in the nature of work;
- a more enlightened (theory Y) view of the workforce.

3   (a)   **What is meant by a hierarchical organization?**
    (b)   **Assess the adverse consequences of a rigid hierarchical structure.**

    (a)   An organization characterized by numerous layers, top-down management and vertical communications.
    (b)   Dysfunctional aspects of a rigid structure include:
        - communication problems;
        - lack of upward and horizontal communication;
        - alienation, low employee satisfaction;
        - lack of flexibility.

4   (a)   **Why are managers often reluctant to delegate?**
    (b)   **Analyse the likely consequences of a failure to delegate.**

    (a)   Reasons include:
        - lack of trust in the workforce;
        - belief that they can do it better or more quickly;
        - fear of loss of power or position;
        - inability to delegate or lack of skills in delegating;
        - realization that responsibility remains with them.
    (b)   Consequences include:
        - overloaded with work;
        - managerial stress;
        - mistakes;
        - failure to consider all factors;
        - employee demotivation;
        - failure to train for succession.

5   **Analyse the advantages of a product-based or divisionalized structure over a functional structure.**

A product/divisional structure results in:

- a focus on product and market;
- autonomy for managers;

- creation of profit centre;
- coordination stems from products and product lines.

But, might lead to conflict between corporate and divisional interest and might lead to the neglect of long-term interests.

The functional structure:

- makes better use of specialist resources;
- establishes clear lines of responsibility, authority and control;
- increases central control.

But, can result in:

- empire building;
- bureaucracy;
- long lines of communication;
- lack of responsiveness to customer needs.

Chapter 4

1   **Discuss the role of communication in relation to the major tasks of management.**

Communication is essential for:

- the formulation of plans;
- the clarification and communication of objectives;
- leading and motivation;
- obtaining feedback;
- coordinating;
- controlling.

2   **New technology inevitably brings an improvement in communication. Discuss.**

New technology brings the potential for improved communications, but, for communication to be effective, the message must be conveyed and understood in the manner intended by the sender. Reference should be made to the problems of encoding, transmission and decoding.

3   **Communication is invevitably more difficult in large organizations. Evaluate what can be done to improve it.**

Answers should explore possible problems concerning:

- organizational structure;
- hierarchical nature;
- distance;
- inappropriate nets;
- the attitudes of senior managers.

Solutions could include:

- flatter structure;
- team briefings/departmental meetings/newsletters;
- greater emphasis on teamworking;
- training management in communication techniques;
- development of more appropriate nets.

4   **Assess the causes and consequences of communication failure.**

Causes include:
- encoding problems, such as inappropriate language;
- transmisssion problems;
- the problem of noise;
- decoding problems – the failure to decode in the way intended by the sender;
- lack of facilities for feedback.

Consequences include:
- problems of communication;
- conflict;
- decline in relations;
- failure to achieve objectives.

5   **Analyse communication within groups in terms of communication nets.**

The criteria for evaluating communications are:
- effectiveness;
- speed;
- ability to deal with complicated issues;
- extent of two-way communication;
- lines of communication.

The wheel and chain are centralized and result in longer lines.

The circle and all channels net are decentralized and encourage a two-way flow.

Chapter 6

1   **Assess the benefits and costs associated with computerization of the office.**

Some of the benefits are easily quantifiable, but others less so. Benefits include:
- increase in volume of work that can be done, more easily;
- increase in speed;
- labour savings;
- greater control possible;
- improves the quality of decision making;
- up-to-date feedback via management information systems;
- desktop publishing improves presentation;
- use of databases;
- e-mail for communication;
- access to the internet.

Costs include:
- capital outlay;
- staff training;
- increased dependence.

2   **Outline and assess the consequences of information technology on working practices in service-sector organizations.**

Most of the consequences are beneficial – others involve costs and problems.

Reference can be made to:

- teleworking;
- e-mail for communications;
- location;
- layout of offices;
- training needs;
- increased dependence;
- IT problems;
- possiblility of power failure;
- eye strain and repetitive strain injury.

3   **Evaluate the use of:**

(a)   **databases**

(b)   **spreadsheets**

(c)   **the Internet**

in business.

(a)   Databases are used for staff records, customer records and stock movements.

Databases can be interrogated to provide different types of information more quickly than is possible when using conventional files. Databases are essential in direct maketing, but the Data Protection Act constrains their use.

(b)   Spreadsheets are an invaluable tool when asking 'What if ... ?' questions and in the production of budget accounts.

(c)   The Internet is a source of information, a means of communication and a way of marketing and selling a firm's products.

4   **The paperless office: a real possibility or a theoretical idea? Discuss.**

Answers should explore the use of IT in the workplace. In theory, all communication – both internal and external – could be by computer screen and all records kept electronically. This would save space and provide accurate, up-to-date and accessible information when required. The development of lap top and palm computers enable executives to access information wherever they are located.

However, at present at least, some records need to be kept in permanent print form. Reading difficult text is easier in printed sources. Eye strain with computers limits their use for long periods.

The Data Protection Act also acts as constraint.

5   **Explain and evaluate the use of IT in manufacturing.**

This question is designed to encourage students to explore CAM, ACAD, MRPI and II and computer-controlled manufacturing. Reference should be made to flexibility, programmable robots, shorter product development times, saving labour costs, increased competitiveness, increased control over stock and use of just-in-time techniques.

Chapter 7

1   (a)   **Identify the components of the external environment.**

(b)   **Analyse ways in which they impact business.**

(a)   Economic, social, political, legal, technological.

Examples should be given for each aspect of the environment.

(b) they entail:
- opportunities for growth;
- constraints on growth;
- threats for the future.

2 (a) **Identify the major demographic trends in the UK.**

(b) **Analyse their likely impacts on business.**

(a) The trends are:
- slow growth of population;
- ageing population;
- changing balance between urban and rural;
- growth of single-person households;
- growth in number of single-parent families;
- smaller families.

(b) The impacts should be manifest as demand for goods and services, size of the market, changing structure, market segments and opportunities for growth of sales. Reference should also be made to the supply of labour. An ageing population with a fall in the number of new entrants to labour markets has major implications for firms' recruitment and training.

3 **Analyse the role of SWOT and PEST analysis in business planning.**

SWOT and PEST provide a means of analysing the current situation – growth opportunities, threats, constraints. A situational audit will then inform the process of formulating objectives and strategies.

4 **Using examples, analyse ways in which changes in the technological environment affect business.**

An open-ended question that students should answer by making reference to:
- new products;
- competition for existing products;
- new processes;
- need for new skills;
- changes in the workforce required;
- competition;
- development of new strategies;
- investment in R&D and in new product development.

5 (a) **Identify trends in the social environment (other than demographic trends).**

(b) **Analyse their likely impact on business.**

This question was designed to emphasize the fact that the social environment is more than just demographic trends. Reference should be made to lifestyles, household size, the geography of populations, culture, religious beliefs and education.

(b) Students should consider:
- market opportunities;
- segments of the market;
- promotional activities;
- constraints.

Chapter 8

1   (a)   Analyse the distinction between civil and criminal law.

    (b)   Explain three circumstances in which a firm selling a legal product might be subject to criminal prosecution.

Civil law covers disputes between individuals and/or business organizations. The purpose is to compensate the person and/or organization harmed.

Criminal law covers wrongs committed against society and the guilty person is punished.

Other differences relate to terminology, the parties involved, the standard of proof and the type of sanction or remedy.

    (b)   This part of the question has been designed to emphasize the fact that some aspects of consumer law are part of criminal law:

    • trade descriptions;

    • product liability;

    • weights and measures;

    • misleading prices;

    • food hygiene.

2   (a)   Describe the essential elements of a contract.

    (b)   Why are consumer contracts and contracts of employment the subject of statute law, which overrides the law of contract?

    (a)   The elements are:

    • offer;

    • unconditional acceptance;

    • consideration;

    • capacity;

    • willingness to be bound by legal agreement.

    (b)   The simple answer is the inequality between the two sides – both consumers and employees are in a relatively weak position and require the additional protection of statute law.

3   (a)   Explain what is meant by vicarious liability.

    (b)   Vicarious liability only applies if the worker is an employee rather than an independent contractor.

          (i)   How would a court determine whether or not a worker was an employee?

          (ii)   In what other aspect of law is it essential to determine whether a person is an employee rather than an independent contractor?

    (a)   Liability for the actions of another person.

    (b)   (i)   There are several tests available to courts:

                • integration test;

                • control test;

                • National Insurance.

          (ii)   Law relating to dismissal. Employees (but not independent contractors) are covered by the Employment Protection Acts.

4   (a)   Explain the difference between unfair and wrongful dismissal.

    (b)   Analyse the circumstances in which dismissal is fair in law.

(a)   Any dismissal that is not fair is, by definition, unfair. Wrongful dismissal is dismissal without the appropriate notice having been given.

(b)   Dismissal is fair in cases of:

- redundancy;
- incapacity;
- misconduct;
- where continued employment breaches the law;
- any other substantial reason.

5   **A threat to jobs or essential protection for the worker? Assess post 1997 measures relating to employment from the perspective of the employer and employee.**

This question relates to measures introduced under the Social Chapter and the Minimum Wage Act. The free market view is that such measures raise costs and make it difficult for UK firms to compete against rivals, especially the 'Asian Tigers'. Against that, it could be argued that these measures are necessary to ensure fairness in the workplace. In reality, it is unlikely that Europe can compete with Asian Tigers on the basis of costs, but it can do on the basis of quality, for which a skilled, well-paid work force is necessary.

6   (a)   **Outline the law relating to consumer goods considered to be of an unsatisfactory quality.**

    (b)   **What redress does a consumer have:**

        (i)   **if the goods are faulty; and**

        (ii)   **if the goods cause injury?**

(a)   This question calls for knowledge of the various Sale of Goods Acts – reference should be made to the phrases 'as described', 'fit for its purpose' and 'of merchantable quality'.

(b)   Faulty goods are covered by civil law – consumers have a right to replacement, refund or correction of faulty goods, but much depends on a variety of factors.

    If goods can be shown to have caused injury, the principle of strict liability applies. The producer, own-brand manufacturer or retailer who fails to name the producer or importer is liable, irrespective of who is the real culprit.

Chapter 9

1   **The demand curve is drawn on the assumption that other things remain equal.**

    (a)   **Why do economists make this assumption?**

    (b)   **Analyse the consequences of:**

        (i)   **a rise in income;**

        (ii)   **a fall in the price of a complementary good;**

        (iii)   **a fall in the price of a substitute product.**

(a)   To identify cause and effect.

(b)   (i)   Rightward movement of demand curve.

        (ii)   Rightward movement of demand curve.

        (iii)   Leftward movement of demand curve.

    In the first two cases, the result is a rise in price and in quantity, while, in the third, both price and quantity fall. In a good answer, there would be reference to income elasticity of demand and cross-elasticity of demand.

2 (a) What is meant by price elasticity of demand and how is it measured?

   (b) Assess the possible price elasticity of demand for:

        (i)   salt; and

        (ii) Ford cars.

   (a) A measure of the sensitivity of demand to changes in price. It is measured by dividing the proportionate change in quantity by the proportionate change in price.

   (b) Determinants of elasticity are:

        • degree of necessity;

        • closeness of substitutes;

        • price in relation to income;

        • extent to which it is habit-forming.

        Salt is inelastic in demand whereas Ford cars face elastic demand. The demand for a particular brand is always more elastic than the demand for the product as a whole.

3 (a) Explain the difference between an extension of and an increase in demand.

   (b) Analyse the likely impact of a rise in income on the demand for each of the following:

        (i)   bread;

        (ii) bus rides;

        (iii) foreign holidays.

   (a) An extension is caused by a reduction in price and is depicted by a movement along the demand curve.

        An increase is caused by some other factor and is depicted by a rightward shift of the curve.

   (b) This question relates to income elasticity of demand (YED)

        (i)   Bread is a necessity and so has low YED.

        (ii) Bus rides are an inferior good and so have negative YED.

        (iii) Foreign holidays are a luxury and so have high YED.

4 A manufacturer has been informed that the price elasticity of demand for its product is –1.25.

   (a) Explain what this means and how it was measured.

   (b) Analyse the significance of this information to the manufacturer.

   (a) The proportionate change in quantity divided by the proportionate change in price.

        A 10% rise in price leads to 12½% fall in quantity.

   (b) As demand is elastic, a price rise will lead to a fall in sales revenue.

5 (a) Using supply and demand graphs, analyse the consequences of:

        (i)   a rise in demand;

        (ii) a fall in supply.

   (b) Analyse the consequences of imposing a maximum price below the equilibrium.

   (a) (i)   A rise in demand leads to a rise in price and quantity.

        (ii) A fall in supply leads to a rise in price, but a fall in quantity.

   (b) Demand will exceed supply. Shortages will result. The price mechanism is prevented from solving the problem. As a result, there will be queues and the development of a black market.

6 (a) A perfectly competitive firm has no discretion regarding price. Explain.

   (b) Referring both to price and non-price factors, explain why monopoly is considered to be harmful to the consumer.

(a) Perfect competition is an ideal devised by economists to provide a yardstick by which to measure imperfect markets. As a result of numerous competitors, homogeneous (rather than differentiated goods) and no personal loyalty, the perfectly competitive firm is a price-taker and has to accept the market price. Any attempt to sell above market price will lead to an immediate collapse in sales.

(b) Monopoly results in:

- higher prices;
- less choice;
- inefficiency and complacency;
- less innovation;
- lower output.

Chapter 10

1 (a) **Explain what is meant by inflation and why it occurs.**

(b) **Analyse the likely consequences of inflation for a firm in the manufacturing sector.**

(a) A rise in the general level of prices. Causes: excess demand, cost-push, excessive growth in the money supply.

(b) Inflation has the following consequences for manufacturers:

- rising costs;
- squeeze on profits;
- loss of competitiveness;
- problems in planning;
- complications for accounting processes.

2 (a) **What are the major features and symptoms of a recession?**

(b) **Analyse the likely consequences of recession on a firm engaged in selling holidays abroad.**

(a) Decline in output, employment, trade, investment and rate of economic growth. The technical definition is two successive quarters of negative growth. Reference could be made to leading and lagging indicators.

(b) As a 'luxury' product, it is reasonable to expect a fall in people's incomes will reduce the demand for foreign holidays. However, a recession will not lead to a decline in living standards for all. In fact, it is possible that demand in some sectors might remain buoyant. Firms will have to compete more agressively.

3 (a) **What is meant by economic growth?**

(b) **Critically assess the benefits of economic growth.**

(a) A rise in real national output (GDP).

(b) The benefits are:

- a rise in production;
- an increase in employment;
- a rise in income per head.

The costs are:

- pollution, depletion of resources, congestion;
- technological change, leading to unemployment;
- rapid growth in the UK results in inflation and a balance of payments deficit.

4 (a) Explain the difference between inflation and reflation.

   (b) Analyse the circumstances in which a government would pursue a reflationary policy.

   (c) What are the likely consequences of a reflationary policy that overheats the economy?

   (a) Reflation is a policy of raising the level of aggregate demand to reduce unemployment. Inflation is a rise in the general level of prices.

   (b) In conditions of unemployment of labour and other resources.

   (c) Reflation to full employment is not inflationary (according to Keynesian theory). Once full employment is reached, any further rise in demand will push up prices.

5 Analyse the consequences for business of a rise in interest rates.

A rise in interest rates:
- raises the cost of borrowing;
- reduces investment;
- raises the cost of stockholding;
- results in destocking;
- reduces consumer demand for products.

6 (a) What are the objectives of governments' macroeconomic policies?

   (b) Analyse the weapons used to achieve these policy objectives.

   (a) Governments' objectives are:
   - economic growth;
   - low inflation;
   - high level of employment;
   - balance of payments equilibrium.

   (b) Weapons used are:
   - fiscal policy regarding tax changes and changes in government spending;
   - monetary policies, concerning interest rates;
   - exchange rate policies;
   - supply-side policies.

   Using examples, students should explain how these policies work. A good answer would focus on monetary policies (interest rates) and the role of the Bank of England in setting rates.

Chapter 11

1 Interference in the operation of markets is unnecessary and harmful to enterprise. Discuss.

The free market approach is based on the belief that an efficient, competitive price mechanism will allocate resources to produce the goods wanted by consumers. Interference will create problems producing a suboptimal situation. For example, maximum prices cause shortages and minimum prices lead to surpluses. The rationale for government intervention is that markets sometimes fail and, instead of a competitive market, we are then often faced with monopoly forces.

2 (a) Explain what is meant by market failure.

   (b) Analyse the ways in which governments seek to correct market failures.

   (a) The failure of the market to provide goods and services at the right quantity and right price. Examples include the failure to:
   - provide public goods;
   - provide sufficient quantities of merit goods;

- take account of external costs and benefits;
- avoid providing demerit goods.

(b) Governments do the following:
- provide goods and services;
- regulate markets;
- tax tobacco;
- subsidize producers of beneficial goods;
- offer grants and other incentives;
- manage the macroeconomy.

3 **Governments should promote mergers, not prevent them. Critically discuss.**

The public case for mergers is based on the economies of large-scale production. With lower unit costs, consumers will benefit in the form of lower prices. Larger firms will be able to undertake more R&D and to fight off overseas competition. The case against is based on the criticisms of monopoly.

4 **Analyse the consequences for business of:**
(a) **a cut in the standard rate of income tax;**
(b) **a cut in the higher rate of income tax;**
(c) **a cut in personal allowances against income tax;**
(d) **the abolition of zero rating for Value Added Tax.**

(a) This will benefit all taxpayers and even remove some from the tax net. Relatively, the gains will be greatest at lower income levels and will thus increase demand for goods and services at this end of the market.

(b) This will benefit high income earners and will increase demand for luxury products.

(c) This represents an increase in tax liability, thus reducing demand.

(d) Again, this is an increase in taxation, which will harm consumers and suppliers of food, children's clothing and so on. A good answer will include reference to income elasticity of demand and price elasticity of demand.

5 (a) **Assess the case for an interventionist regional policy.**
(b) **How would you evaluate the success of a regional policy measure.**

(a) As always, intervention is based on the failure of the market to solve the problem.

(b) Success should be evaluated in terms of:
- the extent to which objectives have been achieved;
- a consideration of costs and benefits, or, cost-effectiveness.

6 **Assess the benefits of:**
(a) **privatization; and**
(b) **deregulation.**

(a) The assessment should include references to:
- price;
- quality of service;
- investment;
- innovation.

It is argued that a privatized concern operating in a competitive environment will be more efficient.

158

(b)   Competition produces benefits in terms of lower prices, greater responsiveness to customers' needs and improvements in quality.

Privatization and deregulation that result in monopoly are harmful to the public interest.

Chapter 12

1   **Assess the consequences of a fall in the sterling exchange rate.**

The consequences would include:
*   UK exports being cheaper for people abroad;
*   foreign imports would be dearer for us in the UK;
*   an increase in the volume of exports;
*   a fall in the volume of imports (in this and the above cases, the extent of the quantity changes depend on price elasticity of demand);
*   improvement in the balance of payments.

However, the problem is that depreciation will add to the UK's inflation.

2   **A double blow to the economy. Assess the consequences of high interest rates pushing up the exchange rate.**

The consequences are a rise in:
*   the exchange rate, which harms UK exports;
*   interest rates, which harms the domestic economy.

3   **Assess the benefits of the UK:**
    (a)   remaining outside the Euro; and
    (b)   adopting the Euro.

(a)   The UK retains control over monetary policy. It is also argued that, as the UK operates on a different business cycle to the rest of the EU, British entry will mean the imposition of economic policies on the UK that, while beneficial to the rest of the EU, would harm the UK.

(b)   The benefits of adopting the Euro would be:
*   elimination of exchange rate risks and conversion costs;
*   UK trade with the EU would grow.

4   **Analyse the consequences for the UK of membership of the European Union.**

Reference should be made to the benefits of the single market:
*   increased trade (trade creation);
*   greater choice;
*   lower prices;
*   larger home market.

Against these points, we should consider:
*   the diversion of trade;
*   we buy from the cheapest EU source where we should be looking for the cheapest world source;
*   the EU is 'second best' to universal free trade;
*   the UK has to accept EU laws;
*   European producers enjoy free access to UK markets;
*   the EU limits the UK's freedom to act.

5   (a)   Distinguish between enlargement and deepening of the EU.

      (b)   What are the likely consequences for the UK of EU enlargement?

      (a)   Enlargement means the accession of new members. Deepening is the development of closer relationships with existing members.

      (b)   The likely consequences are:

- new market opportunities;
- access to cheaper sources;
- investment opportunities.

           However, future enlargement will mean the inclusion of poorer countries from Eastern Europe.

6   (a)   Explain what is meant by an emerging economy.

      (b)   Assess the consequences for the UK of economic growth in the rest of the world.

      (a)   The term can be use to cover less developed countries and countries that are developing their market economies after decades of central planning.

      (b)   The consequences are:

- market opportunities;
- increases in exports;
- rises in output and employment;
- new competitors;
- investment opportunities.

Chapter 13

1   (a)   What is meant by an external cost?

      (b)   Assess the benefits of taxing a polluter.

      (a)   Costs not borne by the firm but inflicted on the community outside the market, such as those relating to pollution, congestion, depletion of natural resources.

      (b)   The benefits are that this:

- 'internalizes the externality';
- encourages cleaner methods;
- provides finance for the clean-up;
- forces consumers to confront the real costs of production.

2   Analyse why it is in a manufacturer's own interest to control pollution and manage waste.

Benefits include:

- cost reduction by means of recycling;
- meeting the demands of green consumers;
- reduction in liability;
- ethical investment.

3   (a)   What is meant by green marketing?

      (b)   Analyse the factors behind the rise of green marketing.

      (a)   Marketing products by:

- appealing to those with environmental concerns;
- making environmentally friendly products;
- reduction in packaging;

- organic products;
- not tested on animals and so on.

(b)   Its growth is due to:
- society's concern about the environment;
- changes in lifestyles;
- improvements in education;
- environmentally conscious population;
- depletion of resources in the late twentieth century.

4   **Evaluate the case for socially responsible behaviour by firms.**

Altruism is only one factor in the rise of the socially responsible firm. Other considerations include:
- customer demands;
- demands of other stakeholders;
- self-regulation before government regulation.

The free market view is that companies have a duty to shareholders to be efficient and profitable.

5   **'Profits are everything.' Evaluate the role and importance of ethics in business.**

In a market economy, profits are essential because they:
- provide a motivating force;
- provide incentives;
- encourage efficiency;
- provide finance for expansion.

However, ethical behaviour is essential:
- unethical behaviour could result in unwanted government regulations;
- customers, suppliers and creditors require it;
- large corporations also have a duty to other stakeholders.

Chapter 14

1   **Marketing is designed to create demand and sell goods that few wish to buy. Discuss.**

This question requires the student to define marketing and explore its elements. The definition should emphasize responding to customer needs, producing products required by customers, getting products to consumers at the right place and at the right time. Reference should also be made to creating value.

The cynical view that marketing is an attempt to manipulate consumers is contrary to marketing philosophy and is based on a depressing view of human nature and a short-term policy.

Marketing should commence with investigating consumers' wants and end with satisfying those wants.

2   **Are the principles of marketing appropriate for a public-sector organization? Justify your answer.**

The simple answer to this question is 'yes'. Even public-sector monopolies need to investigate the market, discover consumers' wants and produce services to satisfy customers. The major differences between private and public sectors concern ownership and objectives, but management functions apply equally in the private sector. Reference could also be made to marketization of the public sector (competition, market testing, contracting out). These trends increase the need to adopt a marketing view.

3   **The marketing department is the focal point of a well-run business. Discuss.**

Kotler stressed that marketing is not just one of four management functions, but is central. An organization seeks to satisfy customers and the marketing function is at the interface with customers.

The production department produces goods and/or services identified by the marketing department. HRM supplies the human resources required.

Accounting and finance provide data for decision making and essential in raising financial resources.

4   **With reference to a variety of examples, explain how and why the marketing mix will vary from product to product.**

Marketing strategy relates to the elements of the marketing mix. In a highly competitive, price-sensitive market, price is a key element in the mix. Elsewhere, quality is of greater significance. For some firms, location and type of outlet are of great significance, but these are less important for others.

Reference should also be made to variations in the promotional mix for differing products. Examples are essential to achieve a high mark.

5   (a)   **What do you understand by a product or brand manager?**

(b)   **Argue the case for the appointment of product managers in a large, multiproduct organization.**

(a)   Note that the question refers to product or brand manager, not production manager.

The product or brand manager is responsible for the marketing strategy of a particular product line.

(b)   The case for appointing such managers is that:

• they are responsible for a consistent, coherent strategy for the particular product;

• the product line can be seen as a profit centre;

• increased coordination is possible;

• identification of responsibility.

Reference could also be made to the problem of coordination across the full product range.

Chapter 15

1   (a)   **Identify the major sources of secondary data available to a small, local retailer.**

(b)   **Assess the value of desk research to business organizations.**

(a)   Internal sources are, for example sales reports.
External sources include:

• market intelligence reports;

• trade associations;

• trade press;

• government sources;

• international organizations.

(b)   Its strengths include that it is

• accessible;

• inexpensive.

Its weaknesses include that it is

• often outdated;

• might not be available;

- no control over method.

Although often criticized, secondary sources provide a framework for later primary research. Electronic sources will result in an increase in the importance of secondary research.

2   (a)   **Explain the differences between probability and non-probability sampling.**

   (b)   **Analyse the causes of sampling error.**

(a)   Probability sampling is the term for those methods where each unit has a known and equal chance of being selected. As a result, it lends itself to statistical analysis based on the central limit theorem.

Non-probability sampling is when researchers use their judgement when deciding on the items to be selected. The validity of research findings depend on the choice of subjects – for example, that quotas conform to the population as a whole.

(b)   Sampling errors are the differences between the estimate of a value obtained from a sample and the actual value.

3   (a)   **Explain the differences between qualitative and quantitative research.**

   (b)   **Evaluate the benefits of qualitative research.**

(a)   Qualitative research is detailed research into the motivations behind the attitudes and buying habits of consumers. It usually involves in-depth interviews and focus group discussions conducted by psychologists.

Quantitative research asks pre-set questions of a large sample of people to provide statistically valid data on, for example:

- what people buy;
- what sort of people buy particular products;
- the features they find appealing.

(b)   Marketers need to understand *why* people do what they do in order to develop products (with an appropriate marketing mix) to satisfy customers. However, qualitative research requires highly trained personnel and will give biased results if answers are given by an unrepresentative group of respondents.

4   **Explain the principles you would use to select a sample of people to question about the quality of service at a fast food restaurant. Justify your choice of sampling method.**

This question requires more than a description of sampling methods. Choice of methods depends on:
- the availability of a sampling frame;
- size of population;
- the extent to which the population is dispersed geographically;
- the extent to which the population is divided into identifiable segments;
- financial resources.

Students should choose a particular sampling method (not to be confused with survey method) and justify it in terms of the above criteria.

5   **Explain and evaluate each of the survey methods.**

Methods used are postal, face-to-face and telephone interviews, the Internet. Evaluation should be in terms of cost, coverage, response rate, speed and reliability of data collected.

Chapter 16

1 Evaluate the role of sales forecasting to a well-run business.

Reference should be made to:

- use of resources – human and non-human;
- planning and decision making;
- setting objectives;
- budgets;
- review and control mechanisms;
- production schedules;
- development of marketing strategies.

As evaluation is explicitly required in this question, reference should be made to the problems associated with forecasting – especially, questioning of the extent to which the future can be forecast from past experience. When Henry Ford allegedly said that 'history is bunk', he meant forecasting the future from past experience is bunk.

2 (a) Explain four major techniques used in forecasting.

(b) Assess the value of forecasts based on past experience.

(a) Reference could be made to:

- panels of experts;
- salesforce composites;
- scenario planning;
- Delphi method;
- moving averages and time series analysis;
- causal method;
- correlation and regression.

(b) Students should address the following issues:

- the extent to which history repeats itself;
- the regularity of cycles;
- random factors;
- quality of the data;
- the length of the forecast;
- the validity of assumptions.

3 (a) Explain the method of sales forecasting based on the extrapolation of moving averages.

(b) What is the basis for choosing a particular time period (say five or six years) for a moving average?

(a) Students need to:

- explain the technique of moving averages;
- explain the process of centering;
- identify the trend;
- extrapolate the trend;
- calculate seasonal/cyclical variations;

Forecast = Trend + Cyclical variation + Seasonal variation + Random variation (the latter is difficult to identify in advance).

(b)   The time period chosen must capture a complete cycle. If we are concerned with fluctuations over the year, we should choose a quarterly or 12-month moving average.

   If we are concerned with cyclical fluctuations, we need a time period that captures a complete cycle of boom and slump.

Chapter 17

1   **Analyse the differences between business-to-business marketing and consumer marketing.**

   Students should explore the differences in terms of the:
   - sizes of the orders;
   - motivations of the buyers;
   - relative importance of elements of the marketing mix;
   - relative importance of elements of the promotional mix;
   - extent to which prices are fixed or negotiated;
   - distribution channels.

2   **Evaluate the contribution of each of the social sciences to our understanding of consumer behaviour.**

   Economists are concerned with price and income. Sociologists are concerned with the extent to which behaviour is influenced by society and groups within society. Psychologists are concerned with motivation and learning behaviour.

   The contribution of economists is in relation to pricing and forecasting. Sociologists can help identify social trends and market segments. Psychologists are important in terms of assistance in understanding *why* people buy the product.

3   (a)   **What is meant by segmenting the market?**

   (b)   **Analyse the benefits of a segmentation strategy.**

   (a)   Dividing the market into distinct groups of buyers. Segmentation is based on age, income group, sex, buyer behaviour, lifestyles and so on.

   (b)   The benefits are:
   - ability to devise marketing strategies to appeal to particular groups;
   - possible to target a particular group;
   - variations in products and other aspects of the mix can be designed to suit different segments;
   - differentiated and concentrated strategies can be developed;
   - appropriate promotional strategies can be devised.

4   (a)   **Explain four ways of segmenting the market other than by age or gender.**

   (b)   **Justifying your answer, state appropriate ways to segment the market for the following products:**
   - foreign holidays;
   - perfume;
   - cars;
   - computer software;
   - public transport;
   - mobile phones.

(a) These are by:
- income or social class;
- lifestyle;
- geography;
- family size;
- buyer behaviour.

(b) In each case, segmentation can be by a variety of methods, but key principles in segmentation are the extent to which a segment is:
- distinct
- measurable
- accessible.

Segmentation is based on the belief that buying behaviour differs from one group to another. Only if *behaviour* is distinctive can a segment be used to develop a market strategy.

5 **Explain why it is beneficial to analyse:**

(a) **the process of decision making within households;**

(b) **why people choose particular brands.**

(a) This question is based on the concept of the decision-making unit. By understanding interactions within the unit, we can identify those with influence, those with the power of veto and those who make the final decisions. Strategies can be developed accordingly.

(b) By understanding motives for buying, we can ensure that a product has its maximum appeal. Hence, such knowledge will influence product, promotion and distribution decisions.

Chapter 18

1 (a) **What is meant by a 'me too' product?**

(b) **Evaluate the benefits of a 'me too' strategy for a firm seeking to enter an established market.**

(a) A new product that is like an existing product, such as Virgin Cola.

(b) Reference should be made to position maps and the difficulties of breaking into an existing market. A 'me too' strategy minimizes risk, but will not produce the high profits that can be expected with a successful new product.

2 **Identify and evaluate five strategies of extending the product lifecycle.**

These are:
- improve the product;
- new promotional strategy;
- change in pricing policy;
- develop a new target segment;
- change the distribution strategy.

Extension strategies will only succeed if a product is suffering a temporary decline that can be reversed. Each of the strategies is based on an assumption that may or may not be valid, such as the existing promotion is ineffective or there are new segments to which to appeal. Each of the strategies will involve a cost and therefore a risk.

3 **Evaluate the product lifecycle as a tool of analysis in marketing.**

This question invites students to consider the notion of the inevitability of decline. Reference could be made to the variety of lifecycles and extension strategies. Even if decline is inevitable in the long run, does the product lifecycle provide a model for identifying the timing of decline?

4   (a)   Analyse the likely causes of product failure.

     (b)   If a product fails soon after launch, there has been a failure in market research. Discuss.

     (a)   Causes include:
            • lack of demand;
            • an inappropriate marketing strategy;
            • failure of market research;
            • competitor products;
            • unexpected changes in the external environment.

     (b)   Market research is a risk-reducing activity and, in an ideal world, it should ensure that there is a market for the product and appropriate strategies are developed. However, unexpected changes in the external environment might result in failure of an otherwise promising product.

5   Why do most product ideas never reach the market?

     Reasons include:
     • lack of demand identified in market research;
     • product lifecycle is considered too short;
     • insufficiently profitable;
     • production problems;
     • changes in the external environment;
     • overtaken by rival product;
     • The product does not 'fit' the organization;
     • lack of resources.

6   Evaluate:
     (a)   the Boston Matrix; and (b) a positioning map; as tools of marketing analysis.

            In both cases, the analytical tools should be explained.

            The Boston Matrix is a device for analysing a firm's product range and developing strategies for products within its product range – for example, identifying potential stars in order to prioritize resources and identify candidates for deletion. It analyses the present, but is it of use in forecasting?

            The positioning map is a device for identifying gaps in the market and the product's close competitors. It is an aid to decision making, but does not replace human judgement.

Chapter 19

1   Evaluate the main advertising media for:
     (a)   a national supermarket chain;
     (b)   a car manufacturer; and
     (c)   an electrical products retailer.

            Criteria for evaluating media are:
            • reach;
            • selectivity;
            • cost;
            • impact;
            • scope for providing information.

2   **Explain how you would evaluate the success of a promotional campaign.**

Evaluation should be in terms of achievement of objectives (sales, revenue, reaching the target, consumer recognition, Dagmar). Reference should also be made to cost.

3   (a)   **What do you understand by the term promotional mix?**

      (b)   **Analyse how it varies from product to product.**

      (a)   The mixture of promotional activities used to promote a particular product. The main forms of promotion should be explained.

      (b)   Advertising and personal selling are the main forms of promotion, but they are backed up by other techniques. Students should use examples to explain and analyse different mixes. In general, the more complicated and expensive the product, the greater the use of personal selling. Reference could be made to Dagmar.

4   (a)   **Explain the terms promotional mix and product lifecycle.**

      (b)   **Analyse the ways in which a promotion changes over the product lifecycle.**

      (a)   The promotional mix is the mixture of promotional techniques used for a particular product. A product lifecycle is the stages through which a product goes from conception through launch to maturity and decline.

      (b)   Using examples, students should explain how:

- promotional objectives;
- choice of promotional technique;
- choice of media;
- choice of message;
- the target audience;
- change over the product lifecycle.

5   **The sole aim of advertising is to increase sales. Discuss.**

The simple answer to this question is 'no'. Increasing sales might be the ultimate aim, but it is likely that there are several intermediate aims, including:

- increasing customer awareness;
- positioning the product;
- supporting other aspects of the mix;
- reminding people of the product;
- providing information;
- creating a favourable impression.

6   **Evaluate the role of personal selling in the promotional mix for:**

    (a)   **cars; and**

    (b)   **soft drinks.**

Although in general personal selling is only of significance for expensive, complicated products (such as cars), there is still a role for personal selling in the drinks market, for example. Sales staff are employed to push the product through the channels of distribution. Reference could be made to the different promotional mixes and different channels of distribution.

Chapter 20

1   (a)   **What do you understand by price discrimination?**

(b)   **In what circumstances is it an appropriate strategy?**

(a)   Selling the same (or substantially the same) product at different prices in different segments. There are similarities with differential pricing at peak and off-peak times, but pure price discrimination means 'same product at same time but different prices'.

(b)   Discrimination requires:

- monopoly power in the market;
- separation of segments;
- different degree of price elasticity;
- ability to maintain separation of segments.

Price discrimination is most common in the marketing of services, which *cannot* be resold.

2   (a)   **What is meant by cost-based pricing?**

     (b)   **Analyse the weakness of pursuing such a pricing policy.**

(a)   Calculation of cost per unit (fixed and variable) plus a percentage mark-up. As a general rule, the size of the mark-up is inversely linked to the speed of stock turnover.

(b)   Such a policy ignores consumer demand and competition.

3   (a)   **What is meant by destroyer pricing?**

     (b)   **To what extent is it in the consumers' interest?**

(a)   Prices are set low in order to destroy rivals.

(b)   It is beneficial in the short run, but destroyer pricing eliminates competition and establishes a barrier to entry. As such, it creates and sustains monopoly power in the market.

4   **Evaluate marginal cost pricing for a manufacturer currently operating at 80 per cent capacity.**

With spare capacity, it is possible to consider marginal cost or contribution pricing. Price must cover marginal costs – that is, extra variable and extra fixed costs. Any additional revenue adds to profits. However:

- operating at close to 100% might be difficult;
- a low marginal cost price sets a precedent;
- it should only be considered if no better offer is available.

5   **Assess the value of an understanding of price elasticity of demand when setting prices.**

Students should define price elasticity of demand and explain the factors that determine it. If demand is inelastic, a price rise will cause only a slight fall off in demand and, as a result, sales revenue will rise. If demand is elastic, a price rise leads to a fall in sales revenue.

6   (a)   **Distinguish between skimming and penetration as pricing strategies.**

     (b)   **Analyse the circumstances in which each is appropriate.**

(a)   Introducing a product at a high price to 'skim' the market or introducing it at a low price to 'penetrate' deep into the market and secure a large market share.

(b)   Skimming is appropriate when:

- the firm enjoys a lead over rivals;
- introducing a fundamentally new product;
- high initial costs require a high price;
- demand is inelastic;
- a high price increases the attractiveness of the product.

Penetration is used to break into an existing market.

7   (a)   **To what extent do firms have discretion over pricing?**

      (b)   **Analyse the linkages between price and other aspects of the marketing mix.**

      (a)   Perfectly competitive firms are price-takers and, as such, cannot use the discretion concerning price. Perfect competition requires:

- many competitors;
- a homogeneous product;
- no personal loyalty to a particular buyer.

The absence of these provides firms with some degree of discretion regarding price, but no supplier is able to ignore demand.

      (b)   This question relates to price and non-price competition. Price is but one element in the marketing mix – firms can choose to compete in other ways. Reference should also be made to the need to ensure consistency between elements in the marketing mix.

Chapter 21

1   **Evaluate the case for direct marketing of products, cutting out all intermediaries.**

Direct marketing cuts out the middlemen:

- profits are not shared;
- manufacturers enjoy greater control;
- facilitates targeting.

TV shopping channels and the Internet provide new opportunities. However, conversely, reference should be made to the beneficial roles of wholesalers and retailers.

2   **Analyse strategies employed by manufacturers to move goods through the channels of distribution.**

Students should consider:

- push;
- pull strategies;

to move goods through channels of distribution.

Push strategies require the deployment of resources for personal selling.

Pull strategies require promotional expenditure.

3   (a)   **Analyse the role of the wholesaler in consumer markets.**

      (b)   **Why has the position of the independent wholesaler been under threat for a number of decades?**

      (a)   The wholesaler:

- breaks bulk;
- provides storage;
- reduces risks;
- assists the liquidity of manufacturers;
- provides credit to retailers;
- provides specialist services;
- undertakes some promotional activity;
- evens out irregular flows.

      (b)   The basic reason is the rise of multiple retail shops, which undertake their own wholesaling.

4   (a)   **What are the main types of retailer in the UK?**

    (b)   **Describe the changes in the market share of each type of retailer and account for the trends that you have identified.**

    (a)   Types of retailers include:
- independent shops;
- multiple or chain stores;
- supermarkets;
- departmental shops;
- variety chains;
- voluntary chains;
- hypermarkets.

    (b)   Trends include the decline of both departmental stores and variety chains, the rise of the out-of-town superstore, the rise of multiples at the expense of independent stores and the rise of franchising.

5   **Analyse the case for employing a variety of different distribution channels.**

Place is one element in the marketing mix. Its role is not passive, but it is used as part of the strategy. Multichannels:
- enable the firm to reach new markets and customers;
- can be used as part of a segmentation strategy;
- can be used experimentally.

Chapter 22

1   **Analyse the ways in which international marketing differs from domestic marketing.**

Reference should be made to:
- differences in currencies;
- differences in lifestyles and cultures;
- language differences;
- differences in legal systems;
- increased transport costs;
- differences in business practices;
- increased documentation;
- differences in buying behaviour;
- differences in living standards.

The EU single market seeks to reduce, but cannot eliminate all, these differences.

2   **Analyse the different market entry strategies available to manufacturing companies.**

Entry strategies include active exporting, passive exporting, contract product, licensing, multinational production.

Choice of strategy depends on:
- degree of involvement in foreign markets;
- cost (and financial resources);
- availability of overseas channels;
- legal and political factors.

3   Analyse the particular risks and problems associated with international marketing.

The risks are political, legal and those relating to the exchange rate. The latter could be explored with reference to movements in exchange rates and the volume and sales revenue derived from exporting. The single currency (and the aborted ERM) reduce these risks.
The problems are the result of the differences between the UK domestic and overseas markets.

4   Standardization or local variation. Analyse the case for each in relation to:
     (a)   the product;
     (b)   promotional strategy.

The case for standardization is based on economies of scale. The case against is based on the continuing differences in overseas markets.

5   (a)   Explain the role of agents in international marketing.
     (b)   Analyse the reasons for long, indirect channels of distribution being especially common in international marketing.

     (a)   This question links international marketing with channels of distribution. Students should define an agent and then identify the roles of agents, which are to use their:
            • expert local knowledge;
            • contacts;
            • expertise in trading across borders;
            • legal knowledge.
            Firms new to exporting and smaller firms rely on agents.
     (b)   Long channels with numerous intermediaries reflect:
            • the costs involve;
            • different degrees of knowledge.

6   (a)   Analyse the long-term impact of the EU single market on UK marketing to the rest of the EU.
     (b)   Analyse the likely impact of possible UK adoption of the Euro on the marketing strategies of UK firms.

     (a)   The single market (especially if completed by a single currency) will:
            • increase trade with Europe;
            • divert, as well as create, trade;
            • reduce differences between EU members;
            • result in a pan-European approach.
     (b)   Adoption of the Euro:
            • eliminates exchange rate risks;
            • eliminates conversion costs.
            It also completes the single market and accelerates the adoption of a pan-European approach.

Chapter 23

1   (a)   With the use of examples, explain what is meant by a marketing objective. Clearly distinguish a marketing objective from a corporate objective.
     (b)   Analyse the role of a marketing objective in the development of a marketing strategy.

     (a)   A target for the marketing department. SMART objectives will be expressed in terms of sales revenue, sales quantity, market share or market growth. A marketing objective is subsidiary to the achievement of overall corporate objectives.

(b)   Objectives are what the firm wishes to achieve – strategies relate to how they are to be achieved. Reference should be made to strategies such as market leadership, market challenging, cost leadership or a focused strategy.

2   **(a)**   **Describe the likely contents of a marketing plan.**

      (b)   **Assess the benefit of drawing up marketing plans.**

(a)   Contents include:
- situational audit;
- marketing objectives;
- plans for product, price, promotion and distribution;
- budgets;
- monitoring and review.

(b)   Plans:
- force decision makers to think through an idea;
- provide a sense of direction;
- motivate;
- provide targets;
- provide a yardstick against which to measure performance;
- ensure that all factors are considered

3   **Suggest and evaluate marketing strategies available to:**

      (a)   **a market leader; and**

      (b)   **a market follower.**

(a)   Maintain leadership by strategies for:
- product development;
- cost advantage by means of economies of scale;
- promotional activities;
- excellence in operations (world class, TQM);
- power in the market.

(b)   A follower can choose safety by adopting a 'me too' strategy and accepting price leadership or can challenge by means of price reductions or product differentiation. Alternatively, it might prefer a market niche strategy.

Chapter 24

1   **(a)**   **Explain the role of financial accounting in business management.**

      (b)   **Analyse what each of the major stakeholders looks for in a set of accounts.**

(a)   Its basic role is that of reporting back to stakeholders on the performance of the company. Reference should be made to the three major types of statement – balance sheets, profit and loss accounts and cash flow statements (not to be confused with cash flow forecasts). Reference should also be made to the stewardship principle and any legal requirements.

(b)   Shareholders look for profit, capital gain, share value, stability.

         Creditors look for ability to repay loans.

         Employers look for profits, security.

         Suppliers look for future prospects and orders.

         The community looks for long-term stability of the business and employment in the area.

2   **Profit figures are not objective but can be manipulated. Discuss.**

This is a question about the subjective nature of accounting and the opportunity for window dressing. Reference should be made to:
- depreciation policies;
- stock valuation;
- the bringing forward of invoices and deliveries into the current year.

3   **Analyse the possible explanations for a satisfactory gross profit figure being converted into an unsatisfactory net profit figure.**

Gross profit = Sales revenue – Cost of sales

Net profit = Gross profit – Overheads

The answer lies in excessively high overheads – rent, selling costs, administrative costs, high interest charges, gearing and electricity charges.

4   **Analyse the factors taken into account in relation to the appropriation account.**

The appropriation account relates to the distribution of net profits. The first claim on profits is taxation – income tax for sole traders and partners and corporation tax for companies. There is obviously no control over tax liability. The remainder is shared between retained profits (added to reserves) and dividends. The balance between the two is determined by:
- directors' decisions;
- need to satisfy shareholders;
- expansion plans;
- alternative sources of finance;
- liquidity position;
- current liability shown on balance sheet;
- dividends policy.

Chapter 25

1   **Analyse the role and nature of the balance sheet.**

It shows what the business owns, owes and is owed. Reference should be made to:
- the stewardship function;
- reporting back to shareholders and other stakeholders;
- fixed assets, current assets, current liabilities, long-term liabilities, shareholders' equity;
- depreciation of fixed assets, but not revaluation of property;
- intangible assets;
- working capital;
- gearing;
- liquidity ratios;
- comparison with other financial accounts and statements;
- the balance sheet as a 'snapshot';
- the question does it reveal the value of a business?

2   **Is the true value of a company revealed in a balance sheet? Justify your answer.**

No, because:
- the net fixed assets figure is not necessarily the same as the market value of the assets;
- except after a takeover, property is not shown as appreciation of assets;

- there are different ways to treat stock values;
- intangible assets are rarely shown.

The value of a business equals the value of assets less current and long-term liabilities, plus goodwill. Answers should explore the meaning of goodwill and ways in which it can be valued (such as a multiple of profits or sales revenue).

3   Analyse the impact of the balance sheet items of each of the following:
    (a)   the purchase of stock on trade credit;
    (b)   the purchase of fixed assets with a long-term loan;
    (c)   revaluation of property to reflect current values.

    (a)   Rise in stocks, rise in current liabilities. The working capital will not change although the ratios will. The acid test will show a deterioration.

    (b)   Rise in fixed assets, rise in long-term liabilities. Increase in gearing.

    (c)   Rise in fixed assets, rise in reserves, increase in shareholders' equity.

4   (a)   Analyse the reasons for subjecting fixed assets to depreciation in financial accounts.
    (b)   Analyse the consequences for the balance sheet and the profit and loss account of using the reducing balance methods rather than the straight line method of depreciation.

    (a)   Accounting for a decline in the value of assets over time. Fixed assets are shown net of depreciation in the balance sheet. Depreciation is shown as a negative item in the profit and loss account.

    (b)   Reducing balance skews the depreciation to the early years. Hence, in the early years, there will be a sharp fall in the net book value of fixed assets and a lower profit figure. The straight line method spreads the charge evenly over the life of the assets.

5   'Tidying up the house before the arrival of visitors' or 'cooking the books'. Evaluate the ethics of window dressing.

Window dressing should be defined and explained. It can be justified in terms of ensuring the completion of both sides of transactions within the accounting period. However, if the purpose is to manipulate profit, liquidity or asset value in order to deceive, then it is clearly unethical and, in some cases, illegal.

Chapter 26

1   (a)   Define working capital.
    (b)   Analyse its importance in the successful running of business.

    (a)   Day-to-day finance for running the business. Current assets less current liabilities.
    (b)   Reference should be made to:
        - purchases of stock;
        - need to finance credit sales;
        - trade credit or overdrafts;
        - liquidity;
        - liquidity ratios.

2   (a)   Evaluate the usefulness of the textbook ideals for the major liquidity ratios.
    (b)   Comment on the relative merits of the current asset ratio and the acid test ratio.

    (a)   The ideals of 1½ and 1 respectively are intended as a rule of thumb. Excessively high figures suggest high levels of stock, cash or debtors – each of which should be investigated. Low ratios suggest the risk of being unable to meet debts.

In evaluating ratios, reference should be made to:

- the date of the balance sheet;
- the nature of the business;
- stock turnovers.

(b)   The acid test is a severe test of liquidity. Disposing of stock to meet current liabilities is undesirable as goods will have to be sold at a discount. The acid test is a measure of the ability to meet current liabilities from cash and from debtors.

3   Analyse the consequences for working capital, the current asset ratio and the acid test ratio of each of the following:

(a)   the purchase of stock using cash;

(b)   the sale of surplus stock;

(c)   the use of cash to purchase a fixed asset;

(d)   the use of cash to reduce an overdraft.

(a)   Working capital and the current asset ratio would be unchanged, but there would be a worsening of the acid test ratio.

(b)   There would be a rise in cash, but the current assets, and so current asset ratio, would be unchanged. There would be an improvement in the acid test ratio.

(c)   There would be a fall in the working capital and current assets ratio. There would also be a worsening of the acid test ratio.

(d)   Working capital would be unchanged as assets rise when liabilities fall.

4   Analyse the consequences of different ways of financing the purchase of stock.

By cash:

- reduces cash reserves;
- discounts for prompt payment.

By trade credit:

- creates a current liability;
- worsens liquidity ratio.

By overdraft:

- Danger of reaching overdraft limit.

5   Analyse the consequences of:

(a)   creditors demanding payment more promptly;

(b)   debtors paying up more slowly.

(a)   Cash flow problems – this can be shown by reference to a cash flow forecast. There would also be penalties for late payment.

(b)   Again, cash flow problems. The firm might need to offer incentives for prompt payment.

Chapter 27

1   Analyse the problems associated with:

(a)   interfirm comparisons of accounting ratios;

(b)   historical comparisons of accounting ratios.

(a)   Interfirm comparisons are only valid if they:

- are similar firms;
- have similar product ranges;

- each use the same accounting policies;
- operate in similar markets.

(b) Again, there are problems of ensuring a comparison of like with like. Over time, a firm's product range will change. Similarly, it might operate in different markets.

2   (a)   **Explain how you would evaluate the profitability of a company.**

       (b)   **Analyse why it is important to treat all profit figures with caution.**

(a) By looking at:
- absolute levels of profits;
- changes in profits over time;
- profits as percentages of sales revenue;
- profits as percentages of capital employed.

Ratios are only meaningful if there is a yardstick against which to measure performance (such as the industry average).

(b) They are of a subjective nature, due to the organizations':
- depreciation policies;
- stock valuation policies;
- window dressing activities.

3   (a)   **Identify the major categories of accounting ratio.**

       (b)   **Justifying your answer, identify the ratios that are likely to be of greatest interest to each of five named stakeholders in a large public company.**

(a) These are:
- liquidity ratios;
- profitability ratios;
- efficiency ratios;
- gearing ratios.

(b) The following are the stakeholders and the ratios of most use to them.
- *Shareholders* are concerned with ROCE, dividend cover, dividend yield and price to earnings ratios. These relate to earnings and share values.
- *Creditors* will be interested in liquidity and gearing ratios as these reflect the ability of the firm to pay.
- *Managers* will be interested in profitability and efficiency ratios, such as stock turnover.
- *Employers* will be interested in profitability ratios and liquidity as they indicate stability and ability to offer pay rises.
- *Suppliers* will be interested in efficiency ratios as they reflect orders for stock.

4   **Comment on and analyse possible explanations for a company recording the following results:**

- **2 per cent return on capital employed;**
- **50 per cent gross profit;**
- **10 per cent net profit.**

The gross profit figure is satisfactory, but clearly a high proportion of gross profit is absorbed by overhead costs.

The ROCE is very low, suggesting that both sales revenue and profits were at a low level in relation to the firm's capital.

5   Analyse the reasons for it being essential to understand the nature of a company before commenting on its accounting ratios.

The ratios are affected by the nature of the firm and its markets. Reference should be made to:
- product range;
- choice of markets;
- accounting policies;
- dating of the accounts;
- the industry average;
- historical comparisons.

Chapter 28

1   Evaluate the role of a cash flow forecast in:

(a)   an application for external finance; and

(b)   the internal management of a business.

(a)   A cash budget is an essential part of a business plan.

(b)   Reference should be made to:
- the distinction between cash and profits;
- the problem of seasonality;
- overdraft limits;
- identifying ways to improve cash flow;
- budgetary control;
- variance analysis.

2   (a)   **Why was the law changed to require the publication of cash flow statements?**

(b)   **Analyse ways in which a cash flow statement differs from a profit and loss account.**

(a)   'After-the-event' cash flow statements are required of all public limited companies. The law was changed as a result of a number of corporate failures (such as Polly Peck), in which companies were 'profitable' but suffered cash problems.

(b)   The differences are that:
- depreciation does not feature in a cash statement as there is no outflow of money;
- sales are only included when there is a movement of cash;
- purchases are only included when there is an outflow of cash;
- cash statements record all cash movements, irrespective of cause.

3   (a)   **Analyse possible reasons for a cash flow problem.**

(b)   **Evaluate possible solutions.**

(a)   Reasons include:
- seasonality;
- slow payment by debtors;
- the need to settle with creditors quickly;
- unexpected downturn in sales.

(b)   Solutions should be related to the cause of the problem, so:
- the problem of seasonality can be tackled by diversification and developing sales out of season;
- the problems associated with working capital can be tackled by encouraging prompt payment, obtaining more credit or by a just-in-time approach to stock holding;

- the downturn in sales might have to be tackled by discounts in the short run and a change in strategy in the longer run.

4   Analyse the consequences for cash flow of each of the following:
   (a)   sale and leaseback of fixed assets;
   (b)   hire purchase rather than cash purchase;
   (c)   an increase in the debtor day ratio;
   (d)   a just-in-time approach to stock purchase.

   (a)   Initially, it will improve the cash flow, but it creates a continual outflow in the long term.
   (b)   Hire purchase phases the payment over time and therefore improves cash flow.
   (c)   Slower receipt of cash for sales worsens cash flow.
   (d)   This improves cash flow by reducing the length of the working capital cycle.

5   (a)   Without a reliable forecast of sales revenue, a cash flow forecast is of little use. Discuss.
   (b)   Evaluate techniques of forecasting sales revenue.

   (a)   The first line in the cash flow forecast is the forecast of sales. The forecast must be based on reliable data, taking into account customer demand, competition, price, marketing mix and the firm's productive capacity.
   (b)   Reference could be made to one or more techniques. Statistical methods (such as moving averages) assume that the future can be predicted from the past by identifying trends and adjusting for regular cyclical and seasonal fluctuations.

Chapter 29

1   (a)   Explain the main sources of long-term finance available to a large public limited company.
   (b)   Analyse the implications of financing expansion by long-term borrowing.

   (a)   Sources of finance include:
      - venture capital;
      - loans;
      - debentures;
      - share issues;
      - retained profits;
      - government grants and loans.
   (b)   Reference should be made to:
      - gearing;
      - the impact on profits available for distribution;
      - retention of control;
      - creation of a liability;
      - the ability to raise further finance by borrowing.

2   (a)   Explain the sources of long-term finance available to a small, family-owned private limited company.
   (b)   Analyse the implications of financing expansion by a share issue.

   (a)   Sources include:
      - savings of owners;
      - retained profits;

- bank loans;
- leasing and hire purchase;
- share issues.

(b)   A share issue threatens the control of the business, but does not create a legal obligation to pay a return. However, shareholders do require a satisfactory return in terms of profit and dividends. As a private limited company, it is unable to make an appeal to the public to subscribe to the issue.

3   (a)   **Explain the difference between authorized, issued and paid-up shares.**

    (b)   **Evaluate the proposition that equity finance involves no cost to the business.**

(a)   Authorized shares are shares that the company is authorized to issue. The number is stated in its memorandum of association.

Issued shares are those actually issued. The total numbers issued might be less than the number the company is authorized to issue.

Paid-up shares are those that have been fully paid for. It is common to collect the finance in instalments. Once the shares have been paid for, no further claim can be made on the shareholder.

(b)   Dividends are paid out of profit. If a firm is unprofitable and no dividends are paid, the shareholders cannot take legal action. Nevertheless, they do look for a satisfactory return and, therefore, there is a cost to the company.

4   (a)   **With reference to the notion of matching sources to purposes explain the differing purposes of short-, medium- and long-term finance.**

    (b)   **Evaluate leasing as a method acquiring assets.**

(a)   Short-term finance is for working capital items, such as stock, debtors.

Medium-term finance is for assets with a life of three to ten years, such as vehicles.

Long-term finance is for long-term assets, such as property.

(b)   The advantages of leasing are that it:

- spreads payments over the years;
- improves initial cash flow;
- reduces capital requirements;
- includes maintenance contracts and updating.

The disadvantages are:

- higher costs in the long term;
- items are not available for use as security for future loans.

5   (a)   **Explain the main sources of short-term finance.**

    (b)   **Evaluate the overdraft as a method of short-term finance.**

(a)   Sources include overdrafts, trade credit, factoring of debts.

(b)   The features of an overdraft are that:

- it is repayable on demand;
- interest is charged on a daily basis;
- it is subject to an overdraft limit;
- it is a flexible method of obtaining bank finance.

6   Analyse the implications for a company's balance sheet of each of the methods of financing expansion.

Debt finance shows up as long-term liabilities.

Loans are used to buy assets that appear in the fixed assets section at the top of the balance sheet, but are cancelled out by the rise in long-term liabilities.

A share issue shows up in shareholders' equity. The rise in fixed assets is balanced by a rise in shareholders' equity.

Chapter 30

1   A firm intends to invest in a computer system in order to reduce costs.
   (a)   Explain how it should set about calculating the (net) annual return on the investment.
   (b)   Propose and evaluate one technique of investment appraisal that it should use.

   (a)   The return on an expansion project is expected sales revenue less operating costs. The return on a cost saving project is net savings.
   (b)   Payback discriminates against projects that only pay back over a long period.
          Against that, it is important for cash flow to get a quick return.
          Alternatively, ARR takes into account the returns over the whole life of the asset, but ignores the timing of the return.
          Another option is discounting methods, which take into account the return over the whole life and the timing of the return.

2   (a)   Explain each of the non-discounting techniques of investment appraisal.
   (b)   Evaluate the proposition that the discounting methods are superior to the non-discounting ones.

   (a)   Payback tells you the time it will take for the asset to pay for itself.
          With ARR, the annual profits are expressed as a percentage of the capital cost.
   (b)   The discounting methods take into account:
          • the return over the whole life of the asset;
          • the timing of the return.

3   (a)   Explain the difference between the net present value and the internal rate of return.
   (b)   Evaluate each of these two methods of investment appraisal.

   (a)   NPV = Discounted cash inflow – the initial cost. Proceed if NPV is positive.
          IRR is the rate of discount at which NPV is zero. Proceed if IRR exceeds the cost of borrowing.
          With NPV a predetermined rate of discount is used. With IRR a process of trial and error is used to identify the rate.
   (b)   They both take into account the size and timing of the return. The weakness of NPV, however, is that the result depends on the choice of discount rate.

4   (a)   With reference to each of the techniques of investment appraisal, analyse how the rate of interest on loans affects investment decision making.
   (b)   When financing investment from internal sources, firms can ignore interest rates. Discuss.

   (a)   In the payback method interest charges will affect the net return on the investment.
          With ARR/IRR, only proceed if the return exceeds the rate of interest.
          With NPV, the rate of discount reflects the rate of interest on borrowed money.
   (b)   No. The rate of interest will influence decisions even if the firm does not need to borrow money. This is because it will take into account the opportunity cost – that is, what it could obtain by investing the money elsewhere.

5   (a)   Explain how a computer program can aid investment decision making.

        (b)   Analyse non-quantifiable factors that should be taken into account in investment decisions.

        (a)   Use of spreadsheets to answer 'What if ... ' questions. Computer programs can also calculate ARR and IRR quickly and accurately.

        (b)   Such factors include:
- life of the asset;
- lifecycle of the product;
- the availability of finance;
- competition changes in the external environment;
- the implications for human resources.

6   (a)   Analyse ways in which expected inflation affects the process of investment decision making.

        (b)   Analyse how uncertainty affects the process of decision making.

        (a)   If inflation is expected and accurately anticipated, it is possible to adjust the figures accordingly. Hence, we could refer to the expected return in real terms.

        (b)   It is necessary to make an estimate of the likelihood of events happening. This is seen in decision tree analysis.

               In general, inflation and other uncertainties are likely to mean taking a more cautious approach.

Chapter 31

1   (a)   Outline the nature and purpose of decision trees.

        (b)   Evaluate the decision tree as a technique of analysis.

        (a)   Decision trees take into account the expected return moderated by the probability of events happening. Expected value = Return × Probability.

        (b)   It is a sophisticated technique, based on a subjective estimate of probability.

2   (a)   Explain what you understand by expected value.

        (b)   Evaluate decision trees as an analytical tool.

        (a)   EV = Return × Probability.

        (b)   It uses subjective probability.

3   (a)   Explain four types of decisions that could be subjected to decision tree analysis.

        (b)   Evaluate the proposition that decision tree analysis is based on sure foundations

        (a)   Examples include:
- new product launches;
- investment in capital assets;
- promotional campaigns;
- investment in human capital;
- any proposal that involves expenditure today for an uncertain return in the future.

        (b)   It is based on subjective probability.

Chapter 32

1   Analyse the role of cost accounting within a business organization.

It is used:
- for planning the production of budgets for control purposes;
- to identify the cost of an activity;
- to aid decision making, such as pricing;
- to ensure accountability (cost and profit centres).

Management accounting involves techniques of analysis and decision making.

2   Analyse the relationship between the level of output and unit costs.

In the short run, a rise in output will ensure that overheads are spread over a larger volume of goods, thus reducing unit costs.

In the long run, a rise in the scale of production leads to economies of scale (technical, managerial, commercial, marketing, research), although, beyond a certain point, there is a danger of diseconomies of scale.

3   Comment on each of the following statements.
   (a)   In the long run, there is no such thing as a fixed cost;
   (b)   Direct cost is just another name for variable cost;
   (c)   Indirect cost is just another name for fixed costs;
   (d)   In practice, most so-called fixed costs are semivariable costs.

   (a)   Costs are only fixed in the short run.
   (b)   Direct costs are directly associated with the production of particular goods and can be fixed as well as variable – for example, dedicated machinery.
   (c)   Indirect costs are usually seen as fixed, but it is possible for some to be variable.
   (d)   Costs are only fixed over a certain range of output.

4   Analyse the problems confronting a plumber when costing a job.

This requires an explanation of costing methods. A plumber has to calculate the cost of materials used, the cost of direct labour (hours × hourly rate) and add in a share of overheads.

5   (a)   Explain the difference between full and absorption costing.

   (b)   Evaluate these methods in relation to marginal or contribution costing.

   (a)   Full costing, allocates the overheads *en masse* over the output. Absorption costing, however, treats each overhead in an individual manner. Thus, the cost of personnel administration is allocated in relation to the size of the workforce in each cost centre, rent is allocated in relation to space used and so on.
   (b)   They ensure that all costs are accounted for to calculate the overall costs associated with each unit of output. However, at times, there is an argument for leaving out fixed costs and making decisions on marginal costs alone – for example, decisions concerning special order contracts, and make or buy in.

6   (a)   Explain what you understand by contribution.
   (b)   Analyse the role of contribution in decision making.

   (a)   Sales revenue – Variable costs.
          Contribution per unit is Price – Variable cost per unit.

(b)   Reference should be made to:
- break-even analysis;
- the special order contract;
- deleting the unprofitable product;
- the make or buy decision.

In each case, the quality of decision making can be improved by leaving out fixed costs. This should be illustrated by numerical examples.

7   **Analyse the circumstances in which a firm might be willing to accept an order in which average revenue (price) does not cover average costs.**

Although apparently making a loss, the contract is worth while if:
- variable costs are covered;
- there is spare capacity;
- no more profitable order is available;
- it does not set a precedent.

If fixed costs are covered by 'regular' orders, any contribution made by the 'special' order will add to profits.

8   **Explain how contribution can be used to answer the following types of business decision:**
   (a)   whether or not to drop a loss-making product;
   (b)   whether or not to accept a loss-making special order;
   (c)   whether or not to make or buy in a component.

   (a)   Provided deletion does not eliminate a fixed cost, it is worth while continuing with the product while it makes a positive contribution.
   (b)   Accept the order if it makes a contribution and spare capacity exists.
   (c)   Make the decision on the basis of which of the two makes the greater contribution.

Chapter 33

1   **Evaluate break-even analysis for business decision making.**

Break-even analysis enables us to:
- identify the output needed to break even;
- decide whether or not a proposed product is likely to be profitable;
- identify a margin of safety.

The major weaknesses of it are the assumption of a linear relationship between output and cost and that sales can be increased at the set price.

2   **Analyse the complications for break-even analysis that result from each of the following features of life for real business:**
   (a)   the non-standard product;
   (b)   the multiproduct firm;
   (c)   the stepped rise in fixed costs;
   (d)   the non-linear cost and revenue curves.

   (a)   The simple break-even graph is only appropriate for standardized products.
   (b)   Non-standard products produced by a multiproduct firm can be subjected to break-even analysis using the ratio of contribution to sales.
   (c)   A stepped fixed cost line can result in multiple break-even points.

(d)   Non-linear curves make it more difficult to identify the break-even points. Moreover, after profit-maximizing output is reached, profits will fall. In the traditional break-even curve, profits always rise with output.

3   Using sketch graphs, analyse the consequences for the break-even point of each of the following:
      (a)   a rise in fixed costs;
      (b)   a rise in variable costs per unit;
      (c)   a price reduction;
      (d)   fixed costs being a high percentage of total costs.

      (a)   A rise in fixed costs will push the total cost line up and raise the break-even level of output.
      (b)   A rise in variable costs will produce a more steeply rising total cost curve – again, the break-even level of output will be greater.
      (c)   A price reduction shifts the revenue curve downwards – again, raising the break-even point.
      (d)   If fixed costs are a high percentage of total costs, then, the break-even level of output is high, and, once the break-even point has been reached, profits will rise steeply.

All these points should be analysed by means of sketch graphs.

4   The margin of safety for a product produced by a firm is currently 5 per cent.
      (a)   Explain what this means and what its implications are.
      (b)   Evaluate strategies to improve the situation.

      (a)   Current output is only 5% above the break-even point.
              Therefore, any reduction in output or sales will soon produce a loss-making situation. The profits are made on only a small proportion of output.
      (b)   Raise prices, assuming that customers will continue to buy. Alternatively, reduce fixed costs, but this is difficult to do in the short run. Otherwise, reduce variable costs by achieving greater efficiency.

5   The standard linear break-even chart suggests that profits will always be increased by raising the level of output. Analyse why this is not true in the real world.

The law of demand demonstrates that, to increase sales, it is necessary to reduce the price.
In real life, increased output will bring about changes in unit costs due to spreading overheads, economies of scale, diseconomies of sale and so on.

Chapter 34

1   Explain and evaluate the role of budgeting in business.

The role of budgeting is to aid:
• planning;
• decision making;
• control.
In the evaluation, reference should be made to the assumptions behind the budget.

2   (a)   Analyse the difference between a fixed and a flexible budget.
      (b)   Which of the two provides the better basis for variance analysis?

      (a)   A fixed budget is based on a single level of activity. A flexible budget is fixed for different levels of activity.
      (b)   Flexible – because variance analysis is based on a comparison of actual costs at that level of activity and what costs should have been.

3   Explain what is meant by each of the following:
     (a)   a sales budget;
     (b)   a production cost budget;
     (c)   a cash budget;
     (d)   a budget profit and loss account;
     (e)   a capital budget;
     (d)   a marketing budget.

     (a)   A sales budget shows planned sales disaggregated by product, region and so on.
     (b)   A production cost budget shows itemized production costs at a stated level of activity.
     (c)   A cash budget is a cash flow forecast that shows the expected movement of cash in to and out of the business.
     (d)   A budget profit and loss account is a forecast of what the profit and loss account will look like.
     (e)   A capital budget shows the planned investment spending.
     (f)   A marketing budget delineates the planned spending on marketing activities, divided into time periods.
            In each case, the explanation should be accompanied by simple examples.

4   Analyse possible explanations for the following:
     (a)   costs being greater than expected;
     (b)   profits being lower than expected;
     (c)   an adverse variance in labour costs;
     (d)   a favourable variance in sales revenue;
     (e)   the quantity of materials used being greater than expected.

     (a)   Costs can be affected by a rise in the costs of inputs or there being a greater than expected use of inputs.
     (b)   Profits may be low due to price reductions, low sales or a rise in costs.
     (c)   Labour costs can increase if there are unexpected rises in rates of pay, more labour was required than was expected or a higher grade of labour was used.
     (d)   Sales revenue can be greater than expected if there are price rises or increases in sales volume.
     (e)   More materials can be required if there is a great deal of waste or a rise in production.

5   (a)   Explain the terms cost centre, revenue centre and profit centre.
     (b)   Evaluate the benefits of organizing a business in terms of profit centres.

     (a)   In each case, the centres are part of the organization (a division, department or other group) for which information is collected on:
            •   costs;
            •   revenue;
            •   costs and revenue respectively.
     (b)   Profit centres are 'businesses within a business'. Those responsible for the centres are held accountable for their results and so on. The system avoids the danger of cross-subsidization.

Chapter 35

1   (a)   Explain the role of a production or operations manager.
     (b)   Analyse the factors that are taken into account in planning the level of capacity.

     (a)   Production or operations management is the specialist management function that deals with all aspects of the production process. This, in turn, converts inputs into outputs. These managers make decisions relating to:

- product design;
- factory layout;
- works organization and method;
- equipment design;
- quality;
- stock levels;
- the scheduling of output;
- cost and waste control;
- maintenance;
- planning;
- capacity.

(b) Such factors include:

- demand forecasts;
- types of processes;
- economic operating levels;
- strategies for dealing with fluctuating or uncertain demand levels;
- reference should also be made to opportunities for buying in (outsourcing).

2 (a) **Analyse the causes and consequences of seasonal fluctuations in demand.**

   (b) **Suggest and evaluate ways in which a production department can cope with the problem of seasonality.**

   (a) Reference should be made to:

- stock levels;
- working capital;
- perishability;
- additional costs associated with peak-time production;
- capacity levels.

   (b) Seasonality can be tackled by pricing policies – peak pricing to shift demand. Non-perishable goods can be stored at off-peak times, but this involves costs and complications for cash flow.

   Peak production requires additional capacity (and, therefore, surplus capacity off-peak) and will raise costs in terms of intensive use of labour and other resources.

3 (a) **Define:**

   (i) **batch production; and**

   (ii) **flow production.**

   (b) **Discuss the implications of these two processes.**

   (a) Batch production is the manufacture of a limited number of identical products. Within each stage of the production process, work will be completed for the whole batch before the next stage is started.

   Flow production is the manufacture of an item in a continually moving process. Each stage is linked either by a conveyor belt or, if the product or constituents are in liquid form, through pipes.

   (b) The choice of method has implications for :

- scale of capital investment;
- labour force requirements;
- the skills base of the workforce;

- layout of the plant;
- standardization versus variation in the product;
- costs and efficiency;
- production times;
- quality control;
- worker motivation.

4 (a) **Analyse the advantages to the production department of product standardization.**

   (b) **Analyse the disadvantages for the organization of concentrating on a standardized product.**

   (a) Standardization facilitates flow production, producing advantages in terms of;
   - lower unit costs;
   - reduction in downtime;
   - easier costing;
   - less variety in, and lower levels of, stocks;
   - long production runs;
   - lower training requirements;
   - reduction in variety of equipment.

   (b) The main disadvantage relates to the marketing function. Production variation enables the organization to target different segments. Standardization increases risks from changes in demand.

5 (a) **What do you understand by batch production?**

   (b) **Discuss the importance of scheduling for batch production.**

   (a) Batch production is the manufacture of a limited number of identical products. Within each stage of the production process, work will be completed for the whole batch before the next stage is started.

   (b) Scheduling allocates start and finish times to tasks. It specifies in advance the programme for all movements in to, and out of, the manufacturing system. It involves:
   - sequencing – the order in which work will be undertaken;
   - resource allocation.

   Because batch production is not continuous, it is essential to plan activities to ensure that resources are available when required and that downtime between operations is minimized. Economic batch size calculations are used to identify optimum batch sizes.

Chapter 36

1 (a) **With the use of an illustration, outline the features of a stock control graph.**

   (b) **Analyse the costs and benefits of a buffer stock.**

   (a) Stock control graphs must be included in the answer and reference should be made to the following:
   - depletion rate;
   - deliveries;
   - reorder level;
   - reorder quantity;
   - maximum stock levels;
   - buffer stock;
   - lead time.

(b) The costs are:
- the storage and security required;
- high levels of working capital are needed;
- costs of trade credit or overdraft;
- it worsens cash flow.

The benefits of a buffer stock are that it:
- reduces the danger of stockout;
- eliminates the need for rush orders at high costs;
- enables economic order quantities to be purchased.

2 **Analyse the factors to be considered by a firm in deciding on its purchasing policy.**

Reference should be made to:
- economic order quantity;
- cost of delivery;
- cost of stockholding;
- working capital requirements;
- suppliers;
- just-in-time versus just-in-case methods;
- the cost of stockout.

In addition to analysing factors relating to size of orders, students could also explore the issue of single and multiple sourcing.

3 (a) **What is meant by the economic order quantity?**

(b) **Analyse the consequences for stock policy of the concept of an economic order quantity?**

(a) The optimum stock order level, taking into account delivery costs and the cost of stockholding. It provides a partial model for stock control and can be calculated using the formula:

$$\text{EOQ} = \sqrt{\frac{2cd}{h}}$$

where c = cost of placing an order
d = annual demand for the item
h = the cost of holding stock

(b) If there is an optimum size for the ordering of stock, then it is advantageous to place orders to this magnitude. This has implications for stockholding policies and might rule out a just-in-time approach. The higher the delivery cost in relation to the cost of holding stock, the larger the order level should be. This would result in a policy of large but infrequent orders rather than small but frequent ones.

4 (a) **Analyse the implications of a just-in-time stock policy on relations with suppliers.**

(b) **Analyse the preconditions for a successful policy of just-in-time.**

(a) Just-in-time methods require:
- sourcing from a limited number of supply firms;
- close, long-term relationships with suppliers;
- partnership with suppliers.

(b) Just-in-time methods require:
- close relationships with suppliers;
- Total Quality Management, zero defects;
- flexibility and a multifunctional workforce;

- dependability;
- demand-pull manufacturing (*Kanban*);
- employee commitment.

5   **Analyse the role of information technology in stock control.**

Reference can be made to:
- calculation of EOQ;
- tracking of stock;
- computer-based ordering of stock;
- material requirement planning (MRP) – this is a computer-based system for managing inventories, designed to ensure that a firm has the parts and materials needed to supply its products at the right time, place and quantity.

Chapter 37

1   (a)   **Analyse the importance of quality control to organizations operating in a competitive market.**

    (b)   **Discuss the problems associated with end-of-the-line quality control.**

    (a)   Reference should be made to quality as an important aspect of competitiveness and the growing expectations of customers.

    (b)   End-of-the-line quality control tends to absolve employees from responsibility for quality. As it involves quality control by sampling, the twin problems of consumers' risk and producers' risk arise.

2   **Should quality be left to a specialist quality control department? Justify your answer.**

No – although there is a role for a specialist quality control department, responsibility for quality should be shared by the entire workforce. Reference should be made to:
- Total Quality Management;
- zero defects;
- the cost of low quality;
- quality as a weapon in competition;
- public demand for quality.

3   (a)   **Analyse the principle of statistical quality control.**

    (b)   **Evaluate statistical quality control as a way of ensuring quality.**

Quality control takes place at the end of the line and usually involves sampling. Sampling is especially necessary where quality testing involves destruction.

The subject of statistical quality control (SQC) can be divided into acceptance sampling and process control. Acceptance sampling involves testing a random sample of existing goods and deciding whether or not to accept an entire lot based on the quality of the random sample. Statistical process control (SPC) involves testing a random sample of output from a process to determine whether or not the process is producing items within a preselected range. When the tested output exceeds that range, it is a signal to adjust the production process to force the output back into the acceptable range. This is accomplished by adjusting the process itself. Acceptance sampling is frequently used in a purchasing or receiving situation, while process control is used in a production situation of any type.

Quality control for both acceptance sampling and process control measures either attributes or variables. Goods or services may be observed to be either good or bad, or functioning or malfunctioning. For example, a lawnmower either runs or it doesn't; it attains a certain level of torque and horsepower or it doesn't. This type of measurement is known as sampling by attributes. Alternatively, a lawnmower's torque and horsepower can be measured as an amount of deviation from a set standard. This type of measurement is known as sampling by variables.

Control charts are constructed to measure deviations from a central line. Warning levels on the control chart indicate when machines need to be reset.

In the case of acceptance sampling, samples that are outside the permitted tolerance will result in:

- further samples;
- rejection.

This inevitably means that some satisfactory goods are rejected (producers' risk) while some defective goods are accepted (consumers' risk).

4 **Total Quality Management (TQM) requires a change in the culture of the organization. Discuss.**

TQM:

- is a total process, involving everyone, and is led from the top;
- places the customer at the centre;
- requires involvement and commitment;
- requires teamwork and creativity;
- results in new perceptions of quality – not as a cost, but, instead, as part of strategic management, and poor quality involves a cost, too.

A contrast should be made with traditional end-of-the-line methods of quality control.

5 **'Quality is free' (P. Crosby). Discuss.**

Traditionally, quality was seen as a cost – the expense of producing quality products. The 'quality gurus', however, stressed the importance of quality and that low quality means:

- loss of competitiveness;
- loss of orders;
- dissatisfied customers.

Philip B. Crosby followed W. Edwards Deming, Joseph M. Juran and others in stressing the importance of changing the culture of an organization to strive for zero defects. This contrasts with traditional quality control, which seems to accept that some defective goods will be produced. TQM 'builds in quality' rather than inspecting out defective goods.

Chapter 38

1 (a) **Explain each of the following terms:**
      (i)   **effectiveness;**
      (ii) **efficiency;**
      (iii) **productivity.**

   (b) **Analyse ways of improving the productivity of labour.**

   (a) Effectiveness is about achieving objectives. Efficiency means using resources to make the best, most cost-effective use of them. Productivity is output per unit of input. Effectiveness is only concerned with output, whereas efficiency and productivity relate to the relationships between input and output. Efficiency is not only concerned with the productivity of labour, but also the productivity of other inputs and the minimization of waste.

   (b) The productivity of labour can be improved by:
      - providing workers with more capital equipment;
      - better technology;
      - training to improve the quality of the workforce;
      - better organization of production;
      - teamwork, motivation and leadership.

2   (a)   **Outline the methods of work study.**

        (b)   **Analyse the problems involved in undertaking work study.**

        (a)   Work study emerged from the work of Frederick Taylor and the scientific management school. It consists of:

- method study – to devise the optimum methods of working,;
- work measurement – to provide a basis for piece-rate payments.

        (b)   Method study is the systematic recording and analysis of existing methods of doing work and comparison with proposed new methods, together with the assessment of easier and more efficient methods. It involves observing work, analysing movement, developing improved methods of working. Method study is based on the assumption that there is a single best method of doing a particular job.

Work measurement seeks to establish standard times for performing a task. These are obtained by time study (for existing tasks) and synthetic timing (for new tasks). This will involve breaking tasks down into their components and building up times for each motion.

Problems include:

- employees' resentment of being timed;
- how to calculate non-existent tasks;
- establishing standard times appropriate for the experienced worker.

3   (a)   **What do you understand by work study?**

        (b)   **Analyse the role of:**

            (i)   **work measurement; and (ii) method study.**

        (a)   As above.

        (b)   (i)   Work measurement is used as a basis for:

- costing;
- planning operations;
- setting piece-work rates.

            (ii)   Method study is based on the belief that there is a single best way to perform any operation. Method studies seek to find what that best method is.

4   **Explain what is meant by business process re-engineering and analyse its role in operations management.**

Business process re-engineering is the search for, and implementation of, radical changes in business processes to achieve breakthrough results in terms of major gains in levels of performance.

Like lean production, it involves the elimination of waste, but it requires dramatic change and a 'clean sheet' approach.

The aim is to:

- reduce waste and cost;
- improve efficiency;
- improve competitiveness.

5   **Discuss ways of improving the productivity of capital equipment.**

Define productivity as the output per unit of input (in this case, per machine per hour).

Productivity can be improved by:

- better technology;
- training to improve the quality of labour;
- waste reduction;
- improved organization.

Chapter 39

1   Waste is defined as an activity that does not add value. Discuss the implications of this statement.

Production involves inputs being transformed into outputs. In the process, value is added to the goods and services. Waste is seen as any activity that does not add value for the customer, such as:
- overproduction;
- unnecessary motion;
- defective goods;
- inappropriate processes;
- wasting time;
- unnecessary movement of goods.

Lean production seeks to eliminate waste, undertaking only value-adding activities.

2   (a)   What do you understand by lean production?

   (b)   Evaluate two aspects of lean production.

   (a)   Lean production is a range of Japanese-inspired measures designed to save on waste.

   (b)   Evaluate two techniques from the following:
   - just-in-time production and stockholding methods;
   - continuous improvement;
   - time-based competition;
   - Total Quality Management;
   - cellular production.

   In each case, an explanation should be followed by some evaluative comment, such as just-in-time methods increase the risk of stockout and require commitment from staff and close relations with suppliers. Continuous improvement has been challenged by supporters of the dramatic breakthrough promised by business process re-engineering.

3   (a)   Explain the following Japanese terms:
   (i)   *Kaizen*;
   (ii)   *Kanban*.

   (b)   Analyse their importance within the lean production philosophy.

   (a)   *Kaisen* means gradual, continuous improvement. *Kanban* is a system of cards used in demand-pull production. They facilitate just-in-time methods.

   (b)   Improvement in technology, processes, productivity and quality take the form of continuous change rather than dramatic breakthroughs. In the Western model, dramatic progress is followed by consolidation.

   Kanban cards are used to pull production through a series of processes. This is the practical means by which just-in-time production occurs.

4   Discuss the benefits of, and the preconditions for, successful quality circles.

A quality circle is a small group of workers who meet to discuss quality, production methods, productivity and safety. The aim is to suggest and implement improvements. The benefits include:
- improvement in work practices;
- increased involvement and motivation;
- job enrichment;
- use being made of shopfloor experience;
- greater awareness of shopfloor problems.

Preconditions necessary for success are:
* commitment and support from senior management;
* a participative culture;
* training of circle leaders;
* involvement of supervisors.

5   **Time is an important weapon in securing competitive advantage. Analyse the principles and benefits of time-based competition.**

Time-based competition requires the elimination of unproductive time, such as:
* overproduction;
* rejects;
* set-up times;
* process waste;
* bottlenecks;
* waiting time.

The benefits take the form of:
* increased flexibility;
* increased customer satisfaction;
* reduction in costs;
* shorter product development times;
* the securing of competitive advantage.

Chapter 40

1   **Evaluate the role of critical path analysis.**

Network or critical path analysis facilitates the planning of operations by:
* identifying the minimum time needed to complete a project;
* identifying critical and non-critical activities;
* providing the basis for decision making relating to the deployment of resources;
* providing a basis for costing.

2   (a)   **Define these terms:**
        (i)   **critical activity; and**
        (ii)   **total float.**
    (b)   **Analyse ways in which identification of float can play a part in project planning.**

    (a)   A critical activity is one that, if delayed, would result in a failure to complete the project within the minimum time period.

        Total float is the spare time you have for each activity before a delay would result. Whereas free float is the overall spare time before the subsequent activity is delayed, total float is the overall time spare if the whole project is not to be delayed.

    (b)   Resources must be prioritized on critical activities. Non-critical activities can be delayed without endangering the project's completion time. Hence, critical path analysis can play a major role in planning activities and the deployment of resources.

3   Analyse reasons for the following.

(a)   It might not be possible to complete the project in the timescale suggested by network analysis;

(b)   a crash programme to speed up the completion of a project might add to costs.

(a)   A network analysis diagram assumes the resources will be available to complete the project on time. In practice, potentially concurrent activities might not occur together if there are shortages of labour or other resources. Most network analysis problems also stem from the assumption that resources can be switched from one activity to another.

(b)   A crash programme will add to costs if the following occur:

- labour is employed at overtime rates;

- materials are bought in quantities other than the economic order quantity;

- additional payments are required to secure the use of capital equipment.

4   (a)   Explain how a Gantt chart is produced.

(b)   With the aid of examples, evaluate the role of a Gantt chart in project management.

(a)   A Gantt chart is a horizontal bar chart in which the activities needed to complete a project are shown in the right order and at the right time.

Such a chart is based on the same data used in a network diagram – that is, durations and, sequences of events.

(b)   The great benefit of Gantt charts is that they make it easy to identify concurrent activities (which compete for resources) and the float available for shifting resources from critical to non-critical activities.

Chapter 41

1   (a)   Explain the role of a personnel manager in a large company.

(b)   Analyse the ways in which personnel work interrelates with other functional areas of management.

(a)   The personnel role consists of:

- employee resourcing incorporating recruitment and selection, job analysis, dismissal, human resource planning;

- training and development;

- performance appraisal;

- reward management;

- job evaluation;

- sickness and pensions;

- employee relations;

- participation;

- discipline and grievance.

(b)   The interaction is in terms of ensuring that the organization has human resources in the quantity and of the quality necessary to achieve organizational objectives. The human resource plan is one component of the overall corporate plan. Hence, to achieve the profit objective it is necessary to produce a target level of output and sales and this in turn necessitates human resources.

2   Is human resource management (HRM) merely a new name for personnel management? Justify your answer.

It is true that HRM deals with the same issues as personnel management and that the old style personnel manager has re-emerged as a human resource manager. However, there are major philosophical differences between the two:

HRM is:

* seen as central to the achievement of organizational objectives;
* of strategic importance;
* based on the idea that employees are the key resource;
* based on commitment rather than compliance.

The objective of HRM is to make the most productive use of human resource.

The final distinction is that whereas personnel management was a specialist activity every manager is a human resource manager.

3   Analyse the differences between hard and soft HRM.

A simple distinction is that hard HRM places the emphasis on the word resource, whereas soft HRM places the emphasis on the word human.

In hard HRM:

* workers are seen as a cost;
* the company outlook takes precedence;
* there is an emphasis on efficiency.

In soft HRM:

* workers are seen as exploitable assets;
* employee involvement and commitment are encouraged;
* there is more concern with the views of employees;
* core workers should be developed.

4   HRM places personnel work at the centre of strategic management. Discuss.

Answers to this question should explore the distinction between personnel and HR management. Old style personnel departments were seen in a supportive role with a "hiring, firing and welfare" slant. Modern HRM is at the centre of the management decision making. Human resources are the key source to modern business organizations and are therefore essential to the achievement of objectives.

5   Employees are the firm's most important resource in modern business. Discuss

Answers to this question should explore the nature of HRM and the ways in which it is philosophically different from personnel work. Reference should also be made to the nature of work especially in the service sectors and knowledge based industry. A better educated workforce utilising its skills and intelligence requires a different syle of management involving leadership rather that direction. Changes in technology require investment in employee training and it is only by adopting a modern approach to the management of human resources that organizations can secure and retain a competitive advantage.

Chapter 42

1   (a)   Outline the principles of scientific management.

(b)   Does scientific management have any relevance to the modern world? Justify your answer.

(a)   These are:

* work study to devise optimum methods;
* work measurement;

- payment linked to output (piece-work rates);
- division of labour leading to 'Fordism';
- pay as the motivator;
- management control over the workplace.

(b) Scientific management is still found in the workplace. There is still a role for work study and work measurement. Incentive payments are still found in industry, but employee motivation is more complicated than Frederick Taylor envisaged. Reference should be made to later theories of leadership, motivation and teamwork.

2 **Evaluate the contribution of Elton Mayo to our understanding of people at work.**

Mayo taught us that man is a social, as well as an economic, animal. He was the founder of the human relations school. He showed that employees' motivation is affected by social factors, including the role of the social group. Social scientists still refer to the Hawthorne effect. Finally, he played a major role in the development of research methods.

3 (a) **Compare and contrast the theories associated with Maslow and Herzberg.**
  (b) **Suggest and evaluate strategies that apply Herzberg's theory in the workplace.**

  (a) Herzberg's maintenance factors correspond to the lower-order needs of Maslow's theory. The motivators correspond to the higher-order needs.

  Both stressed the importance of satisfying lower needs before the higher-order needs. Maslow envisaged motivation as steps rising upwards, whereas Herzberg's contrasted the negative impact resulting from the absence of hygiene factors and the positive impact of the motivators.

  (b) Herzberg did not dismiss the importance of pay in motivation. Unsatisfactory pay levels will result in a demotivated workforce. However, the real motivators are intrinsic to the job. As a result of Herzberg's work, there has been an emphasis on job redesign and job enrichment.

4 (a) **Outline both equity and expectancy theories.**
  (b) **Discuss how these theories can be applied to the work situation.**

  (a) Equity theory teaches us the importance of fairness in human motivation. A perception of unfairness results in a demotivated workforce.

  Expectancy theory relates rewards to the subjective probability of achieving the rewards.

  (b) Pay and promotion should not only be fair, but be seen to be fair.

  Incentive pay should be set such that the rewards are considered worth while, are achievable and there is prompt feedback of results and rewards.

5 **Discuss the principles of job enrichment.**

The term should be defined and reference should be made to Frederick Herzberg's theory.

Richard Hackman and Oldham, building on Herzberg, saw enrichment in terms of:

- skill variety;
- task identity;
- task significance;
- autonomy;
- feedback.

Each should be explained with examples and explanations of the ways in which they enrich a job.

6 (a) **Outline McGregor's Theory X and Theory Y**
  (b) **Did McGregor produce a theory about different types of workers or different types of management? Justify your answer.**

(a)   Contrast the two in terms of:
- attitudes to responsibility;
- need for control;
- attitudes to work;
- types of control.

(b)   McGregor was not arguing that there are two types of worker – instead, he was arguing that if workers are assumed to correspond with one set of assumptions (Theory X) they will behave and have to be controlled accordingly. He was concerned with management's attitudes rather than those of workers.

7   (a)   **Outline two approaches to the study of leadership.**

   (b)   **Is there a single best style of leadership? Justify your answer.**

(a)   Reference could be made to:
- the traits approach, which falls down because there are always exceptions to any rule ;
- the styles approach.

Modern theories emphasize situations and contingency.

(b)   No, it all depends on the situation, the organization, the task and the personalities involved.

Chapter 43

1   (a)   **Distinguish between a team and a group of people.**

   (b)   **Analyse the benefits of working in a team.**

(a)   A team is a group of people selected to achieve a particular goal.

(b)   The benefits are that team working:
- satisfies social needs
- allows individuals to gain from the strengths of others;
- delegation of responsibility is facilitated;
- provides scope for job enrichment via the Hackman-Oldham principles.

2   (a)   **What do you understand by an autonomous work team?**

   (b)   **Analyse the benefits of organizing work in this way.**

(a)   Reference should be made to the features of a team and the benefits of granting greater autonomy to the workforce. This should be supported by reference to human relation's theory.

(b)   The benefits are:
- social;
- sharing of work and responsibility;
- those that stem from empowering workers;
- job enrichment;
- increased motivation.

3   **What makes for effective teamworking? In your answer, make reference to appropriate theories.**

Reference could be made to R. Meredith Belbin, group formation, management, social dynamics, objectives, communication nets and so on.

4   (a)   **Outline the phases in the development of a group or team.**

   (b)   **Discuss the relevance of this line of enquiry.**

(a) The phases are:
- forming – coming together;
- storming – disagreements emerge;
- norming – develop 'norms' of acceptable behaviour;
- performing – cohesion, now working as a team.

(b) It provides a better understanding of group dynamics and illustrates the early problems that can occur within groups or teams.

5   **Evaluate the relevance of Belbin's theory of group roles.**

Belbin identified the essential roles that must be fulfilled if the group is to be effective. Successful groups or teams are essential in modern business and managers need to be aware of how groups work.

Chapter 44

1   **Evaluate the role of job descriptions and person specifications in recruitment and selection.**

Note, this question is limited to recruitment and selection.

The two documents should be described before their roles are evaluated. For the candidate, they give information on the type of person the firm is seeking and on the nature of the job. This is important when deciding whether or not to apply and when preparing for the application and selection processes.

The production of the documents:
- facilitates the shortlisting process;
- forces the employer to clarify their ideas on what they are looking for;
- facilitates a more objective approach to selection by use of ranking systems at interview stage.

2   **Critically analyse the modern trend towards a slimmed down core and large group of periphery workers.**

A large group of periphery workers provides numerical flexibility. It reduces costs by ensuring that employees are used only when required.

Alleged drawbacks include:
- high turnover of periphery staff;
- differences in degree of commitment;
- difficulties in organizing teams and holding team meetings;
- increased cost of administration.

3   **Evaluate the interview as a method of selection. Suggest ways in which the interview can be supplemented by alternative methods of selection.**

The interview remains the basic method of selection. There is no real alternative to a structured interview with candidates, although it is known that it has major weaknesses:
- some good candidates perform badly at interview;
- some candidates are able to impress by providing answers they perceive as being sought;
- interviews are subjective and interviewers can be swayed.

Although the interview remains the basic selection device, it has been supplemented by:
- intelligence and personality tests;
- group interviews;
- group tasks;
- assessment centres.

4 (a) Outline the principle of human resource planning.

   (b) **Assess the value of human resource planning.**

   (a) Forecast:
        - demand for labour;
        - supply of labour (internal and external).

        Devise strategies to meet the gap:
        - recruitment and selection;
        - succession;
        - training and development;
        - downsizing.

   (b) The basic purpose is to ensure that the organization has the human resources it needs to achieve its production, sales and profit targets. Planning ensures that there is concern about the future, rather than moving from one crisis to another. Reference should be made to the components of all plans – answers to the questions. 'Where are we now?'; 'Where do we want to go?' and 'How are we to get there?'.

5 (a) **Analyse the likely causes of high labour turnover.**

   (b) **Suggest and evaluate solutions to the problem of high labour turnover.**

   (a) Causes include:
        - low pay;
        - demotivated staff;
        - working conditions;
        - supervision;
        - lack of job satisfaction.

   (b) Investigate causes of the high turnover, then evaluate the problem and devise appropriate solutions, which could be to:
        - increase pay;
        - improve conditions;
        - effect job enrichment;
        - change methods or levels of supervision.

        Any solution should be related to the causes of the problem. The cost of implementing the solutions should be considered as well as the benefits.

6 (a) **What factors should be considered before making workers redundant?**

   (b) **Evaluate the alternatives to redundancy.**

   (a) Factors to consider include:
        - thinking about the question 'Is redundancy necessary?' – whether it is a temporary recession or a permanent downturn;
        - the cost of redundancy;
        - the loss of trained, experienced labour;
        - disruption to teams;
        - conflict, fears, impacts on those remaining;
        - the need to consult;
        - the legal aspects of redundancy selection methods.

   (b) Alternatives include:
        - natural wastage, not recruiting when people leave;

- early retirement schemes;
- voluntary redundancy;
- short time working.

Each of these alternatives has its own problems, of course.

7   (a)   **What should be included in a programme of induction?**

     (b)   **Evaluate the benefits of a formal programme of induction.**

     (a)   Induction should include information on:
- the task requirements;
- workplace layout;
- key personnel;
- safety procedures;
- arrangements for breaks;
- holiday entitlement;
- arrangements for paying workers;
- grievance and discipline procedures.

     (b)   The benefits are in terms of increased output, lower employee turnover and reduced costs. A good induction programme will result in employees reaching high levels of performance sooner. It will also reduce the risk of employees not settling in and, therefore, leaving – the so-called induction crisis.

8   (a)   **Explain how you would set about evaluating a programme of training.**

     (b)   **Discuss the benefits to an organization of recognition as an Investor in People.**

     (a)   Reference should be made to training needs analysis, the setting of objectives for training, closing the skills gap and a comparison of costs and benefits.

     (b)   An employer can be committed to training without gaining the Investors in People award. However, gaining the award:
- forces the employer to plan training;
- forces the employer to consider the needs of employees;
- ensures that the mission statement is communicated and understood;
- forces a systematic appraisal of methods;
- is recognition of the firm as an investor in people – a recognition that might be important in securing contracts.

Chapter 45

1   **Discuss the principles of reward management.**

Reference should be made to pay as part of human resources management and the securing of strategic objectives. The system should be fair and be perceived to be fair. Payments should be related to skills, supply and demand in the marketplace, responsibilities. They should also be designed to motivate employees.

2   **Evaluate piece rates in comparison with time rates.**

Piece-work rates reward people in relation to their individual or group output. Hence, such rates are seen as motivating. However, they are only appropriate where:
- output can be attributed to an individual or small group;

- the product is standardized and can be measured;
- the emphasis on speed does not endanger safety or quality.

Time rates do not motivate – in fact, when combined with overtime premiums, they can demotivate. However, they are necessary where piece-work rates are inappropriate.

3   (a)   **Explain what is meant by new (as opposed to old) pay.**

       (b)   **Evaluate two of the features of new pay.**

       (a)   Old pay is hierarchical and consists of collectively negotiated salaries or time rates.
New pay is:

- linked to performance;
- market-driven;
- flexible;
- broadbanded.

       (b)   Broadbanding is a feature of new pay in delayered organizations. There is also performance-related pay, which is linked to a subjective appraisal of performance.

4   (a)   **Explain the differences between piece rates, commission and performance-related pay.**

       (b)   **Discuss the problems associated with performance-related pay.**

       (a)   Piece-work rates are objectively set against measured output.

Commission is linked to sales performance (over which the individual has some, but not total control).

Performance-related pay involves a pay bonus that is linked to a subjective evaluation of performance, say by a manager.

       (b)   Problems include that it:

- is subjective;
- can cause resentment if unfair;
- involves appraisal systems, which are often resented.

5   **Evaluate profit-related pay as a way of motivating the workforce. In your answer, make reference to appropriate theory.**

It gives employees a greater stake in the organization and should motivate them to the achievement of profit targets, but:

- the bonus is unrelated to individual performance;
- 'profit' is a subjective notion;
- the bonus is paid out long after the effort is required.

Reference should be made to equity theory (is it fair?) and expectancy theory (which stresses the need for prompt feedback).

6   (a)   **Explain what you understand by:**

           (i)   **delayering; and**

           (ii)   **broadbanding of pay.**

       (b)   **Evaluate broadbanding in the light of the trend towards delayering.**

       (a)   (i)   Removal of layers from an organization's hierarchy.

           (ii)   Pay rates that cover a wider band of staff than before.

       (b)   With fewer promotion opportunities, it is necessary to offer a broad band of pay to a wide range of people.

Chapter 46

1   (a)   Explain what you understand by a claim and an offer in collective bargaining.

    (b)   Analyse the factors that each side takes into account in collective bargaining.

    (a)   Employees and their union make a claim, while the employer makes an offer. Collective bargaining involves the search for common ground between a claim and the offer.

    (b)   Factors taken into account include:
    - supply and demand in the labour market;
    - company profits;
    - inflation – unions seek a rise in real terms;
    - other pay rises;
    - relativity and comparability;
    - productivity gains.

2   Analyse the cases for and against:
    (a)   individual rather than collective bargaining;
    (b)   local rather than national bargaining.

    (a)   Individual bargaining might suit those with scarce skills, but most people prefer the strength of collective bargaining. More people are covered by collective agreements than are in trade unions. Some firms might prefer individual bargaining to reward the exceptionally talented, but disputes and resentment can result.

    (b)   Local and plant bargaining relates to pay to cover local conditions in the labour market. In areas of labour shortage, firms will want to pay higher rates than those nationally negotiated to retain staff.

3   Trade union protection for workers leads to job losses. Discuss.

    The rationale for trade unions is strength in numbers. It is true that economic theory points to the danger of excessively regulated labour markets, but UK competitiveness requires skilled, motivated workers.

4   Analyse the cases for and against trade unions in the twenty-first century.

    New unionism involves:
    - a more professional, managerial outlook;
    - cooperation between the two sides of industry;
    - a search for agreement – trade unions remain important for the protection of the workforce.

    Old-style trade unionism – involves conflict, demarcation and restrictive practices – leads to job losses.

5   (a)   Evaluate the benefits of different schemes of employee participation.

    (b)   Discuss the preconditions for a successful scheme of participation.

    (a)   Different schemes include:
    - worker directors;
    - works councils;
    - consultative committees;
    - quality circles;
    - team briefings.

    Evaluation of such schemes should cover representation, coverage of issues, decision-making powers and the communication of information.

(b)   The preconditions include:

- provision of information;
- trust;
- willingness to work towards common goals;
- coverage of topics;
- nature of representation;
- time allowance.

Chapter 47

1   (a)   **What do you understand by organizational culture?**

      (b)   **Analyse the factors that influence the culture of an organization.**

      (a)   Culture is the beliefs and values that affect attitudes, decision making, leadership styles and so on. It has been defined as 'the way we do things around here'.

      (b)   Influential factors include:

- history;
- size;
- attitudes of senior managers;
- beliefs of the founder;
- leadership style.

2   **Analyse ways in which the culture of an organization influences the behaviour of people within the organization.**

Culture affects:

- management style;
- the ways in which decisions are made;
- attitudes of employers;
- motivation;
- attitudes towards change;
- corporate mission and objectives;
- ethical and environmental behaviour.

3   (a)   **Account for the accelerating pace of change in business.**

      (b)   **Analyse the causes of resistance to change.**

      (a)   The rate of change is accelerating because of the:

- speeding up of developments in technology;
- explosion of knowledge;
- increase in competition;
- single market in the EU;
- rise of the Asian Tigers.

      (b)   Change is resisted because it:

- is seen as a threat to livelihoods;
- threatens existing social groups;
- is a threat to self-esteem;
- induces fears of being unable to cope.

4   Suggest and evaluate ways of getting employees to accept change within the organization.

A judgement is required on each of the following strategies:
- negotiation – this involves compromise;
- pay rises – increases costs;
- education – assumes that it will be accepted if people understand the reasons for change;
- threats – might lead to conflict;
- participation – chances of acceptance of change are greater when employees are involved in planning change.

5   Using appropriate examples, analyse the relationship between:
(a)   organizational culture and organizational objectives;
(b)   organizational culture and organizational ethics/social responsibility;
(c)   organizational culture and the history of the organization.

(a)   Culture influences corporate objectives – attitudes to profit, control, stability, growth. A simple distinction could be between the proprietorial business, which aims at survival and retention of control, and the entrepreneurial business, which seeks growth at all costs.

(b)   Culture also affects the ethics of an organization. Values and beliefs determine what is acceptable and what is not acceptable. Culture is reflected in the behaviour towards stakeholders.

(c)   Culture is, in part, affected by the history of the organization, the views of its founders, the ways in which it has been managed over the years, and the attitudes of staff towards the organization who are greatly influenced by how they have been treated in the past.

6   Japanization is defined as the integration of Japanese management techniques into UK firms. Analyse the problems of introducing Japanese management styles into:
(a)   an existing UK firm;
(b)   a newly established business operating on a greenfield site.

(a)   The attitudes, beliefs, values of the existing management and employees might run counter to Japanese ideas. It is likely that some of these ideas, at least, will be resisted.

(b)   A greenfield site is seen as a new beginning without the baggage of existing culture. Newly appointed staff are more likely to accept new ideas as a condition of employment than existing staff at an established site.

Chapter 48

1   With the use of examples taken from the functional areas of management, analyse the differences between strategic and tactical decisions.

Strategic decisions	Tactical decisions
Product/market decision	Pricing policies
Product development	Choice of media
Entry in to markets	Distribution
Positioning	Packaging
Labour requirements	Production scheduling
Major investment decisions	Recruitment and selection
Raising finance	

2   (a) Explain the generic strategies identified by Professor Michael Porter.

      (b) Analyse the factors that should be taken into account when selecting each of the generic strategies.

      (a) These strategies are:
- *cost leadership* competing by being the lowest-cost producer;
- *differentiation* competing by producing a distinctive product;
- *focus* this could be either one of the above, but aimed at a particular target;

      (b) Cost leadership is only available to firms that enjoy economies of scale and are able to produce at lower unit costs than their rivals.

Differentiation requires a reputation for quality and distinctiveness.

A focus strategy might be suited to a small firm aiming at a particular niche.

3   Evaluate the case for both internal (organic) growth and external growth.

Internal or organic growth is slow, but based on existing areas of expertise.

External growth involves the instant acquisition of labour, plant, products and a customer base. Although faster, it sometimes fails because it takes senior management into areas where they lack expertise.

4   (a) What do you understand by:
      (i) demerger; and
      (ii) core activities.

      (b) Analyse the reasons for demerger being a strategy favoured by some business organizations.

      (a) (i) Demerger involves selling off parts of the organization – in particular, profit centres or product divisions.
            (ii) Core activities are those considered to be central to the organization's future strategy.

      (b) Demerger is favoured when an organization wants to:
- concentrate on core activities;
- divest itself of activities that do not fit in with the rest of its activities;
- eliminate activities not seen as being especially profitable;
- eliminate activities outside the expertise of senior management;
- raise finance for strategically important activities.

5   Account for the disappointing results that often follow a merger or takeover.

Disappointing financial performance in these cases is the result of:
- an ill planned acquisition;
- the search for power and larger volume rather than profits;
- a failure to integrate organizationally;
- a failure or inability to change the culture of the organization;
- an inability to achieve substantial economies of scale.

6   Adapting the concept of the product lifecycle, analyse the ways in which an organization is likely to evolve as it moves through history. Your answer should include reference to organizational structure, organizational culture, product range and human resource management.

We can visualize a newly established organization, a developing organization, a mature organization and an organization in decline. In its early stages, a firm is owned and managed by its founder(s). The emphasis is on personal control, flexible structure, a limited product range and close relations with staff.

As it matures, it is likely to 'import' senior managers. The organization is likely to be more structured and bureaucratic. Relationships between managers and employees are likely to be less close and more formal. The product range will be extended.

7   Analyse the intensity of competition in the:

(a)   motor industry;

(b)   perfume industry; and

(c)   retailing of records (CDs).

with reference to the:

*   bargaining power of suppliers;

*   bargaining power of buyers;

*   threat of substitution of rival products;

*   ease of entry of newcomers;

*   market share of existing players.

(a)   Motor manufacturer are in a strong position with reference to suppliers. There is little threat of rival products (except rival brands of cars). The cost of entry is prohibitive to newcomers. Market share is dominated by a small number of players.

(b)   Perfume producers are also in a strong position – these dominate their own suppliers, there are rival brands, but considerable customer loyalty. The entry of newcomers is possible, but reputation is a key factor in the continuing success of existing players.

(c)   Independent retailers are in a relatively weak position in relation to suppliers. In smaller towns, the retailer enjoys a considerable hold over the market (especially if they are the sole specialist seller). However, the entry of newcomers is relatively easy and competition from rival products (such as downloading from the Internet) poses a real threat in the future.

Chapter 49

These questions require answers that draw from two or more areas of the subject:

*   objectives and the external environment;

*   marketing;

*   accounting and finance;

*   human resources in organizations

*   operations.

Within and between each of the major division of the subject, students should develop the ability to link topics to produce rounded answers. There is no 'right' answer to any of the following questions and students should explore all appropriate linkages.

1   **Suggest and evaluate strategies to cope with the problems of a rise in the value of the country's currency against other major foreign currencies.**

The starting point is loss of competitiveness as exports are then more expensive to foreigners and imports penetrate deeper into the UK market.

Strategies to consider include:

*   a reduction in profit margins by absorbing the currency movement;

*   competing on other aspects of the marketing mix;

*   concentration on quality;

*   measures to increase competitiveness, including lean production, business process re-engineering, increase in labour productivity, greater automation;

*   human resources strategies to increase productivity.

2   **Suggest and evaluate strategies to cope with the problem of seasonality in sales.**

We should distinguish between seasonality in terms of supply and seasonality in terms of demand. The former is limited to agriculture, but seasonality in terms of demand is common. Strategies include:

- marketing strategies to develop off-peak demand (such as Bernard Matthews and turkey products);
- production and human resources strategies to increase output at peak times, although this has problems in terms of cost and the availability of resources;
- all-year-round production, coupled with long-term storage, although this creates problems in terms of working capital and cost flow, and long term storage is only possible in the case of non-perishable goods.

3   **Analyse the implications of, and problems associated with, the introduction of new labour-saving equipment.**

Reference should be made to costs of production, investment appraisal and the human resources implications of the equipment's introduction. The management of change should be explored. Operations issues such as stocks, production layout, batch sizes, quality and training should also be analysed.

4   **Analyse the impact of telephone banking on retail banking in the UK.**

Reference should be made to:

- changes in technology;
- changes in the social environment;
- competition in financial services;
- location;
- investment in equipment;
- human resources, issues such as redundancy, training and job design,;
- the cost implications;
- marketing issues, such as satisfying the customers who prefer face-to-face banking.

5   **Analyse possible causes of a decline in profitability.**

Declining profitability might be the result of rising costs:

- rise in unit cost of labour or materials;
- decline in productivity;
- rise in overhead costs;
- failure to control costs;
- rise in the quantity of waste.

Alternatively, it might be the result of:

- competition, forcing price reductions;
- a decline in sales volume.

6   **Suggest and evaluate both short- and long-term strategies to cope with the problem of shortage of skilled labour.**

Short-run strategies include:

- the use of overtime labour;
- rise in pay rates to attract additional workers;
- use of lower-grade workers.

In the longer run, the solution lies in:

- training employees;
- capital investment to reduce the dependence on this scarce resource.

The implications of these strategies should be considered – on costs, productivity, quality, waste, human resources problems, job redesign (deskilling).

7   Analyse the likely consequences of a diversification of a firm's product range.

Consequences should be analysed in terms of:

- spreading risks – using the Boston Matrix;
- marketing consequences – of promoting a range of products;
- the cost of producing a range of goods;
- investment in productive capacity;
- the need for new skills and expertise;
- organizational design, such as profit centres.

8   Suggest and evaluate strategies to cope with the problems resulting from a rise in interest rates.

A rise in interest rates raises the cost of borrowing and reduces demand for the firm's products. The impacts on the cost side include:

- changes in the criteria for investment – ARR, discount rate, IRR;
- increases in the cost of stockholding, perhaps leading to destocking;
- an incentive to reduce liabilities.

The strategies to cope with falling demand might include:

- a reduction in profit margins;
- targeting a new segment;
- changes to the marketing and promotional mix;
- an increased desire to export goods.

9   Suggest and evaluate strategies to cope with a rise in labour costs.

Reference should be made to:

- profit margins;
- competitiveness;
- marketing strategies;
- strategies to raise the productivity of labour;
- automation/CAM to substitute labour with capital;
- changes in organizational structure;
- human resource strategies to increase productivity.

10   Analyse the likely impact of a new competitor on the financial performance of a company. Suggest and evaluate strategies to maintain market share.

The impact of competition is likely to be felt in terms of:

- sales volumes;
- sales revenue;
- downward pressure on price;
- loss of market share;
- reduction in profits and/or profit margins;
- deterioration in ratios.

Strategies to be considered include:

- marketing strategies to maintain competitiveness;
- destroyer pricing;
- strategies to raise productivity;
- development of new markets and/or new products – Ansoff's Matrix.

11 **Analyse the impact of the accelerating pace of technological change on each of the functional areas of business management.**

Marketing:
- investment in new product development;
- short product lifecycles;
- increase in competition.

Accounting and finance:
- short time period to enjoy profits from each product;
- implications for stockholding;
- investment in research and development;
- raising finance.

Operations
- investment in new equipment;
- shorter production runs;
- need for retooling;
- flexibility at a premium.

Human resources management:
- training;
- multiskilling;
- the flexible firm.

12 **Analyse the consequences for UK business of each of the following:**
    (a) EU enlargement to include Eastern Europe;
    (b) acceptance of the Social Charter.

(a) New market opportunities have emerged and will continue to do so in Eastern Europe, including:
- exports – multinational marketing;
- investment and multinational production in these areas;
- source of materials and components;
- as citizens of an enlarged EU, Eastern Europeans will have the right to work in the UK, thus enabling firms to access a larger pool of labour;
- if Eastern European producers increase their efficiency, they will be a great threat as they enjoy the advantage of lower-cost labour.

(b) The Social Charter has the potential of raising the cost of labour and reducing the competitiveness of EU industry. Against the adverse cost considerations, a good case for the Social Charter exists in terms of human resources implications and the need for the EU to compete on quality of goods and the skill of its workforce.

13 **A single market with a single currency. Analyse the impact of these developments in the EU on each of the four functional areas of management.**

The single currency completes the single market and achieves the ideal of intra-EU trade being no more difficult than domestic trade. Both developments create market opportunities, but also a greater threat of import penetration.

- *Marketing* reference could be made to pan-European marketing, price transparency and the need to be competitive.
- *Accounting and finance* reference should be made to the cost of conversion, accounting in Euros and the consequences for the financial performance of a business.
- *Operations* students should refer to output levels, production runs, competitiveness, quality, waste and productivity.
- *Human resources management* students should refer to human resources implications in terms of free movement of labour, the Social Charter, competitiveness, training and productivity.

14 **Analyse the consequences of the adoption of total quality for the management of a firm's resources.**

TQM requires a change in organizational culture. It shifts responsibility for quality from a specialist team at the end of the line to the whole workforce. It requires commitment, enthusiasm and a responsible attitude. In this respect, students' answers could link TQM with theories on motivation and leadership.

Other issues to explore include:
- purchasing policy;
- inspection methods;
- teamwork;
- stock levels;
- production methods.

15 **Analyse the implications of flow line production techniques on the other functional areas of management.**

Human resources management implications include:
- changed labour requirements;
- training;
- motivation.

Marketing implications include:
- costs and therefore pricing;
- product variations;
- altered delivery times.

Accounting implications include:
- changes in costs of production;
- investment;
- raising finance;
- changes in working capital requirements;
- stock levels.

16 **Analyse the consequences for the marketing and other departments of a move away from premium pricing.**

Such a move suggests a reduction in price and quality.
Marketing consequences include:
- changes in a key element of the mix;
- changes in positioning;

- targeting a new segment;
- changes to a promotional strategy;
- possible changes in channels of distribution;
- need to ensure consistency within the mix.

Accounting and finance consequences include:

- lower profit margins;
- consequences for profit and loss account;
- changes in financial performance.

Operations consequences include:

- retooling for new products;
- renewed search for cost reductions.

Human resources management consequences include:

- renewed search for ways to increase the productivity of labour.

17   (a)   **What do you understand by a divisionalized business organization?**

       (b)   **Analyse the implications of divisionalization for the way in which the firm is managed.**

       (a)   Each division, responsible for a range of products, will be a profit centre. Organization is by product rather than function. Each division is therefore a business within a business.

       (b)   The implication for accounting and finance is that accounts are produced for each division as if it were a separate business.

           For Marketing, the implication is that each division is responsible for its own marketing.

           In operations and human resources, again, each division will be given considerable autonomy on these matters.

           Divisional managers are set targets, but are given autonomy to devise strategies to achieve the targets. Demerger or divestment is made easier if an organization is divisionalized.

18   **Shorter production runs and shorter product development times. Discuss the implications of these trends on the management of resources.**

Shorter production runs:

- raise the costs of production;
- provide for greater product variation;
- necessitate greater flexibility in terms of equipment and human resources.

Shorter product development times mean:

- increased investment in R&D;
- time-based competition;
- shorter product lifecycles.

19   **Discuss the implications of a strategy of demerger to concentrate on core competences.**

Demerger or divestment became a common strategy in the late twentieth century. Firms identified core activities (those seen as an essential to the future of the organization) and eliminated non-core activities. This means:

- concentrating on the area of expertise;
- downsizing the workforce;
- greater use of subcontractors;
- reductions in stocks;
- less diversity in activities;

- greater control over core activities;
- an additional source of finance.

20   Analyse the implications of, and the constraints imposed on business by, the Data Protection Act.

Students should refer to the principles behind the Act and the implications for personnel and customer records.

Reference should be made to market research and direct marketing.

21   Analyse the implications of the development of the Internet for business organizations.

The uses of the Internet to be explored include:

- market research;
- promotional activities;
- direct marketing;
- access to secondary data;
- home working.

Implications to be explored include investment, training, the nature of work, location, the revolution in knowledge, competition and globalization.

22   Analyse the factors that will have been taken into account in the formulation of a strategic objective of a 5 per cent increase in the volume of sales in the coming year.

In devising the growth target, top management should have considered:

- demand;
- competition;
- price;
- incomes;
- the state of the economy;
- productive capacity;
- labour supply;
- labour skills;
- financing working capital and fixed assets.

23   Analyse the internal and external constraints on a business organization.

Internal constraints include:

- capital equipment;
- labour;
- skills, expertise;
- financial resources;
- access to materials;
- management;
- technology.

External constraints include:

- customer demand;
- the state of the economy;
- competition;
- government policies, such as taxation;

- legal constraints;
- the EU;
- social and cultural factors.

24   Analyse the consequences of the adoption of a policy of differentiated marketing in which a number of market segments are targeted.

Differentiated marketing requires a different marketing mix for each segment. This makes the firm's products attractive to different segments but:

- requires different marketing strategies, in terms of product, promotion, price and distribution channels, for each segment;
- shorter production runs will raise costs;
- greater flexibility is required in terms of capital equipment and labour.

The result will be a rise in costs, but, perhaps, also a rise in sales revenue and profits. This will be reflected in the final accounts.

25   Suggest and evaluate strategies to cope with the problem of recession.

Marketing strategies include:

- changes in products;
- changes in promotion;
- changes in targeted segments;
- changes in prices;
- changes in channels of distribution.

All these strategies will involve costs. If the recession is perceived as being temporary, the firm might prefer to see a reduction in sales volume or profit margins.

Operations strategies include:

- cost-cutting measures, including waste reduction;
- downsizing;
- increase in the productivity of labour;
- substituting expensive labour with capital.

These changes take time and are therefore not appropriate if the recession is estimated to be short-lived.

Human resources management strategy is:

- downsizing, leading to redundancy.

An accounting strategy is:

- cost reductions, especially in terms of stock.

Another strategy to deal with the problem is to seek export markets.

26   Suggest and evaluate strategies to cope with a shortage in an important raw material.

A shortage of a vital input will constrain production or add to costs. Solutions to consider include:

- the development of alternative materials;
- product redesign;
- increasing the price of the finished goods;
- reducing other costs.

27   Analyse the implications of just-in-time approaches to manufacturing.

Just-in-time manufacturing and stockholding mean:

- less investment in stock;

- lower working capital requirements;
- improved cash flow;
- less need for storage;
- single sourcing based on cooperation;
- demand-pull production;
- employee commitment;
- Total Quality Management and zero defects.

28   Analyse the consequences of a move to 24-hour working.

Around-the-clock working, was in the past, confined to manufacturing, but is now found in retailing, telephone banking and other financial services.

It makes more efficient use of space and capital equipment. Moreover, it aims at improving the service to customers and is, therefore, part of firms' competitive strategies. However, there are cost implications – premium pay for working unsocial hours, for example.

A human resources implication is that more staff are required. This necessitates increases in training and supervision.

29   Discuss the implications of changing from selling exclusively own brand products to selling a range of branded products.

'Own branders' exert considerable control over the suppliers producing items to specifications. They enjoy a monopoly situation regarding their own-brand products and control the marketing process.

Moving to selling a range of branded goods involves very different relationships with suppliers and removes the advantage of exclusivity. Firms doing this have to change their culture as a result and this has human resources management implications.

30   Analyse possible explanations for an adverse variance from a cash budget (cash flow forecast).

Possible explanations include:
- lower than expected levels of sales;
- enforced price reductions;
- credit customers paid after a longer than expected time lag;
- rises in costs of materials or labour;
- creditors required prompt payments;
- greater than expected seasonal fluctuations in sales.